IT'S ONLY A MOVIE

IT'S ONLY A MOVIE

A MEMOIR

Bruce Joel Rubin

Sticking Place Books
New York

This book is dedicated to my Mom and Dad,
and my wife Blanche

Also by Bruce Joel Rubin
Three Visionary Screenplays

© Sticking Place Books 2024
Cover image by Joshua Rubin

www.brucejoelrubin.com
www.stickingplacebooks.com

All rights reserved.
No part of this book may be reproduced, stored in or introduced into a retrieval system, or transmitted, in any form or by any means (electronic, mechanical, photocopying, recording or otherwise) without the written permission of the publishers, except in the case of brief quotations embodied in critical articles or reviews.

ISBN 978-1-942782-44-5

CONTENTS

Foreword   vii

1 Emergence – Detroit   1
2 Blinking – Early Moments   15
3 Glancing – Vernor Elementary   21
4 Looking – Mumford High   35
5 Thinking – 678 West Warren   47
6 Wondering – NYU   61
7 Seeing – LSD   77
8 Searching – Journey to the East   91
9 Exploring – Lord of the Universe   109
10 Finding – Blanche-Rudi-Joshua   133
11 Doing – The Screen Trade   159
12 Hoping – Big Indian   175
13 Witnessing – Death and Rebirth   189
14 Teaching – *Brainstorm* – Ari   203
15 Fearing – Writing My Way Out of Hell   215
16 Arriving – Hollywood   231
17 Sharing – *Ghost* and *Jacob's Ladder*   243
18 Transformation – Openings   277
19 Certainty – *My Life*   293
20 Struggling – *Deep Impact*   311
21 Grace – *The Last Mimzy*   323
22 Questioning – Gun for Hire   331
23 Knowing – The Power of Now   339
24 Enlightenment – Awakening   353
25 Being – *Ghost the Musical*   363
26 Knowing Nothing – Grandkids   379
27 Mortality – Clarity   387
28 Love – It's Only a Movie   399

Foreword

I don't know who I am writing this book for.

I have had what would be considered a successful Hollywood career. I have also been a spiritual seeker and meditation teacher for over fifty years. Although gay, and closeted most of my life, I have had a wonderful marriage to my wife Blanche. I have two remarkable sons Joshua and Ari, two exceptional daughters-in-law, and two incredible grandchildren. In my mind these worlds have blended and reinforced one another for decades, but as a book I have only hazy ideas about how these disparate life stories combine or who my reading audience might be. I would be satisfied to let this manuscript sit in the closet until my grandchildren want to see it. But if you are reading it, that clearly didn't happen.

It's Only a Movie began because one of my meditation students, Joseph Maddrey, asked if he could interview me. He's a deeply sincere person, the author of several books about people in the film industry as well as many true crime shows on television. I said sure. We recorded a lot of conversations, interweaving my spiritual journey with my Hollywood career and how the combination led to movies like *Ghost* and *Jacob's Ladder*. Joe edited the transcripts into a manuscript, which I waited a long while before reading. The problem was that while my Hollywood career had mostly ended and I was able to consider writing about it as a book, my spiritual life was still moving forward. I kept feeling that I needed to arrive at some kind of perfect awareness, some ultimate state of enlightenment, before I could present a finished work to the world. That part of my journey, full of profound revelations and insights, did, in fact, lead to what might be called enlightenment. (Having given away the ending of this book, perhaps I may have saved you from having to read it.)

Recently, several years after putting Joseph's draft on the shelf, I got a call from one of my son Joshua's friends, Paul Cronin, an author of several books on prominent filmmakers. He had, unbeknownst to me, asked Joshua if he could read the edited interview transcripts, and shortly after that I got a call from him saying he needed to see me. He had recently bought a house with his wife Gabrielle not far from Blanche and I, and he came over to visit. His first words were that he had read the manuscript, that he felt it was an exceedingly important work (I may have added the word "exceedingly"), and that it needed to be finished. His big question to me – *Where is your father in all this?* – I considered a surprising but important one. It was enough to allow me to move forward with the book once again. I didn't need to arrive at an ultimate spiritual apotheosis to make it worth sharing. It also helped that Joseph and Paul had met one another as Blanche and I were packing up and leaving California (during which boxes of material from my home office were shipped to the Academy archive). Knowing that they could work together to help me with this new draft was encouraging. So I set out to write it.

My spiritual journey may be of limited interest to certain readers. I think you will smell these sections coming and can skip them if you like – though I feel they are at least as important as the Hollywood stories that dominate the book. Your call. I name names throughout, hoping, I suppose, to make this a popular autobiography and of interest to readers outside of my immediate family. Whether I have succeeded in this remains to be seen. All I can tell you is that the assembly of all these facets of my life, including my large and very close family, which has been the centerpiece of my life, comprises a full picture that is, for better or worse, *me*.

Bruce Joel Rubin
Red Hook, New York
December 2023

One

Emergence – Detroit

The middle of WWII would seem like an odd time for my parents to conceive a child, since the world was falling apart and America wasn't yet winning the war. My dad Jimmy was in the army but never left the country, and was discharged from somewhere in Louisiana for reasons I never really understood. My mom, Sondra, and I were thrilled to have him home.

I don't know how I ended up in Detroit. I always assumed that the stork was heading to New York but somehow I fell out of the blanket, and in March 1943 was dropped headfirst into the Midwest, a thousand miles short of my planned destination. I would spend much of the rest of my early life trying to make my way east, to Broadway and Times Square, which my child-self believed to be the center of the world. As it turns out, that journey would take years. I did, luckily, end up in a wonderful family. Two families really – my mom's and my dad's.

My mother's birth name was Sonia, which she changed to Sondra for some unknown reason, but many people called her Sandy. My dad was born Steven Irving Rubin but changed his name to James Irving. I find this all significant. Perhaps it has something to do with a lack of respect for the status quo, a kind of free thinking and self-determination on their part. My mom's dad, Abraham (Abe) Baliber, had two brothers, each of whom changed the spelling of their last name when they were young men in Russia, since the Czar was conscripting men into military service but allowed the first born to remain at home. So all three brothers – Abe, Joe and Max – had slightly different last names (Balibier, Balberor, Baliber), and no one in our family ever knew how to spell any of them consistently or correctly. But it did save their lives.

There are stories about where the family name comes from. Russia is the easy answer, Belarus possibly, where my grandfather remembered at age eight picking up dead bodies in his little wagon and pulling them out of the town square after Cossacks had killed some requisite number of Jews. Years later, he fled to America with his father Morris and two brothers. They moved to Detroit, where Abe became a construction worker and then a building contractor. My dad was brought into the building business after his wedding to my mom, and it ultimately became his lifelong career.

My grandmother Minnie came from a town called Halopenicy, near Minsk, the capital of Belarus (formerly White Russia). I found it once on the internet. One viewing was enough for me to see why anyone would want to leave the place. She came to America along with her mother Esther and four sisters. I know nothing about her father except his name, Jacob Eber. Unfortunately, when they arrived at Ellis Island the youngest sister had pinkeye and the authorities wouldn't let her enter the country. My grandma and her other sisters, Ida and Rose, disembarked, while my great grandmother heroically took her youngest daughter back to Russia, where they perished in a pogrom. I learned all of this in bits and pieces as I was growing up. It was rarely part of our family discussion, as if the old world had been erased.

My dad's side of the family were less colorful personalities. In those days, there were two kinds of photographic film, Kodak and Ansco. Kodak was packaged in a bright yellow box with red and green colors mixed in. It was lively and encompassing. Ansco was blue and white and dull. I always felt my mom's family was the Kodak family and my dad's was Ansco. My dad's father, David, who lived to 103, was often dry and sullen, perhaps because as a child he was left in an orphanage by his father after his mother's death. There were brothers and sisters as well, all in different orphanages, who later reconnected, I am told, and may even have rejoined their father's second family. I'm not a terribly good historian and didn't even know that his birth name was actually Rubinski until it was acknowledged at his hundredth birthday party. Although raised in Brooklyn, he worked most of his life as a furrier in Detroit and an inventor of sorts. He created a plastic bag for storing furs that pulled dirt out of the coats via static electricity and deposited it at the bottom of the bag. It was an odd claim to fame, except that his invention really worked – at least it did in our closet at home. His favorite story was that he once saw John Phillip Sousa march in a parade when he was still an orphan in Brooklyn. My lasting image of him was as a gardener, wearing a suit and tie, in his tiny allotment in Palmer Park, across the street from his apartment.

His wife Dora liked telling stories about her family, the Cohens, who were rather prosperous and accomplished folks in New York. Her brother, Abe Broderick Cohen, was a professor at Barnard and the only family member in *Who's Who in America*. It was claimed that he had come up with the idea of the sabbatical year for university professors. My grandma's real gift to me was that she had a first cousin, Bessie, who married Al Warner, one of the Warner brothers. Being somehow related to Warner Bros. was foundational for me. I used to go to Saturday matinees at the Royal Theater in Detroit. When the cartoon cavalcade began the show and the Warner logo popped up, along with Bugs Bunny, Daffy Duck and Porky Pig, I would always yell, "That's my cousins on the screen!" I thought having a direct family line to one of the great film production companies would open doors for me. This,

4 It's Only a Movie

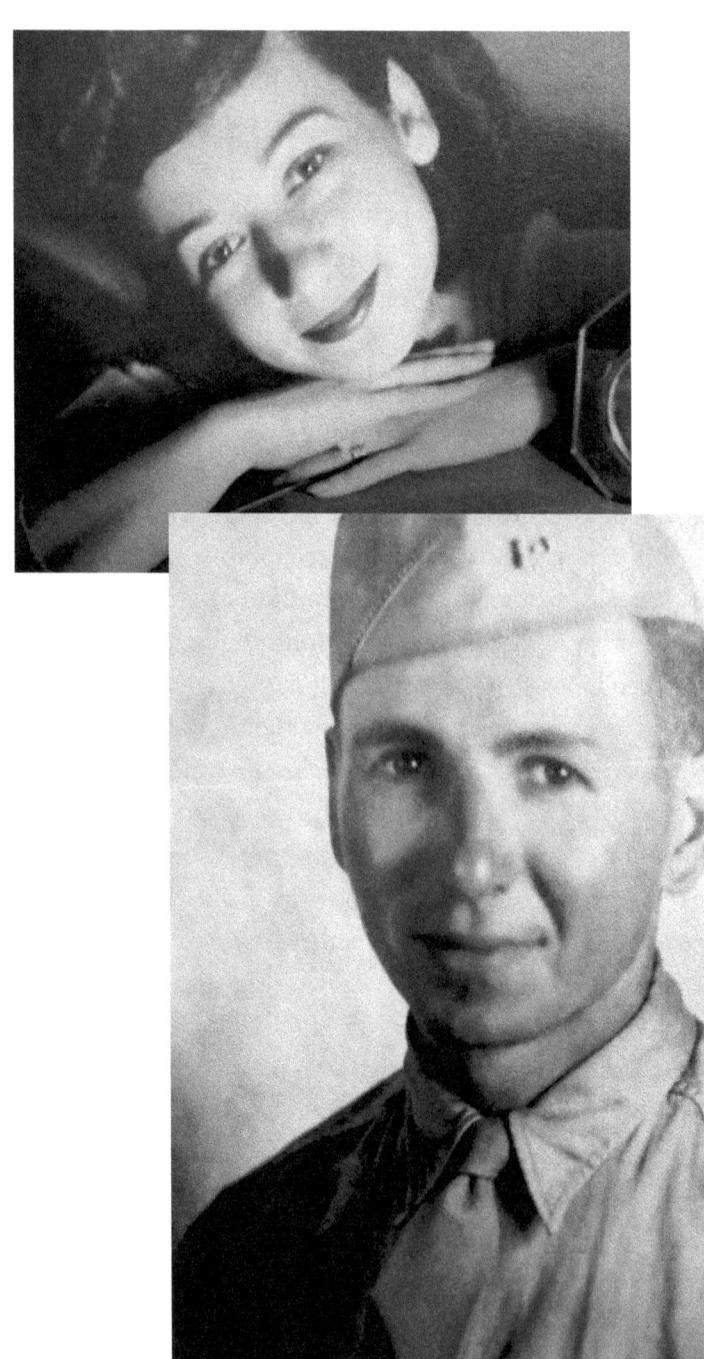

of course, proved to be a pipe dream, but what did I know? I was already famous in my own mind, connected to movie royalty, and a true annoyance to everyone in the auditorium around me.

I once visited my grandparents with my dad, carrying my favorite companion, a soft brown teddy bear that went with me everywhere. When my dad and I left I realized that my teddy was missing, so we went back to get it. Grandma Dora insisted that I hadn't brought it with me. I knew I had. I cried for days, maybe weeks. It was only years later I realized that she had hidden it from me, believing, I suppose, that I was too old for teddy bears. Part of me never forgave her, but it was also my first introduction to the Buddhist idea of impermanence. For that, I guess, I'm grateful.

I loved elevators, until the one in the building where my grandparents lived got stuck between floors. It was the first time I saw my dad frightened. (The other time was on a Ferris wheel when the operator had to take a leak and left us all stranded, my dad and I at the top, for ten minutes.) Seeing that fear in him made an indelible impression, and to this day I am claustrophobic. I had only one childhood excursion with my Grandma Dora. We went downtown to see a double bill of two inappropriate movies when I was eight years old. *The Golden Horde* was a huge Christian epic about conquering Asian barbarians. *Sunset Boulevard*, on the other hand, was a revelation to me. It was clear as I watched, in both dread and fascination, that I was clueless about the adult world and had no idea where human life was heading. William Holden lying dead, face down in a pool, and yet narrating the story, was a seminal moment for me and perhaps an unconscious motivation for my writing career. My fascination with death can most likely be traced to that movie. I do owe my Grandma Dora that. There was also another redemptive moment. For my bar mitzvah, Dora and David gave me my first portable typewriter. In many ways my creative life goes back to that gift. Although I had little skill in using it, the next year, in high school, I took a typing class and practiced with a vengeance. Other than creative writing, typing became my one and only employable skill.

My dad's baby sister Clara was an inventor like her dad. Her claim to fame, true or not, was inventing the hair curler. Supposedly she had suggested the idea to Charles Revson, head of Revlon. There is also a story about her "inventing" the packaging for Kleenex tissues by putting wrapping paper over the old utilitarian box and giving it a colorful, home-friendly look. I have no idea how she may have presented this to Kimberly Clark, but I wouldn't put it past her. That lovely packaging has since defined Kleenex tissues and I feel like part of my Aunt Clara is in my house every day, especially when I sneeze.

Clara's husband, Al Altman, was a dentist. I still have a big gap between two upper teeth, a reminder of my dad taking me to him to save money on braces. He was a good dentist, but not an orthodontist. My dad was always trying to save money, just as my mother tried to spend it. I remember him telling me that the photographer at my bar mitzvah had lost his photos. It dawned on me only later that my dad didn't want or wasn't able to pay for them, so I have no photographs of that event. I hated that my dad lied about it, but his subtle subterfuge also made me aware of a slippery and questionable morality in adults. When there was a flood in our basement, I called my dad and told him I was evacuating everything, taking it upstairs. He told me to stop and take everything back down, then to grab my mom's mink coat and throw it into the rising water. Six months later, after he got the insurance money, we made a major new addition to the house. It changed the entire dynamics of our home and our lives. Everything became expanded and spacious. It was a complex lesson for me.

My Uncle Al was the most adult and forthright of all my uncles. Unfortunately, he had no idea how to deal with anyone under the age of thirteen, so I never really connected to him until I became older, at which point we got to know each other. He understood my evolving love of musical theater and bought me a copy of Leonard Bernstein's *Candide* for my sixteenth birthday, an unexpected and affecting gift. *Candide*, which pays homage to the absurdity of our world, has had a lifelong impact on me and my best friends, who continue to reference it to this day. Voltaire's ultimate theme, "Make Our Garden Grow," set a philosophical note for us that inspires even now. Richard Wilbur's lyrics were especially haunting.

> You've been a fool and so have I,
> But come and be my wife,
> And let us try before we die,
> To make some sense of life.
> We're neither pure nor wise nor good.
> We'll do the best we know.
> We'll build our house and chop our wood
> And make our garden grow.

Al's and Clara's kids, Burton, Marjorie and Joanie, were central to my childhood. Burton developed epilepsy after a head injury as a child, although I didn't know that until later in life. I never witnessed an attack, but his condition had a profound and debilitating effect on his family, who never talked about it. When Burton and I spoke in later years, it was clear he had a penchant for inflating or distorting his life story. It was just who he was. Burton was the first of my cousins to die, a possible epileptic attack while driving. At his funeral several of his friends spoke, telling stories about him I had never heard before. I suspected they were just made-up stories that Burton had told them. I sensed that we were burying someone we never really knew.

Marjorie married Billy and had three kids, each of whom had three kids of their own. They all still live in Detroit, all within walking distance of one another. She is the one cousin who stayed behind. Her life is always a mirror of who I might have become if I had never had the urge to leave. The kind of family proximity that Marjorie has enjoyed her whole life wasn't for me at that time. I would have drowned in it, especially in Detroit. Now, of course, in old age, I've come to treasure it. The communal quality of her life is worth celebrating.

Joanie, the youngest, moved to New York with her first husband Jack. She was the last person I ever expected to leave home. She was afraid to take the bus to school as a kid and seemed the most cautious of all my cousins. But when her marriage ended and she was left alone to support her two children, she began photographing homeless women in New York. Her empathy was potent. In later political action that I would never have anticipated, my innocent Detroit cousin became an advocate for the homeless and a celebrated photographer of their travails. Her interests expanded over time to include the emerging women's movement and then to documenting Jewish women around the world, in places like Russia and Ethiopia. Joanie had never been someone to step out of her house alone. Now she was traveling the world. We were among the few Detroiters I knew at that time who made it out of the security zone we had been born in. Her friend Gloria Steinem celebrated her in a recent documentary devoted to her career. I feel nothing but pride.

My dad's brother Harold lived in Cleveland with his wife Dorothy. She was the saintliest person in our family, until she died of cancer when her kids were small. It was a tragic absence for all of us. I wonder how much saner our lives would have been if she had lived. Harold's family was bigger than life and full of strangeness, like the pet monkey he would bring to our house on Tracy Street. My mom was horrified. It climbed all over her beautiful curtains and nearly destroyed our living room. At age five, Harold's son, my cousin Larry, drove his dad's car straight through the garage and into the middle of the kitchen, and also once snuck into the giraffe cage at the local zoo. He soon had a gaggle of siblings, Cindy, Mickey and Greg. My outlier cousins. I was fascinated by them.

My mother had two sisters, Pearl and Esther. They all grew up in a large, comfortable home on Atkinson Street in a fashionable part of Detroit, but when the Depression hit, they were forced to move into smaller quarters in the northwest suburbs. The loss of wealth and stature was always a part of their story. Both sisters were married and had three children, all of whom were my constant playmates. Pearl and her husband Ben Sax lived two houses down the street from us. Esther and her husband Mike Rosenthal lived a few miles away. Mike died of cancer when I was eleven, days before my cousin Stuart's bar mitzvah. It hit everyone hard but also woke me up to the immediacy of manhood. Stuart had lost a father and become a man at the same time. Esther had to become the wage earner for the family and became the traveling salesman that Mike had been. It was a profound change of persona for her. I was proud of her ability to adapt to tragedy, but was confused by the cards life had dealt her, and became aware that it could happen to any of us at any time. We all grew closer as we welcomed her kids, Marilyn, Stuart and Ilyse, more fully into our lives. I saw them grow up fast. That's when I began to understand the full impact of family and community. My dad was a special hero here, and I was awed watching him become a surrogate dad to Esther's kids. I had never imagined that part of him.

Pearl's husband Ben was really dashing, the best-looking man in our family. I loved having him and my aunt Pearl living just houses away from ours. My cousins, Wendy, Betsy and Margy, were like sisters, and we were always together. There was no ringing of doorbells in our family – we just walked in and out of each other's homes. Then, one dramatic day, Pearl and Ben announced they were moving from our cozy Detroit neighborhood to Beverly Hills with another couple, close friends of our families. Watching the three sisters, Sondra, Pearl and Esther, crying on the porch steps in front of Pearl's house saying goodbye, cut a hole in my heart. I was learning about sadness and loss and their overwhelming power to shape a life. With no more cousins appearing in the kitchen to say hi, their departure emptied our day-to-day lives. It was an incomprehensible loss. We eventually discovered that Ben and the other couple's wife, Dorothy, were having an affair that broke up the marriage and ravaged Pearl's life. The divorce became a family scandal. We children weren't allowed in the room when it was spoken of. In those days, divorce was a thing of shame in the Jewish community.

Our house was always the gathering space for the family, especially after my uncles were no longer part of our lives. We lined the extended dining table at my parents' house for birthdays, Passover, Thanksgiving, Christmas and Hannukah (we were very ecumenical). At my dad's 75th birthday, my cousin Stuart said that my dad had really married three women – my mom and her two sisters. There was some truth to that.

My brother Gary is three years younger than me. When he was born, my mom first introduced him to me as *my* brother. There was an immediate sense of ownership and possession, and I felt an implied need to serve as his caretaker along with my parents, a need that has never gone away. Not that he needed caretaking. He was expansive and joyful and made more friends than anyone I ever knew, and still has them to this day. He's had a fascinating life. His early years centered around the creation of Pioneer Recording Studios, on James Couzens Highway, not far from our house. His journey into that business started with a tape recorder I got for Christmas some years before, which he began using to record musicians in our basement. He graduated out of the basement as his business grew. Pioneer became a kind of back-up to Motown, and many notable recording figures produced records there. But in the end, it was Motown that took off as the defining Detroit studio. After several exciting years, Gary closed shop and joined my dad in the construction business, becoming a builder in Detroit. Years later he and his entire family, his wife Suzy and two kids, Shoshana and Jay, left Detroit and became our neighbors in Los Angeles.

My sister Marcy (later Marci) was born five years after Gary and eight years after me. Other than my mom, she was the first true love of my life. That has never changed. As kids, Gary and I became her protectors and though she married Alan Goldman, a Detroit surgeon, and moved to Atlanta, where she has five grown children, Gary and I still feel an abiding sense of being Marci's caretakers. Once, during a hard financial time for our dad, Gary and I pooled our own money and went downtown on the bus (an hour ride, but only ten cents each way) to buy additional Christmas gifts for Marci, since it was clear there wouldn't be much for her to open on Christmas morning and we didn't want her to go without.

In many ways I was a prime mover among the kids in the family and friends on the block. I was good at inventing games and things to do, an early indicator of a certain creativity to come. We often had afternoons, long summer days and weekends of highly orchestrated play, with me calling the shots. We built a stage in our basement to put on plays, drew elaborate drawings and mazes on the driveway, spent time on the garage roof overlooking our neighborhood, and donned capes like Superman to jump off the porch railings. If we ever ran out of distractions or something exciting to do, my mom would pile us into the car and say, "Let's go get lost." We would drive into the hinterlands surrounding Detroit until we were worried that we might never see home again, then begin the joyful journey back into the realm of the increasingly familiar.

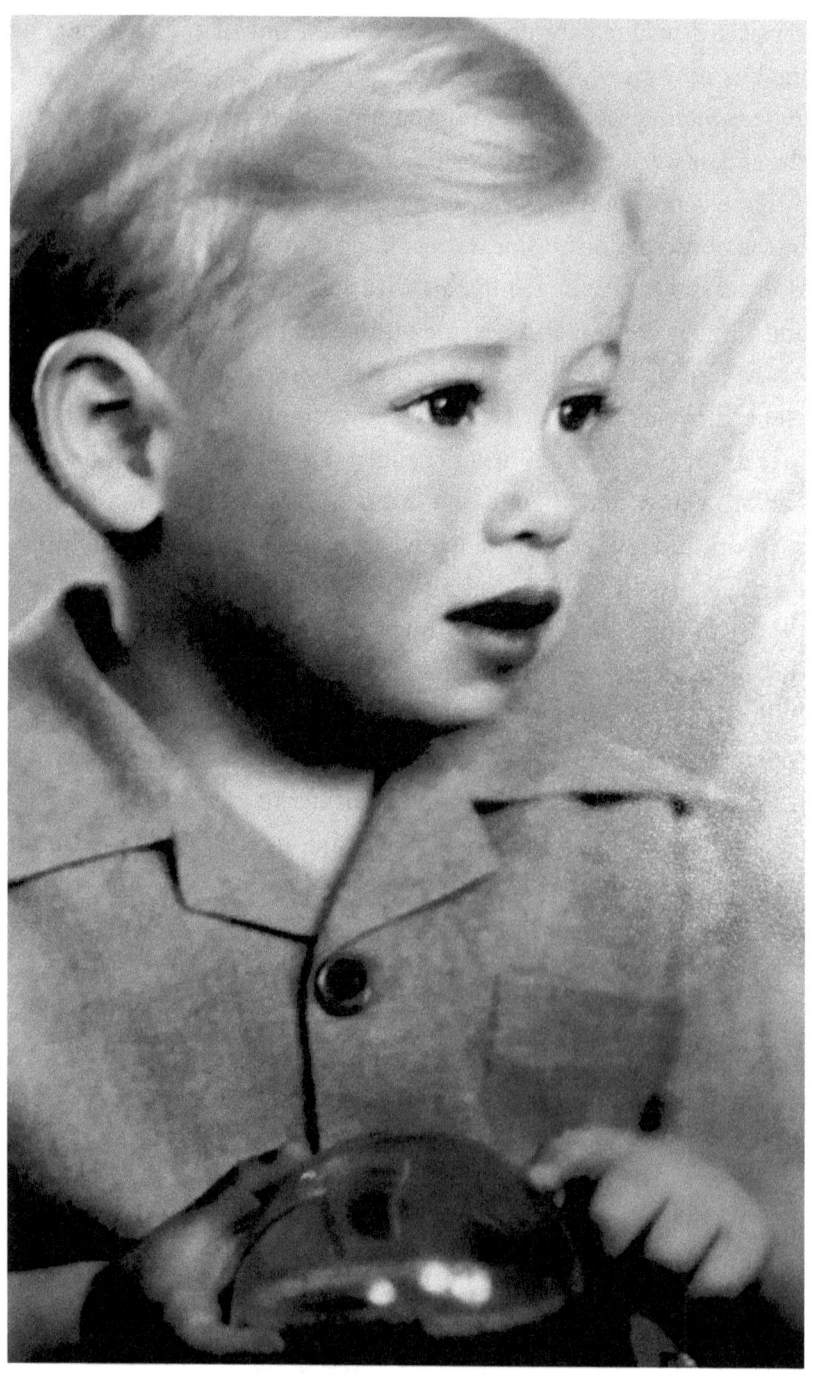

In the end, it was my mom who was my main inspiration. She knew and loved me to the core, and I was devoted to her. Among many qualities, she was stunningly beautiful and attracted boatloads of friends and admirers. One year, when I was working in summer stock, I introduced her to Tony Randall, who told me that she was the most beautiful woman he had ever met – and that he had been in a movie with Marilyn Monroe. My mom enjoyed that. When the play *Auntie Mame* was appearing at the Shubert Theatre downtown, she let me skip school so I could go with her to see it. She was, in a sense, *my* Auntie Mame. The beating heart of our entire family, both immediate and extended, she was also the only person I could really talk to in my life. There was little judgment. I know she was pained when I put on weight as an eight-year-old, and she would tell me how often her girlfriends said how handsome I would be if I were thinner, but her love of sweets, including the candy she hid around the house, didn't inspire me to lose weight. Her love of theater was infectious and her involvement in our local theater became my introduction to a world that would define me. Helping her learn lines was one of my happiest childhood experiences. She was an effervescent glow that illuminated every stage of my life.

As I consider the impact of my parents, I have to acknowledge that my dad was always taken for granted. He supported and loved us, but didn't really know us. I suspect it began with not knowing himself. He wasn't a curious man. He loved cars, gadgets and my mom. I think he felt he had won the jackpot with her, and in a sense he had. I could always tell how much he loved her and how lucky he felt that she had married him. He was a beneficiary of everything she brought into our lives, and he seemed appreciative of it all. But mostly he was a background character to my life. He was a good guy, well intentioned, but a bit of a Willy Loman. I would have had trouble writing a movie about him. If I were a better writer, I might have found a more profound voice for him in this book. As much as he would have liked it, he wasn't a star. My mom was the central character. He married the star.

In a defining way, my dad wasn't a great provider, but he always did the best he could. Money was always an issue with him. The first play I wrote in elementary school, *Bills! Bills! Bills!*, was inspired by his financial angst. His biggest dream was to find money lying around. In later years I would watch him stoop down to pick coins up off the ground, and to this day when I see change on the ground, it feels like a way of connecting with him. Sometimes, when I'm missing him, I bend down to pick it up. My brother and sister do, too. It's our childlike way of honoring him.

Two

Blinking – Early Moments

I remember playing in a sandbox with my cousin Wendy in an empty lot next to her house. I was about four years old. Suddenly I became aware that the sky had turned completely black, even though it was the middle of the day. I looked up into the dark nighttime sky and saw what looked like thousands of multicolored pinwheels spinning around me. Then I realized that I wasn't seeing the wheels but that the top of my head was completely gone. The dome of the sky had replaced the entire top of my head. The planets, the Milky Way, all the galaxies were spinning in the absence of my brain and skull. There was no separation. I was the totality, the whole universe. The experience was so big, so simple and so obvious that it barely registered. I kind of nodded my head. A moment later I was back in my body, playing in the sandbox.

When I was five, I went to the hospital for a tonsillectomy. In those days they did tonsillectomies *en masse*, so I started out in a room with fifteen or twenty other kids. I had never been separated from my parents before and had no idea what was happening. The doctors said they were going to put me to sleep and then do something that would hurt a little and I was going to wake up with a sore throat. They said that when it was all done, I could have some ice cream. The nurse asked, "What kind of ice cream do you like?" I said, "Chocolate." "Well," she said, "when you come out of this, you'll have some chocolate ice cream." They took me into an operating room and put a mask over my nose. It was filling with ether, which was the most noxious odor I had ever experienced. I gagged. I fought. I tried to get away from it. Then I was asleep.

I woke up with the most horrible pain in my throat. I was miserable but satisfied with the fact that at least I had chocolate ice cream coming. And then I looked down, and in front of me was a dish filled with strawberry ice cream. "Sorry, sweetheart," said the nurse. "That's all we have."

I was suddenly filled with a sense of betrayal. I sensed that life as it had been presented to me up to that point was dishonest and that it was going to disappoint me in a big way. Up to that moment, I had been a trustful person. I was now becoming someone else. I knew I couldn't believe anyone.

The next morning, all the other kids were being picked up by their parents. One after another they went home, until there were only two kids left. I was one of them. And then I was alone. At that moment, I experienced a sense of isolation and uncertainty that was overwhelming. I felt terrified, completely abandoned, and wondered how I would survive alone in the world without my parents. After what seemed like hours, they showed up bearing gifts. But by this point such things were meaningless to me. That feeling of abandonment has never fully left me. At that moment I learned to start fighting against a terror of aloneness and all the emotions that come with it. I had to learn to embrace solitude and accept the truth that everything – family, friends, community, a sense of connectivity – can be taken away.

One day when we were riding in the car, my dad pulled over because he saw a crowd of people gathered on the side of the road. He grabbed my hand and we got out to see what was going on. My eyes fixated on a little girl, about my age, lying on the ground not far from an empty car that had swerved onto the sidewalk. Her body was covered with a wool blanket. Splotches of bright red blood were seeping through it. It was clear to me that she was dying. The adults around her seemed horrified and helpless. People were standing around, hovering over her, but no one was comforting her. I couldn't remove my eyes from the fear and confusion radiating from her face. My first experience of mortality.

The idea that someone my age could die was shocking to me. I didn't really understand what had happened to this girl, but it was obvious that she was suffering. She seemed shockingly alone. At least, that's how I remember it. I was distraught. I realized, for the first time, that no one, not one of us, was safe. From that day forward, I couldn't understand why no one ever talked about the fact that we're all going to die. It seemed to me like the one inescapable thing in life – but nobody ever addressed it. Everybody was busy trying to make money and have a good time. To me, it was hauntingly clear that everything was temporary. *Don't they get it?* I kept thinking.

My parents weren't particularly religious. In the Reformed Jewish tradition, people often experience religion only on High Holy Days. We had Passover meals that were comforting and embracing, but I never much liked going to temple. I found it dry and boring. It seemed mostly about people parading their status, their latest fashions. My mom always commented on what so-and-so was wearing. But my parents still sent me to Sunday School, and at first I hated that too. I used to pretend I was sick or hide under my bed to try to get out of going. But when I did go, I was really taken with it, especially the stories. An entire sea parts so that a chosen people can walk through it. A bush burns but is not consumed. The rational mind hears these things and says, "Really? That can happen?" It's hard to accept, so what follows, for most people anyway, is a form of belief. I suspect we develop faith in these things because our ancestors lived and died for these stories. We believe them because we heard them from our parents, who heard them from their parents, and so on. That gives these stories real weight and significance. And the more faith we have in them, the more secure we feel in life. Stories have a grounding effect. I could feel that. I loved stories. But I didn't believe them.

I began to realize that every one of us has our own story, which we start putting together very early in life. Your parents give you a name, and you identify with that name. You begin to identify with a body that works or doesn't work in particular ways. Your friends tell you who you are. Your teachers tell you who you are. You get an A+ on this paper and a D- on that paper, and suddenly you're brilliant in one way and not brilliant in another. People accept you. People reject you. All these experiences become linked together, and the story gets bigger and bigger until you're seeing everything through the lens of that story. Your story becomes your identity. Mostly it's a story other people tell you. But soon we're creating our own.

When I was five, my next-door neighbor, a young boy, also five, took me up to the attic of his house. He told me to take off my shirt and then tied me up in a chair with some rope. I was intrigued. It was like being in a cowboy movie. When he wouldn't untie me, I got scared and cried. He smiled. Eventually I made my way downstairs to his very surprised mom, who undid the knots. I went home crying, but something about the experience took hold – a strange, sexual kind of identity. I had no idea what to make of it, but it was the beginning of an undercurrent in my life. That was the birth of my hidden stories, of stories *not* told. I became aware

of dimensions of my own narrative and our collective narrative. I sensed that this was something private, not to be shared or talked about.

Sometime later, I was playing in my cousin Wendy's basement. There were toys everywhere. I asked her and her sisters, Betsy and Margy, to pile all the toys on top of me as I lay on the couch. They thought it was funny. I pulled down my pants under the toys and began playing with myself, masturbating before I knew what that was. Suddenly I heard my Aunt Pearl coming down the basement stairs. "What's going on?" she yelled. "What do you think you're doing?" The girls kept laughing, but I felt the first surge of true judgment and shame and suffering I had ever known. Pearl didn't let up on condemning what I thought was innocent play. I was clearly a sick person. Something was terribly wrong with me. I had been discovered and would forever be shunned and abandoned by the world. My worst fears – being perceived as less than human – were inserting themselves into the core structure of my being. I began to sense the dark layers of my own story and the complexity of all our lives, although it wasn't so easily articulated at that time. I mostly fought to bury it away. Even writing it here is a source of old pain. Some things are hard to erase.

At the age of eight, I came down with a huge fever. The mercury went to the top of the thermometer, topping out at 108 degrees. My mom called the doctor and asked if they should take me to the hospital. The doctor said that with a fever so high I wouldn't survive the ride. He told my parents to put me in a tub full of cold water, get ice cubes from every neighbor, and put as much ice into the water as the tub would hold. I was already shivering from my fever, but the ice water and cubes put me over the edge. I couldn't stop shaking and only wanted to jump out of the tub. I felt naked, exposed and terrified. The bathroom was filled with people arriving with more ice, and finally the doctor appeared. I discovered that if I didn't move, I could begin to accommodate the cold, but the doctor constantly reached into the tub to stir it up. It was horrifying. I spent hours in that tub, many of them in an altered state. Was this really happening? Was I going to die? Eventually the thermometer began to go down and my temperature gradually returned to normal. I was put back into my pajamas and my mom and dad sat beside me on my bed. They were in tears the whole time. The drama of a near-death experience registered more for them than for me. All I could think was that I never wanted to be so cold again. I've had a fear of cold weather ever since. What I didn't know was that I also had a really good scene for *Jacob's Ladder*, a movie I would write decades later.

Three

Glancing – Vernor Elementary

On reflection, one of the defining moments of my childhood was a demonstration of my power, my capacity, to *believe*. I had heard that when you wish upon a star, your dreams come true. I decided to test that theorem in first grade by wishing for a circus to appear in my backyard the following morning. "Star light, star bright, first star I see tonight, I wish I may, I wish I might, have the wish I wish tonight." I went to bed so excited I could barely sleep. When I woke up and ran to my bedroom porch overlooking the backyard, I was disappointed to see nothing there. I wondered what I had done wrong. And then it hit me. By wishing for the circus to be there in the morning, I hadn't given the circus people enough time to set it all up.

The following night I wished again, but this time for the circus to appear when I got home from school. So completely did I believe it would show up in my backyard that I announced to my entire class that they should all come visit after school to see it. We had a substitute teacher that day. She innocently asked me to write my address on the blackboard, and the kids were told to copy it into their notebooks. I never ran home so fast, my heart pounding with excitement. Of course, the empty backyard sent me into a state of deep despair, amplified by the fact that fifteen of my classmates appeared with their moms all wondering where the circus was. My mother was clueless to explain to those who gathered what had happened – as was I. I disappeared into my bedroom. Nothing I could say helped my mother understand how this huge assembly had come about. All I know is that I lost all faith in wishing that day and in any pronouncements of magical thinking. That can be a hard lesson when you're small. As I recall, Santa fell by the wayside shortly after.

At summer day camp that same year, the counselors said to all the kids, "Okay, everyone who wants to catch frogs, go down the hill. And everyone who wants to be in a pageant, run up the hill." I wanted to catch frogs, so I ran up the hill – which is typical of me: not following directions. When I got to the top of the hill, I said, "I want to catch frogs." And they said, "Sorry, honey, you ran the wrong way. And you can't go back down by yourself, so you're going to have to be in the pageant."

We started practicing for the pageant, which was basically just a bunch of kids walking in a circle holding flags. I wasn't happy. Two days later our parents came to see us perform. As we started walking around with our flags, I became aware that the parents were paying very close attention to us and radiating a sense of love and pride I hadn't experienced before. I felt engaged. I felt excited, like I knew who I was. And that was when I realized I wanted to be an entertainer. I wanted to be in show biz.

That fall, my Aunt Pearl took me to see my very first play. I remember sitting in the auditorium at Cooley High School in Detroit, staring at this huge proscenium arch in front of a firewall painted to look like cement, and wondering why every seat was facing such a big imposing wall. I had never been to a play, so I was in a state of wonder and confusion. *What is this? What are we doing here?* After about five minutes, that huge firewall started to move. I had never seen anything like it. It rose up, up, up and disappeared, revealing a gorgeous purple velour curtain. The magic of a solid wall moving was almost more than I could handle. But to discover a purple curtain behind it made absolutely no sense. Then the curtain became flooded with light. It was overwhelming. The world of solid form was changing before my eyes. I surrendered to the magic. Then the lights went down and we were in pure darkness. I could barely breathe. Slowly, the curtain parted, opening onto a brilliantly lit stage. And what did I see at the center of the stage? My mother and two little kids.

My mother was playing Mrs. Banks in *Mary Poppins*, and the children were the Banks children. I began hitting the chair in front of me and saying, "That's my mother! That's my mother!" My aunt had to pull me back. Then I started asking her, "*Why* is my mother on that stage?" I was told, "Shh!" I kept watching, and as I watched, she became someone else. She transformed into Mrs. Banks, and I watched her carrying on this relationship with these two little kids, who were only slightly older than I was. It was like they were her *other* children. I didn't know she had any other children, besides my brother and me. And the young boy on stage was very handsome. When the play was over, I went backstage and met the kids. I felt like I was meeting my own brother and sister. And I was in awe of them. I wanted to be them. I wanted to be loved by them.

Another formative moment of my early childhood occurred not long after seeing my first play. My parents took me to see my first movie, at the Michigan Theater, one of the most beautiful theaters in downtown Detroit (today a parking garage). The movie was *The Al Jolson Story* starring Larry Parks, which I watched as an out-of-body experience. There was no separation between me and the screen. I was transported, living in that world. I *became* Al Jolson, singing "Swanee" and crying through "Danny Boy." When the film was over and it was time to go, I absolutely refused to leave. I clung to the chair, demanding to stay and see it again. It turns out there was another showing, and my parents reluctantly settled in so I could watch it twice. I now had a full-blown love affair with both theater and film. I wanted to be on stage, and I wanted to be in movies. The only question was how to make that happen. Remembering that my grandma's first cousin was married to Al Warner made me feel that I was somehow connected to Hollywood, that I had direct access, and I could one day be an actor up on the screen. I felt empowered.

One day a band from the local firehouse performed at my elementary school. I was impressed. The entire time I watched them play I was thinking about how I could get them a contract at Warner Bros. I wanted to be a deal broker. I wanted the power to make things happen. I wanted that advantage. I felt driven to stand apart from the crowd, and couldn't accept that I was just another Detroiter. There was nothing I could do, of course, no one I could call. In the end I *was* just another kid destined for mediocrity. The only thing that kept me going was a desire to be recognized, to be set apart, to be special. Besides performing plays for the captive audience of my relatives, I discovered that I liked to write poetry. None of it was any good, but my mom celebrated my efforts, effusing over every poem and reading them to her sisters over the phone. I would sit beside her and bask in the predictable reactions as my aunts raved about my talent. Those reactions had a programmable effect on my psyche and drove me to think of myself as a creative being, for whom there could be recognition and something approaching love for his efforts. It seems like a shoddy way to motivate a child, but encouragement and praise are powerful forces in shaping the human mind.

As a child, I began writing plays for us kids to perform in the basement. We even had a stage that my dad built out of 4'x8' plywood, with a curtain made from a sheet that hung on a clothing line. I would write plays or make them up on the spot, engage my cousins as actors, then demand that assembled relatives come down to the basement at the end of the evening to see our performance. I remember copying *Bills! Bills! Bills!* by hand and hoping to perform it at school, but Mrs. Bruner, the auditorium teacher, didn't see it as worthy of a school production. I hoped she would live to regret it.

I loved attending Vernor Elementary, which was named after the creator of a popular soft drink in Detroit. We were served cups of Vernors Ginger Ale every Christmas, along with candy canes. It seemed that we were the luckiest named school in the city. I was a fairly good student, a bit of a performer, and in love with my classmates. My first girlfriend, in second grade, Rona (born the same day as me and in the same hospital), remains a friend to this day. She was very proud of her grandfather, a member of Detroit's famous Purple Gang, a Jewish crime organization known for armed robbery, bootlegging, extortion and violence. I found it all fascinating and sensed that even villains could come from real families with nice people in them. Rona's presence in my life added a degree of color, a sense that life could have dark shadings and still be beautiful. Her divorced mother was glamourous, and her older brother Alan was amazingly handsome.

Another lifelong friend, Mark Greenberg, five days my senior and a mentor in many ways, figures mightily in my development as a human and socially conscious being. Because neither of us were athletes, we arranged to be on alternate sides during football games in elementary school so we could block each other, which also meant we could talk through the entire game while everyone scrambled around us. Mark was the one who convinced me to skip school for the first time. He always stopped at my house on the way, and we would walk the last two blocks together. One day, when we were running late, he suggested that since we were already in trouble, why not just skip the entire day? "If you're going to be executed for killing a lamb," he said, "you might as well kill a sheep." I don't know why I found that such good advice, but we had the best day ever, walking to the local mall, Northland Center, one of the first in America. Classmates saw that we were skipping school, and somehow it became a subject of conversation in class. In a funny way, we were celebrated for breaking the rules. I hadn't anticipated that reaction.

Mark and I became close friends. His mother Lona and father Lester were like second parents, and his sister Carol and Grandma Dora were my second family, along with all his aunts, uncles and cousins. A true expansion of my world at the time. We shared a group of friends all the way through the first years of college, and in many ways Mark influenced most of the important decisions of my childhood. He was fundamental in making me aware of the social/political world as we grew into teenagers together, encouraging me to campaign for Adlai Stevenson in 1956. We were just kids. One time Mark pulled me into the front row when Stevenson was speaking at a Labor Day rally in downtown Detroit. We were inches from the candidate. I could feel the power. I slept over at Mark's house every election night and twice watched Stevenson lose to Eisenhower. Mark was fascinated by Czarist Russia, and we both were taken with Nicholas II and the fall of his empire. When we were eleven, we watched a TV documentary called *Nightmare in Red*, about the Russian Revolution. The lifestyle and pageantry of the monarchy – all monarchies, really – was mesmerizing. While I aspired to one day own a castle in Scotland, Mark flirted seriously with Communism and tried to bring me along for the ride. By high school, his bedroom wall was festooned with political posters, and he spoke of revolution and transformation. But I didn't get it. I was a committed capitalist. Making money and getting famous were too high on my list to support a socialist revolution.

Politics exerted some kind of hold on me in the sense that, along with my parents, I was a Roosevelt Democrat and felt an underlying obligation to do something more than just talk the talk. I knew I had to stand up for other human beings, so I joined Mark

in the occasional political demonstration. As teenagers we marched together in front of Woolworths, trying to get them to integrate their Southern lunch counters, and later, following Castro's revolution, in support of Fair Play for Cuba. Mark loved Fidel and his battle to oust the notorious dictator, Fulgenicio Batista. For me, the capitalist, it wasn't hard to see the corruption of Batista's regime, and his overthrow seemed like an important step forward. It was like the Russian Revolution writ small, and much closer to home. Also, like the Russian Revolution, it was extraordinary to watch what appeared to be a noble and righteous battle – Fidel's ousting of Batista – transform itself into just another dictatorship. It was my first sense of how good and evil oscillated rhythmically throughout human history. I almost lost my college job doing publicity for the Cass Theater in downtown Detroit after the Fair Play for Cuba march. It turned out that a reporter had followed me from the march several blocks to the theater, then called my boss, Kenny Schwartz, and told him he had a communist working for him. Kenny didn't fire me. He just asked where I had been and said that my politics were my own business, and that I shouldn't bring them to the office.

Perhaps most heroically, when Mark and I were about sixteen, we were involved in a campaign to integrate Crystal Pool, a segregated public swimming pool on 8 Mile Road, close to our homes in northwest Detroit. With a long line of mostly black protesters behind us, Mark and I bought the first admissions to the pool at 9am to prove it was open for business. We changed into our bathing suits and jumped into the huge circular pool to swim. That was the signal for the protest to begin. The pool was shut down and the owners' sons dragged us from the water and forced us outside. We grabbed our clothes and joined the picket line.

When Mark and I were around twelve and walking to the Mercury, a movie theater that had been built by my grandpa Abe (I always felt his presence there, especially radiating from the glowing murals that lined the walls), I found myself in a confessional state. The conversation veered toward sex, and, feeling strangely open, I admitted being aroused by naked men. I had never told anyone before. Mark took it all in and then announced, "You know what you are? You're a 'homosexual.'" "A what?" I asked. He said it again. I had never heard the word "homosexual" before. "A homosexual is a man who loves men, who wants to sleep with men. They're outlaws. They go to jail. You're a homosexual. So was Tchaikovsky." I always knew I was different, or sensed I was, but I never knew there was a name for it. "Look it up," he told me. I couldn't continue the conversation, and we walked in silence the rest of the way. I only wish that Mark had told me then that he, too, was gay, something I wouldn't learn for ten years. It would have changed my life.

It took me weeks before I had the courage to check a dictionary. Just seeing the word sent shivers up my spine. I discovered I was abnormal, something "other," something less then human – an outlaw, a sick and despicable human being. I spent weeks processing the diagnosis and felt increasingly separated from the world by it. I experienced the horror of possible rejection, especially by family and friends. The loneliness was overwhelming. But then a phrase from Mark's statement began to reverberate: "So was Tchaikovsky." I loved Tchaikovsky. He made beautiful music, especially his violin concerto and the *1812 Overture*, which I would play endlessly at home. Somehow there was a saving grace, an unspoken connection between my sexual depravity and the world of music, art, even beauty. Maybe being different would let me see the world differently. This was an astounding realization for me. It became my only hope, my daily prayer. Maybe being different made you special.

One friend from that period, around the seventh grade, was a neighbor named Harvey. He lived down the block, just across from the school. His mother, who went to work every day, was the only working mother I knew. I don't remember how we met or became such close friends, but something drew us together. At some point we began having sleepovers and discovered that changing into our pajamas was a meaningful moment. Our nakedness aroused my earlier memories of being tied up by the boy next door. Interestingly, being naked with Harvey was never sexual. Mostly we played out various movie scenes, trying to get information from one another while tied up, naked, although usually it was me who was tied up. We would see how long I could keep from talking. We would go into my basement, where there was a small room that could be locked. Our code – "Do you want to do something?" – signaled a visit to the basement room. The sexual subtext was always present, but we didn't fully understand it. It was just forbidden play, an examination of dominance and submission, tiptoeing around sado-masochistic ceremonies.

This went on for about four years and might easily have morphed into true sexual engagement, but one day, when I was twelve or thirteen, my parents came home while Harvey and I were playing. That was the beginning of the darkest days of my life. My brother found me tied up in bed and alerted my mom and dad, who didn't know what to say or do. I quickly put on my clothes and Harvey ran home. He never came over again. I spent three days in my bedroom. I didn't eat or talk. The discovery was so painful and intimidating that I was suicidal. My parents were at a loss and frightened at my total speechless withdrawal. No one knew what to do or how to address the situation, until my mother devised a solution.

My Aunt Pearl and her kids were moving back from Los Angeles to Detroit, and my mom suggested that they could use someone to help them with the drive, packing and unpacking, carrying suitcases. I couldn't wait to go. Within days I was on a flight to LA and sitting next to a woman I was told was a famous movie star. Her name was Frances Langford. I had no idea who she was, but she mothered me the entire flight. It was the start of healing and a major turnaround in my life. Being with Pearl and my cousins was also a gift. They were almost as close to me as my own siblings, and their move to LA had been such a loss that their return represented healing on many profound levels.

After three weeks driving across the country, seeing Las Vegas for the first time, the Grand Canyon, the Petrified Forest, I was becoming a new person. We arrived in Detroit the night of a party my mom and dad were throwing in our backyard. The entire event was suddenly a celebration of our return. We were embraced with so much love and excitement that I remembered who I was and where I belonged. The power of family. My previous episodes with Harvey were never spoken of again, although my parents did arrange for me to see a therapist, who in many ways reformed my life journey. I learned about how openness and honesty released the deeper tensions of my long masquerade. I discovered the power of talking, sharing, speaking the truth, uncovering the hiddenness that had been lurking. It was transformative. My therapist accepted all of me, letting me know I was part of a much larger world, that being queer is no sin or abnormality, that it has been part of the human journey from the very beginning. He got me through high school.

After one session I stumbled into my cousin Wendy in the waiting room. Our therapist had no idea we were related, or he would never have booked us back-to-back. But it was, in fact, a great gift. We were surprised to see each other and became aware that we weren't alone, that our family wasn't a sacred ground of perfect beings, that there were oddballs, outsiders, like us. I didn't exactly come out to her there and then, but the depth of our newfound affection was unbreakable.

There were so many formative, defining moments for me at Vernor Elementary. I was drawn to the compartmentalization of knowledge and activity, the art and social studies, the library, gym, auditorium, shop, science, music and homeroom. I was comforted sensing that life followed a knowable and predictable formula, and that school defined it. All the educational elements wove into a lovely tapestry. I knew school was exploratory and that I couldn't excel at everything, but giving each subject space and time allowed me to witness myself, to know who I was. I felt at home.

My family wasn't well off, but well off enough. Some of the kids in my class didn't have many changes of clothing and I remember some of them getting very little for Christmas. I had an emotional reaction to their poverty and a sense of social inequality, but felt helpless around it. I saw some teachers mentally placing us into groups and hierarchies. The judgment upset me, but at the same time I knew I wanted to be on the higher end of the scale.

One teacher changed everything. His name was Eugene McCarty and I had him for half of sixth and all of seventh grade – an exceptionally long time with one teacher. He did many things that stood out, including introducing us to the larger world. We would start each homeroom class with fifteen minutes of discussion about global events. One day the conversation, about Joseph McCarthy and the probe of suspected communists, got so heated that he didn't interrupt it. Everyone in the class had so much to say. Everyone was passionate and well spoken. No one was afraid to raise their hand. Mr. McCarty made everyone equal. The passion was so strong that we skipped English, we skipped math, we skipped everything. We broke all the rules of homeroom, of school. I felt the liberation of dialogue, of sharing, of giving in to the energy of the moment. Mr. McCarty was treating us like adults. It was thrilling to see everyone having an opportunity to express themselves without judgment.

Mr. McCarty also introduced us to his passion, Greek and Roman mythology. We read Edith Hamilton's book, which began to elevate our sense of history as myth, as story. Whenever he said, "Okay, get out your Edith Hamilton," my heart fluttered. I loved the stories she fed into my life. I witnessed an ancient world as though it were still alive. I fell in love with stories. We read Norse myths, particularly *Heroes of the Kalevala*, which I strongly remember wanting to engage with in some way. I wanted to *dramatize* it. Mr. McCarty suggested that I turn it into a play and that the class could then read it as drama. I rose to the occasion. It was my first adaptation, although I mostly just copied the dialogue from the book and wrote it out in script form. I also brought a record to class, Tchaikovsky most likely, and played it over the early part of the reading. The moment the music started and the words were spoken, I felt the thrill of becoming a dramatist.

Another lesson from elementary school was running into a teacher of mine, Mrs. Sutton, at Hedge's Wigwam, a favorite family restaurant. I was around nine years old and was stunned to see her there. Amused, she said, "I bet you think that teachers are just hung up in the closet at night and left over the weekend, like coats, waiting to come out when the kids return. We're people too!" And it dawned on me that this *was* exactly how I felt. I never imagined my teachers as people with lives outside of school or the classroom. That moment opened my eyes to my own self-centered being. I have never looked at a teacher the same way since.

I had a recurring dream that my family moved into Vernor Elementary, that we lived in the homemaking room near the stoves and refrigerators and tables and counters, that we set up couches and beds and showers. I wanted to spend my life living there. I wanted to be so immersed in the school that all I had to do was walk out the door and my world of friends, endless knowledge and exploration were just steps away. Moving in never quite materialized, but, in the metaphoric sense, the idea of school being all around me, everywhere, has proven to be one of the deeper truths of my life.

Four

Looking – Mumford High

I barely remember ninth and tenth grade. I took Latin because Mark suggested it would be helpful in understanding other Romance languages, but, in fact, it didn't help me on any level at all. I moved on to French, which I loved but wasn't very good at. I mostly loved swim class because it was all boys, and we all swam naked. Whose idea was *that*? I also took a tumbling class, where we would topple all over one another and create pyramids. It's where I met a very handsome guy named Larry White. He was unaware of his looks and wasn't a great gymnast, but when we occasionally spoke, he was open, authentic and articulate. It wasn't until a year later and we were both in the Radio Broadcasters Guild that we began to dialogue. Mark was in the Guild, too, and a few other people – Gayle Pearl and Paula Brose among them.

Gayle was a tall girl with a beautiful face and an even more beautiful voice. In a sense I met her when she was sitting in the row behind me and I heard her speaking for the first time. Her voice was commanding and gentle at the same time. I was fond of her immediately. She was also brilliant and articulate. Paula was warm, full of laughter, and very smart. We became a strange and compelling group, outsiders whose only connection was strong and dramatic voices that sounded good on the radio. Our job, to give early morning greetings to the entire school, gave us, in our own minds, some celebrity. The five of us would gather to talk after school and consume plates of French fries and ketchup at Fredson's, the local deli on Wyoming Avenue, a few blocks from school.

The stereotypical view of high school students in the waning years of the Eisenhower administration was portrayed decades later in films like *American Graffiti* and *Grease*, and the television series *Happy Days*. But not every student graduating from high school in 1960 was interested in cruising, rock 'n' roll, cashmere sweaters and white buck shoes. In fact, in just about every urban high school in the country there were groups of kids like us who couldn't dribble basketballs or dance the Chicken. We weren't invited to pledge sororities or rush fraternities. (Yes, we had them, even in high school.) We were victims of a hidden class structure. We either lacked the looks, the parents, the money, or the cars to be granted admission to the "in" crowd.

Within this high school sub-culture, this mass of perpetual outsiders, we formed small protective circles of close friends. We were generally intelligent, possessed of a world view, and sensitive to the inequities of the prevailing social order. In other words, we were aberrations in the late 1950s high school environment. We read Camus and Sartre. We listened to the folk music of Pete Seeger and Theodore Bikel. We were card-carrying members of the NAACP. Some people in school referred to us as "beats," as in "deadbeats" or "beatniks," which later came into vogue, just before "dropouts" and "hippies" took hold of the culture. Fellow students who could pronounce the word called us "existentialists." The word "queer" was also used, although it wasn't clear if sexual innuendo was implied. "Non-conformist" described the more radical fringe elements, a group of diehards who still supported Adlai Stevenson over Jack Kennedy for the 1960 Democratic ticket. It was a major derogatory label, and Mark, Larry, Gayle, Paula and I were at the epicenter of this group.

And yet, by the time we graduated, we had somehow become the coolest kids in school. I don't know how it happened. We just joined the social and political clubs, worked on the school newspaper, and performed in school plays. We weren't afraid to be outspoken. We were becoming comfortable in our skins. And people took note. The world was changing around us. Social movements were erupting and to be engaged was meaningful. We were on the front lines of change. It was a great time to be "other."

Mumford, the name of our high school, was the only high school in Detroit, and I suspect in the world, painted pale blue and purple. You turned to look at it when you drove by. A lot of wonderful people graduated from its halls, but its claim to fame may be its contribution to the movie business. Filmmakers like Bob Shaye, the founder of New Line Cinema and the producer of *The Lord of the Rings* trilogy went there, as did Jerry Bruckheimer, who produced *Top Gun*, *Pirates of the Caribbean* and *Beverly Hills Cop*. Eddie Murphy wears a Mumford T-shirt in that movie.

When I was in tenth or eleventh grades, I started acting in school plays. I would also direct little plays for theater class. My high school had a 1,600-seat auditorium with a massive stage. It was bigger than the school gymnasium, and I loved it. That was my altar. The thing that got me most excited was standing on the stage in the afternoon when nobody was around – with one little light bulb shining down on me. I would do things like grab an A-frame ladder, pull it into the middle of the stage, and open it up to face hundreds of empty seats. I would climb the ladder and start talking, then climb down, walk around it, hug it, treating it as if it were a character. My instinct was to try to create something out of nothing. I didn't know how to do it, but the instinct to fill this huge empty space has been a strong motivating force in my life.

In the eleventh grade, Mark began writing for the school newspaper, *The Mumford Mercury*, and Larry, Gayle, Paula and I all joined the drama club. It was a unique kind of identity, a group of disconnected unathletic kids who found one another. We did plays like *Harvey* and *I Remember Mama*. Helaine, who played the nurse to my doctor character in *Harvey*, gradually joined our group and became my girlfriend for many years. She was vibrant and vivacious and made everyone laugh. Most of us found our love of theater spilling over into the weekends and we would make our way downtown to usher at one of the two (later three) theaters in Detroit – the Shubert, the Cass, and then the Riviera. We saw endless shows there and waited by the stage door to get autographs. Alfred Lunt and Lynne Fontanne were among the highlights. Their production of Friedrich Dürrenmatt's *The Visit* was a transformative theatrical moment. The other was O'Neill's *Long Day's Journey into Night*. I remember thinking that I had walked into the theater a boy and left as a man. I had looked directly into the truths of the human condition. (My first and only play to be on Broadway, *Ghost the Musical*, appeared at the Lunt-Fontanne Theater. That felt like a real blessing to me.)

Two other shows had a profound effect. When I was twelve my parents took me to see *The King and I*. I had been begging to go to the theater for years, but my mom kept saying that if she took me when I was too young, I would have nothing to look forward to. I endlessly disagreed with her. Seeing *The King and I* with my parents at the Shubert Theater was breathtaking. Watching the curtain rise on the ship approaching Bangkok and hearing the music swell from the orchestra pit, I was as smitten as I had been watching *The Jolson Story*. If they had performed the show again, I would have stayed. In some ways, I never left the theater after that night. It took hold of me that evening and has never loosened its grip. If I hadn't later been seduced by movies, I would never have left that magical world. The other theatrical experience that became a seismic shift for me, one I absolutely wasn't prepared for, was *West Side Story*. All of us were sobbing by "Somewhere." That song in particular captured all our dreams and fears. I didn't know a musical could do that. It was a hymn to my entire high school life.

When I was in tenth grade, Northland Playhouse, a summer stock theater at the shopping mall that Mark and I had visited when we skipped school, put up a notice: "Apprentices wanted." It had a huge theater, a massive geodesic dome designed by Buckminster Fuller, with five hundred seats. Gayle and I joined up, as did my old girlfriend Rona, who had ended up in a different high school. It was heaven to all be together. We got to run props, build sets, help with lighting and sound, and occasionally appear in the plays. During those years I worked with Gypsy Rose Lee, Tony Randall, Raymond Burr, Ramon Novarro, Betty White, Robert Goulet, Joan Fontaine, Ida Lupino, Howard Duff, Howard Keel, Walter Pidgeon, William Bendix, Susan Strasberg and James Garner. Michael Moriarty was a fellow apprentice. I would drive many of these actors around, have meals with them, even visit them years later in New York and Los Angeles. Working with so many movie stars gave me confidence that I might become part of that world. I didn't just want to be *close* to that universe, I wanted to be *in* it.

One relationship that evolved during my three summers at Northland Playhouse was with publicity agent Joseph Heidt, who for years worked with the Theatre Guild in New York. He was responsible for promoting many famous shows, but jokingly said that his claim to fame was adding the exclamation mark to *Oklahoma!* He had endless stories about the world of theater and his friendship with Rodgers and Hammerstein, most of them eye-opening, some quite shocking – especially those about his years with Eugene O'Neill and his wife Carlotta. Their marriage seemed as complicated and sad as was Joe's to his wife Joan, who separated from Joe while I was working for him. It was no wonder he was an alcoholic. We spent hours in bars talking late into the night. I was too young to drink, but not too young to see the many ways that the lives of accomplished and notable people could unfold. I soaked up every detail. Most of my theater illusions flew out the window, but the dramatic world Joe painted for me only grew more enticing. It became clear that being a publicist for Northland Playhouse in suburban Detroit wasn't where he had hoped to end up. When a job as the head of publicity opened up at the Fisher Theatre, the brightest and biggest new legit theater in Detroit, Joe was passed over for head publicist. I was supposed to pick him up one morning to take him to work, and when I couldn't get him to answer his hotel room door, a member of the staff let me in. I found Joe lying dead on the floor, surrounded by empty bottles of gin. I was devastated. The takeaway was indelible: a celebrated life in theater, in film, in the arts, wasn't a guaranteed doorway to joy. If anything, it was the opposite. I had thought I was on the path to certain happiness, but now wondered if such a thing existed at all.

A minor subplot to my time at Northland Playhouse was the men – famous movie and TV stars – who wanted to seduce me. I was so uncertain about my sexuality that I didn't know how to respond and was shaken up by the experience of being desired, especially by older men. My sexual identity was a source of terrible fear and depression. In my private moments I felt very alone, so *other*, with no one I could talk to except my therapist. Mostly, he kept me sane.

Around the age of sixteen, I woke up one morning and felt that something fundamental and essential was missing. Part of me, my childhood perhaps, had totally fallen away. It was a life-altering sensation. I was no longer the person I had been. The feeling of absence, of strangeness, of aloneness, was overwhelming.

I had felt whole as a child. I remembered having a joyful life, free of self-consciousness. Suddenly, without preparation or warning, I was alone, cut off, turned away from everything that had been. All my life, family had been a cocoon of comfort. I knew myself because I existed within that context. But that morning, age sixteen, something hit me. I realized that my parents weren't all that much older than I was and were only slightly ahead of me on life's strange journey. I was following people who actually had no idea where they were headed. It was totally shocking. It dawned on me that my mom and dad were no different from the kids around me who were struggling in school, and yet I had entrusted to them the direction and the choices of my life. They were figuring things out for the first time, too, just like me. They didn't have the answers. No one, including me, had the answers. I knew I was loved and cared for, but it no longer seemed enough.

I was a gay man in a straight world, and there was no one I could tell. Guys were beginning to get serious about girls, people were dating. Even our group of non-conformists started to branch out. I felt I had to lie, to go out with girls, to make out. I wasn't good at it. I was desperate to be like everyone else, yet I was like no one. I was looking to be accepted by others, but had no idea how to accept myself. Swimming class was really difficult. Like most teenagers my hormones were in full gear and swimming with naked teenage boys was a challenge. I still don't know how I kept from having a hard-on throughout high school.

Some teachers helped me assimilate. Miss Olmstead, an English teacher everyone revered, had an enormous impact on my sense of identity. Her class had all the smartest people in it – gifted, articulate, straight-A students, the intellectual elite of the school. Given that I was more of a B student, I wasn't quite sure how I ended up in that mix. I labored over one assignment she gave us, to write a short story. I thought it turned out well, but wasn't sure, and was terrified by what Miss Olmstead might think of it. A couple of days after we turned them in, she stood in front of the class and spoke about what it meant to be a good writer, to finds one's voice, to find the poetry of words, the clarity of good sentences. She seemed deeply critical and judgmental. As she spoke, I felt myself trying to disappear into my chair.

Then she started handing the stories back to us with grades that were clearly upsetting to people, at least judging by their reactions. I could barely breathe. For some reason mine was the last story, and she stopped before handing it over. "Now I want to read what a good story sounds like, what real writing can be. This story is by Bruce Rubin, and it's called *Daughter of the Moon*." I stopped breathing. As she read my story out loud to the entire class, everyone in the room was silent, entranced, admiring. I had never felt like that. I had never been *heard* like that. And when it was over, there were glances – of admiration and perhaps envy – from every corner of the room. That's the moment when I became a writer.

But that wasn't the end of Miss Olmstead's influence on my life. At one point I directed a scene from Bernard Shaw's *Caesar and Cleopatra* in that 1,600-seat high school auditorium. I also played the part of Caesar opposite Diane Stern's Cleopatra. I don't remember much about the production or even why I chose that scene to be staged, but afterward Miss Olmstead came up to me, and said, matter-of-factly, "You know, you're really a terrible actor, but a really good director." I never got past the words "terrible actor." It took me years before I registered her telling me I was a good director. I just knew I felt dismembered.

The thing that brought me back to creative life, to seeing myself as part of a creative world, was the discovery of film. One night some of our group went to see a movie we had been hearing about, by a relatively new filmmaker named Ingmar Bergman. It was called *Wild Strawberries* and was playing at the Krim, a movie theater I had never visited before. Most of the movies I had seen up to that point were showing at the local neighborhood theaters like the Royal, the Mercury, or occasionally the Varsity. As young kids we went to Saturday matinees to see movies like *Scaramouch* or *At Sword's Point*, or cowboy movies with Roy Rogers. Later we went to see Doris Day/Rock Hudson movies, which were diverting, but hardly compelling. *Wild Strawberries*, however, was staggering. My mouth hung open the whole time. It had a literary richness, depth, meaning. It was intellectually stimulating and visually dynamic. Ingmar Bergman became an exciting challenge for me. I started thinking, *I'm headed in the wrong direction. The future is movies.* I decided I wanted to study film instead of theater. The casual idea of "movies" exploded into clarifying words like "film" and "cinema." A new world had arrived. Even Hollywood changed for me. *On the Waterfront* was at my local movie house. I went downtown to see *The Bridge on the River Kwai*, *North by Northwest*, *Rear Window*, *Stalag 17*, and sought out other Bergman films like *The Seventh Seal* and *The Magician*. It was a wonderful awakening. I knew where I was headed.

When I was preparing to graduate high school, I was intimidated by the idea of walking across the stage to get my diploma and hearing only my family and small group of friends applaud, so I decided I would try out for class speaker. That way I was likely to be applauded and have at least the *appearance* of being loved and embraced by my fellow students. The graduating class was so large – 1,200 students – that we actually had four class speakers and divided the graduation ceremony in half, with two speakers at each ceremony. There was competition for the four slots, but I was determined to win one of them. And I did. I delivered a traditional, nicely written speech about how we all had to strive to be artists, to design, structure, color and create our own lives. It could have worked in any high school in America.

Speaking at my graduation became a moment of total wish fulfillment. I remember sitting onstage, just a few feet away from the school principal, Colonel Clark, and other dignitaries. When the Colonel got up to speak after my speech, he surprisingly singled me out as a representative of everything that was great about Mumford High School. He noted that I was president of the Drama Club, vice president of the Radio Broadcasters Guild, and a member of several other clubs that I had hoped would look good on college applications. I was floored by his remarks because I didn't sense that the principal had any idea who I was. My parents were proud. I couldn't help wondering how I had turned my fear of being unnoticed into that moment in the spotlight. I sensed that I had somehow engineered the moment myself, but also that there were other forces at work. I wondered if there was something else out there, some universal force, that arranged time and space to provide this moment of fulfillment for me. How did that happen? It seemed to me that something much greater than myself was involved on my behalf. Was I being singled out? Or does that "something greater" work for everyone? The search for the "what" and the "why" would become my greatest pursuit, even greater than the pursuit of a filmmaking career.

There is a footnote to my personal sense of accomplishment and temporary bliss. Some of my friends criticized me because my talk was so traditional, so generalized, and didn't reflect the politics of the moment, including the civil rights movement and other developments. It had never dawned on me to write that speech, to reflect the specific political drama of our time rather than offer polite generalities that are generally expected at a graduation address. I felt, in a sense, judged and diminished, as if I hadn't measured up to my peers. More interesting was that Richard Wishnetsky, another of the four speakers, *did* make that speech to the other session. He spoke with passion and outrage about the world around us and how we all had to make a difference.

I admired Richard's speech but struggled with his anger. I always liked Richard and felt that I was somehow not part of that elevated, politically awakened world. But there was more to his story that continues to haunt me. He belonged to Shaary Zedek, a conservative Detroit schul, where Morris Adler was the rabbi. Rabbi Adler had moved to Detroit in 1939 and my parents were the first couple he married there. I knew him personally. He and his wife Goldie and daughter Naomi lived across the hall from my Grandpa Abe for many years, and we would sometimes have the Passover seder in his apartment. Occasionally his family would visit our home. I adored them. One Friday evening, about four years after graduation, Richard Wishnetsky attended one of the Rabbi's services, stood up in the middle of it and made an angry speech of his own, calling the congregation an abomination and a travesty. Brandishing a gun, he shot Rabbi Adler in the head five times then killed himself in front of his parents. Our separate graduation pronouncements were about living a creative life versus a political one, and what actions our words and thoughts could lead to. Richard's actions ended two lives, unsettled a community, and rattled my world. Even today I look at underlying anger as it mixes with political action and fear the consequences. I love Hollywood because it offers us happy endings. But often, in real life, there are no such endings. It's simply over – gone.

I had been a heavy kid since I was eight. My mom discovered a pill (today we would call it a drug) called Dexedrine, which reduced appetite. I convinced her to give me some and then took it the summer after high school. My baby fat dropped away and I became a somewhat good-looking young man. My self-image was always of an overweight kid, but things were different now. The boy who was heading off to college looked nothing like the kid who had just left high school. I was a new person. I didn't know what to do with this new look. It opened doors emotionally and sexually that I was afraid to enter.

Five

Thinking – 678 West Warren

I applied to two colleges, Wayne State University in downtown Detroit and the University of Michigan at Ann Arbor, and was accepted to both. Larry had already been at Wayne for half a semester and Mark had decided to go there as well. Here, finally, was my opportunity to set out on my own, but nothing in me wanted to do that. U of M offered more prestige, but I was terrified of dorm life. I didn't know how to be a hidden gay person in that world. I felt safer driving down to Wayne every day, a 45-minute ride from my home, than being in a room with handsome men talking about getting laid every weekend. I didn't think I would survive that.

It wasn't an easy decision to make. Mark had begun to smoke, then so did I, quickly surpassing him, getting through four packs of Lucky Strikes every day. My parents were both smokers too – almost everybody was. I became so addicted that my first and last breath of the day often started with a cigarette. It was calming and satisfying, and ashtrays were a huge part of my life. I started with small 8mm film cans and ended up using bigger 16mm cans to hold all the debris I was creating. A gray haze of smoke followed me everywhere. But at least I was calm. Four years later, after a French class at NYU, I took my pack of cigarettes and threw it into a wastebasket as I walked out of the building. It was a totally unpremeditated act and I still have no idea what led me to do it. It just happened. Other than marijuana years later, I never smoked again. I was fascinated that life changes, even addictive behavior like smoking, could be enacted in such an instant. It suggested an inner power I didn't know I had.

In the middle of the summer before starting at Wayne, one of Mark's friends at the bookstore where he was working, Don Goldenbaum, announced that he wanted to move into an apartment on West Warren, close to Wayne, and wondered if Mark would move in with him. Mark was worried about the cost and asked if I wanted to join them. The offer terrified me. I wasn't someone who moved beyond the known and familiar. But then he asked Larry, who thought it was a great idea, and a third friend, Arnold Kessler, who also jumped at the prospect of apartment life. Arnold was Mark's closest political friend, a committed communist, but a Trotskyite opposed to Mark's Leninist leanings. They had endless political arguments, usually as I sat silently on the sidelines. I remember always wanting to say, "You're both wrong," but could never find the courage or argument that would derail their certainty. Arnold had gone to Cuba just after the Castro revolution, driven a tractor there, and was our main inspiration for marching in downtown Detroit on behalf of Castro. "Cuba si! Yanqui no!" was the chant that nearly got me fired from my publicity job at the Cass Theater. With Larry and Arnold on board, my interest in moving heightened.

My parents thought I was crazy and tried to persuade me to save money and live at home, but I felt safe moving in with people who had been my friends for years. Mark knew I was gay and never questioned me on the subject. I assumed he was straight since I walked in on him one evening in bed with Julie, a mutual friend of ours. I was shocked but happy that he was getting laid. He hadn't spent a lot of time with girls but did take Loretta, a beautiful black girl, to the school play I was in. I was awed by that. Mixed race

Thinking – 678 West Warren

dating didn't happen much in those days, and I was happy to see him live the talk. That was heroic to me. Larry and I talked about girls, but because I was dating and so was he, my sexuality wasn't a cause of concern. My girlfriend, Helaine, was a kind of decoy, although I hate to describe her like that. She was such a caring, life-giving person. I loved being with her. Like most girls of that time, she didn't believe in sex before marriage, which kind of saved me from having to disclose my secret self. I liked making out with her, so it wasn't hard to stay hidden. Besides, she went to Michigan State in Lansing and our time together was limited. More importantly, I really enjoyed her company, and, in truth, I even loved her. But whenever she announced that she loved me, I would always reply "ditto." I could never say "I love you" back. Decades later that exchange became a key ingredient in my film *Ghost*.

678 West Warren was two blocks from campus, three blocks from Detroit's cultural center (essentially the public library and art museum), and in the heart of one of the worst neighborhoods in the metropolitan area. For Mark, Arnold and Don, the move was an act of political consciousness, expressing a desire to escape from the bourgeois sensibilities of our parents and peers and to get closer to "the people." For Larry and me it was our first taste of freedom, our first flight from the nest, and our first exposure to life in the urban slum. The arrival of Jim Vaccaro, a pre-med student in need of a place to live, completed our takeover of two apartments on the upper floor of the building. My parents were horrified when they first saw the condition of the apartments. We had no shower, a ceiling that was falling down, and a linoleum floor that was coming up. The refrigerator was decorated in four colors of exotic mold and the stove appeared to have last been cleaned in the 1940s. My dad said that the bed he brought down for me to sleep on would never be allowed back in his house. I went home on weekends to enjoy the comforts of middle-class life. Larry decorated the apartment

with posters of France and was responsible for introducing us to Edith Piaf, whose inspirational "Non, je ne regrette rien" became a theme song of our year in the apartment and was often sung out loud at the dinner table.

It was with unexpected joy that I discovered that the mysterious church next to our apartment was, in fact, the university film studio. It felt like fate. I immediately applied for a job as a production assistant in the editing department. My first assignment in the glamorous world of movies didn't live up to expectations. It seems that while making a film about the university's basketball team, the sound equipment stopped working. My job was to record basketball dribbles at the university gym and add them to the soundtrack, one synchronized dribble at a time. The assignment lasted two agonizing months. It was my first experience of assembly line dehumanization, at only sixty cents an hour. Mark and Arnold were thrilled that I was beginning to sense the meaning of the word "exploitation."

I wasn't an especially good student at Wayne. I took German, although I don't know why. I was terrible at it. I'd had an occasional habit of writing answers to exams on the soles of my shoes, crossing my legs, and looking down at them during the tests. I had to be especially careful walking to classes not to step in mud or water. During a chemistry class in high school, Mr. Strepek, the teacher, interrupted an exam to say, "How inspiring it is to gaze across the room and see some of my worst students searching their soles for answers." There was a dead silence in the room, punctuated only by the sound of my foot crashing to the floor. Luckily it was the only time I was caught cheating, and my punishment never went further than his brilliant retort. I had figured I would never any use for

math or science, so cheating didn't matter, but out of some kind of karmic sensitivity, I never cheated again. The result of giving up crib sheets was that I nearly failed my German final exam and went back to studying French the next semester.

Two classes at Wayne were empowering. The first was an art appreciation class for juniors and seniors that I had to beg the professor to join. He was resistant to having a sophomore in his class, but I somehow persuaded him to let me attend. My analysis of El Greco's "View of Toledo" got me an A+ in the course, compliments from the professor, and an intuitive sense of the energy of a pictorial image that blossomed in my later years as a photographer. The other foundational course, one that changed my whole understanding of cinema, was film history. For the first time, I understood that American film was a rich mine of brilliant art, that there was more to it than the usual Saturday matinees. *Citizen Kane*, which I had never even heard of, became and remains among my favorite films. It may seem odd that I needed to go to a university to discover what had always been there, but in those days where else would I have seen such films? There were no venues in town that screened classic and "underground" movies. It was only in a university setting that I was able to discover the full range of filmmaking surging around me. It was there that I was introduced to Fellini's *La Strada*, Kurosawa's *Rashomon*, and the work of a host of other filmmakers that further cemented my desire to follow in their footsteps.

Sometime after leaving 678 West Warren, I wrote a movie treatment that attempted to capture the essence of that year and some of the prevailing joy that suffused my life at the time. I had no idea what a treatment was, so it had no structure to speak of and failed to ignite anyone's interest in hiring me to write it, but after uncovering it while writing this book, it seems appropriate to include an extract here. It depicts the first Marxist meeting in

Mark's apartment across the hall from Larry and me, and typifies the confrontations that occurred when the dictates of a proletarian life began to collide with our bourgeois origins.

Many people are filing up the rickety stairs to Mark's third floor apartment. Bruce hears their feet from his apartment across the hall, the unmistakable sound of army surplus boots. Suddenly there is a knock at his door. It's Mark asking to borrow some chairs. Bruce stares at him, groggy-eyed.

"Are you crazy? It's Sunday morning."

"It's the meeting. I thought you were coming," Mark answers.

"The meeting?" Bruce glances at the scruffy beards filing into Mark's doorway. "Oh, yeah, the meeting. Goddamn, why can't Marxists teach their courses in the afternoon like normal people?"

"Can I borrow the chairs?" Mark asks again.

"Chairs? Oh yeah, sure. Take all you want. I'm just gonna get dressed. I'll be over soon."

"Better hurry. It's getting crowded," Mark tells him as he commandeers men in army fatigues to help him with the chairs.

Larry is sound asleep in the dining area, which also serves as his bedroom. The sound of six men dragging chairs from the room does not wake him. Bruce shakes him on the shoulder.

"Hey, Larry, the meeting's starting. Wake up. Come on, you said you didn't want to miss it."

But it's all to no avail. Nothing short of an atomic blast will wake him.

Bruce dresses quickly and then barges in on the lecture in the apartment across the hall. He wasn't prepared for it to be already underway. Everything stops as he tries to find a seat. The room is packed and there is no aisleway between the chairs. The only available seat is in the front of the room next to Mark. The lecturer holds out his hand and invites Bruce to sit there. The approach is impassable, and Bruce seems hesitant to try. The lecturer seems unwilling to continue until Bruce is sitting. Everyone glances at him, wondering if he will dare to make the trip. He does, and everybody in the room shifts to let him by. When he finally reaches the chair, he discovers that it was vacant for a reason. It's broken. Embarrassed and afraid to attempt a return trip, Bruce leans up against the wall and positions himself behind a tall floor lamp. The lecturer looks at him to see if it's all right to continue. Bruce nods, partly hidden by the lamp shade, giving him the go-ahead.

Although it's a sunny morning, the room appears dull and smoky. The reading lamp on the dining room table has been switched on and the lecturer seems almost lost in the shadow behind it. The room is quiet, like a morgue. The only sounds are the lecturer's soft voice and Don's bed squeaking rhythmically in the bedroom down the hall. Occasional squeals of pleasure punctuate the squeaks. All eyes migrate in that direction.

Suddenly the phone rings. The lecturer glances at it, disturbed. He continues speaking, pausing only for the rings. The boy sitting near the ringing can't find the phone and gives an awkward shrug. The phone is persistent. Finally, Mark calls out, instructing the boy to look in the bottom drawer. The boy tugs at the drawer, but it won't open.

"You have to kick it," Mark calls out, interrupting the lecturer.

The boy kicks it, but can't get it to budge. Several others get up to help him, but they seem to make it worse.

"Lightly," Mark says, demonstrating with his foot and kicking the girl next to him in the shin.

"Sorry."

"It's okay," she assures him.

The phone stops ringing. Everyone relaxes. Then it starts again. The lecturer looks annoyed. The team of young men kick the drawer lightly and suddenly it gives. One of them reaches in and grabs hold of the phone. By this time the lecturer is standing silently, watching.

"It's your mother," the boy calls out to Mark.

"My mother?" Marks says, turning bright red.

"You're Mark, aren't you?"

"Tell her I'll call her back."

"He'll call you back," he repeats. There is a pause. "She says she wants to talk to you. You haven't called her in a week."

"Tell her I'll call her back later." There is another pause. "She says you always say that and she's been waiting for a week without a word and do you want her to die an early death worrying about you walking around in this terrible neighborhood where God knows anything could happen and she would never know."

Mark shakes his head as the boy holds up the phone.

"I think you better take it," he says.

Mark looks apologetically at the lecturer and then confronts the mass of bodies between him and the phone. There is a communal groan as everyone in the room shifts to let him by. Mark takes the phone and answers it quietly while trying to carry it out of the room. He tugs at the cord, but it won't stretch. He covers the receiver and tries to dismiss his mother, but she won't let him off the phone. Mark is forced to give her a quick rundown on the week's events, to tell her what the dentist said, and to apologize for not sending a thank-you note to his Aunt Rita. The lecturer tries at first to talk over Mark's conversation but finally gives up. The group waits silently for him to finish. At long last he hangs up, says he's sorry, and promises it won't happen again. He nods for the lecturer to continue and the phone rings. Mark quickly lifts the receiver.

"Call back later!" he whispers angrily and hangs up.

The lecturer smiles politely and goes on with his reading. He has completed no more than two sentences from *Das Capital* when the phone rings once more. Mark lunges at it.

"What do you want?" he yells angrily. "Who is this?' There is a brief pause.

"He's sleeping. He'll call you back later."

There is a loud voice at the other end that projects loudly into the room. Mark lets go of the receiver.

"Damn it!" he says, as he storms down the hall to Don's room. The bed is still squeaking but stops abruptly when he knocks. Don and a young lady are disentangling themselves as Mark barges in.

"There's a call for you, he says emphatically. "They said it's important.

"Tell 'em I'll call back."

"*You* tell 'em," Mark says angrily as he marches out of the room.

The lecturer has started up again when Mark returns. He squeezes past the phone and takes a position standing in the far corner. Don appears, moments later, stark naked. Needless to say, he is surprised by the crowd in his living room, but they seem far more surprised by him. The lecturer's mouth drops open.

"Oh Jesus!" someone says as they glance out the window. "FBI!"

Several suited FBI men are on the sidewalk photographing license plates of cars parked on the street. A camera can be seen in the window of the building across the street aimed right at them. The man at the window slams it shut and draws the blinds as the room erupts in a frenzy.

"Where's the back door?" someone calls out, and before anyone has time to answer, people are rushing toward it. The lecturer is among the first to vacate the premises and seems skilled at this type of exit. Others are more clumsy. Within moments the apartment is vacant. Only Mark and Don, still naked, remain.

"Some party," Don says.

That was life at 678 West Warren. I still think it would make a fun movie, but without a Marvel comic hero coming through the window to save the day, I don't know if anyone would make it.

The second year at Wayne State, Mark and I moved back home. Don was told that if he stayed in an apartment filled with communists, his father, who worked for NASA, could lose his job. Jim got another apartment and Larry decided to take a year off and go to Paris and Israel. He invited me and Mark to join him, but we didn't have the money or motivation. The truth is, I was scared. Leaving home, leaving Detroit, was a terrifying prospect. I was afraid of the world. Larry took a menial summer job at Trojan Lake Lodge in upstate New York to earn enough money for the trip. I was awed by his courage. I went back to Northland Playhouse for my final summer there and Mark went back to working at the bookstore. Old high school patterns returned. I was going backwards.

Our sophomore year at Wayne was awful and lonely. I took two of my classes over the radio, so was rarely on campus. Larry wrote wonderful letters from Europe and I kept wishing I'd had the courage to join him. In reality, as I found out later, he wasn't having a very good time. He ran out of money and ended up living on a kibbutz in Israel because he was broke and didn't know where else to go. The film *Exodus* had just come out, and the theme music brought me to tears thinking of Larry's bold adventure. Little did I know how unhappy he was. It was at this time that Mark announced that he had decided to go to the University of California in Berkeley. The announcement took me by surprise and changed the trajectory of my life. I was devastated, terrified of being alone in Detroit. I didn't know what to do. There was a strong pull to stay in safe and familiar territory. Helaine and I had finally had the conversation where I told her I was gay. She said I could get that fixed and was determined that we could make a life of it. I wanted to believe her. I loved that she thought it was possible, but I didn't think so. The more I mulled the decision, the more tempted I felt to look for a new beginning.

What I wanted more than anything, if I was to leave home, was to go to film school. There were four that attracted me: IDHEC in Paris (but I would have had to speak fluent French), USC and UCLA in Southern California, and NYU in New York. I had been to New York twice by that point. I once drove from Detroit with Mark and his parents to visit his Aunt Rita and Uncle Jay. We both stayed at the YMCA on 34th Street, where a guy tried to pick Mark up in the shower, something he seemed proud of. I was oddly jealous. No one had ever tried to pick me up, other than a few aging Hollywood actors long past their prime. All I ever wanted was to live in New York. Times Square was the center of the universe for me and had always been my dream, my destiny. I couldn't believe the joy, the fullness I felt standing below the statue of George M. Cohan. But it wasn't quite enough. I wanted to be "on" Broadway, not just standing in the middle of it. Later, our graduating class took a senior trip to D.C., but our group – Mark, Larry, Gayle, Paula and I – decided to go by ourselves to New York instead. We took the train and stayed at YMCAs and YWCAs and went to every play we could get tickets for. We usually ended up sitting at the back of the balcony or even standing, which was all we could afford. New York felt like it had been destined from the beginning. But at the same time, deciding between the East and West Coasts was a monumental decision. A new group of filmmakers was emerging. Had I decided on Los Angeles, I would have probably been in classes with George Lucas and Walter Murch. As it turns out, I chose New York, and ended up in classes with Brian De Palma and Martin Scorsese.

Six

Wondering – NYU

My parents drove me to New York. My dad had been born in Mineola, on Long Island, before the family moved to Detroit, and visiting his family there was a joy for him. One of his many cousins I had never met was a real estate agent who found me an apartment on 15th Street between Sixth and Seventh Avenue in Greenwich Village. It was a tiny, one-room, first-floor space, a short walk from Washington Square Park and NYU. I went shopping for furniture in New Jersey with my mom and dad, who had very little money to support my move, so the furniture was beyond basic. It was understood that I would try to find work to help pay for tuition and living expenses. That wasn't easy, but I managed to find a job at the Longines Wittnauer watch company on Fifth Avenue. My job was to process the inscriptions written on the back of watches for people who were retiring from what often sounded like fifty years in dead-end jobs. It was odd to be focusing on retirees when I was just starting out.

I entered NYU as a junior in 1962. I couldn't have cared less about the academic classes I had to take. I only wanted to be up on the eighth floor in the film department, which in those days was relatively small. The Tisch School of the Arts, with film as its centerpiece, was a few years away. When I arrived there were only a few dozen film students. Video technology wasn't yet on the scene. We used 16mm cameras and primitive Moviola editing machines.

New York itself was an explosion of possibilities. Everywhere I turned there was the revelation of new cinema. Truffaut had just made *The 400 Blows* and *Jules and Jim*, and Antonioni's *L'Avventura*, Fellini's *La Dolce Vita* and *8½* and David Lean's *Lawrence of Arabia* were new on the scene. I fell in love with *Ballad of a Soldier* by Grigory Chukhray. I could walk or take a subway to see any of them at the Bleecker Street Cinema, the Fifth Avenue Cinema, the Paris or the Thalia. But most exciting were my film classes and fellow students.

There were three who grabbed my attention from the get-go. One guy, the smartest dresser in the group, never to be seen without a sports jacket or suit, was named Marty Scorsese. He spoke faster than anyone I had ever met and with such clarity and constant laughter that it was a joy to be around him. He also seemed to know more about movies than anyone else alive. He could name every Hollywood movie ever made, along with its director, cinematographer, writer, editor, even the script coordinator. His passion was contagious. I felt lucky just to be in the same class with him. Marty and I became close. I would go with him to visit his mom in Little Italy, and I met many of his friends from the neighborhood, including Harvey Keitel and Dennis Hopper. The fact that nearly a quarter of a century later he and I would be nominated for Oscars the same year would never have crossed my mind.

Brian De Palma was another unforgettable classmate. He was a graduate of Sarah Lawrence College when it was an all-girls school. How he had pulled that off was both incomprehensible and admirable. It also seemed that he may have slept with half the student body, but separating fact from fiction with Brian was often hard. He was a big talker, a larger-than-life character, and something of a celebrity because he had already made an independent film called *Wotan's Wake*, which had been celebrated at Cinema 16, a downtown film club run by Amos Vogel, who later founded the New York Film Festival. Brian lived in a basement apartment at 65 Bank Street, which later became my home. The large bedroom that I moved into was furnished with a glorious oriental carpet that, rumor had it, Brian and his roommate Jared Martin had removed from the Columbia University library. The story was that they simply walked into the building, told people to move, pushed aside tables and chairs, rolled up the carpet, and carried it home. No one stopped them. I was awed by this story. Brian's celebrity and capacity for living on his own terms pushed a button in me, and I very much wanted to work with him.

The last essential person in my NYU days was a classmate named David Moscovitz. He didn't go on to have a Hollywood career, but he did become one of the most open, joyous, loving human beings I've known in this lifetime. David had written a script that got a lot of attention while we were in film school and I longed to talk to him about writing, to learn the game from him. We would go out to a local restaurant, the Waverly Diner on the corner of Sixth Avenue and Waverly Street, for lunch. Five hours later, in the same corner booth and still talking, we would order dinner. We talked about everything, from his childhood as one of the few Jews growing up in Jacksonville, Florida, to his family (his father was the editor of the *Southern Jewish Weekly*), his love of movies and his passion for writing. David's view of the world was eye-opening for me. I remember him looking out the window and marveling at the sight of "strange beings" walking up and down the street. I only saw everyday people. He didn't take our existence for granted and made me rethink my acceptance of the world as it appeared. He made everyday life seem odd and fascinating in ways I never imagined.

64 It's Only a Movie

Brian directed my first script at NYU. It was originally called *Hide and Seek*, although the title was later changed to *Jennifer*. I remember working on it day and night, smoking pack after pack of cigarettes. It was originally about a boy whose mother dies. He runs out of the hospital and ends up falling asleep in the doorway of what seems to be a deserted building. A young girl appears, awakens him, and invites him inside. It's a sweet fifteen-minute script about how she revives his spirit and brings him back to life. In the end, they play a game of hide and seek, but he never finds her. It seems questionable that she ever existed at all. Brian cast a young actor named Scott Gehman and a friend from Sarah Lawrence, Jennifer Salt, whose father, Waldo Salt, was a blacklisted Hollywood screenwriter who gained fame as the writer of John Schlesinger's *Midnight Cowboy* and Hal Ashby's *Coming Home*, both of which won him Oscars.

Brian shot the film in dilapidated buildings around SoHo and the East Village. It was such a fulfilling experience to see my words spoken, my images rendered on film. Looking back at the original script, all five pages of it, I'm struck by the writing, especially the dialogue, which had an emotional maturity I wouldn't have expected from that period. I don't remember whether I ever saw the finished film, but what happened to it was one of the most shocking experiences I ever had in the movie world, and, in a strange way, prepared me for the Hollywood years to come.

After having completed the film, Brian disappeared for a while. As I remember it, he was shot by a policeman while trying to get into a vacant building he was checking out as a location. He had a minor gunshot wound but managed to avoid prosecution. Nothing about the story surprised me. That was Brian. But what did surprise me was what happened next. Brian decided that the cut of the movie was too traditional, too predictable for him. He didn't like it. Without asking me, he took the negative, cut it into many disparate and dismembered pieces, then reassembled it, willy-nilly, out of any predictable order, except for the end. The result was an inexpressible mess. I understood his instinct to try and make the film into something more abstract, more contemporary, but what he did to my story seemed unforgivable. In the long run, the ego-crushing experience that I learned from Brian was important preparation for the kind of spiritual journey I embarked upon decades later. I worked with Brian for many years after that incident, so I guess I did forgive him at some point, but Haig Manoogian, the head of NYU's film school, who had loved my script, did not. He felt

Brian had behaved recklessly and thoughtlessly. Shortly afterward, Brian was no longer in the film program. My first movie was never screened or heard of again.

Disenchanted with my experience on *Jennifer*, I contemplated leaving film school, and connected with a group driving cross-country to California. I decided to go see Mark, and possibly Raymond Burr, star of the hit TV series *Perry Mason*, who I had worked with at Northland Playhouse and had once said he would be happy to help me get work in Hollywood. I think it was more of a seduction attempt than a real offer, but I had to start somewhere.

I started out in Berkeley, hoping to stay with Mark, but learned shortly after I arrived that he had come out as gay and didn't want anyone staying in his apartment. I wasn't as shocked by Mark's announcement as I was by how he and I could have been such close friends, and yet he hadn't shared the deepest parts of himself with me during our teenage years, even labeling me a homosexual years before. His awkward coming out didn't bring us closer together. Mark seemed transformed by his emergence, almost a different person. He exuded a confidence and happiness that had eluded him in his younger years. And he looked great. He was clearly emerging as a player in Berkeley. He encouraged me to come out too, but I remained closeted. I never felt I could be a player in the gay world, and mostly we didn't talk about it. The truth is that much of my gay side had a sadomasochistic aspect, going back to being tied up in a chair as a kid, and I never saw a path to that life. It was just too alien, even more than just being gay. I closed the door to that closet and remained alone and envious for years.

Mark's cousin, Bobby, had come to San Francisco with his friend Jim and offered me a bed at his place in the city when Mark's apartment became unavailable. I was annoyed with Mark, but Bobby was a good guy, an excellent photographer and a great roommate. It was lucky for me he was there. I was dirt poor and couldn't have afforded an apartment on my own. What I didn't expect was how cold San Francisco was. Mark Twain said that the coldest winter in his whole life was San Francisco in the summer. We heated the apartment using the gas stove in the early morning and I would climb on a stool to catch the heat from the upper burners as it rose up toward the ceiling. Then I went out in my short sleeve shirt, the only kind I had brought to sunny California, to get an open cable car to the end of Market Street, where I had a job selling cameras in a local camera store.

"Herr" Filgus, the German store manager, watched the sales counter from a window high above the main floor. If ever the salespeople touched the counter, he would call on the phone and yell at us to step back. "No touching!" He was scary. But he did teach me one thing that was worth the cold weeks I spent traveling to the job. He taught me how to sell. It was all very simple. He said that to sell a camera, you had to hold it like the Crown Jewels. You had to stroke the camera continually, as though it were the most precious thing in existence. While the customer watched, you had to present the camera to them, holding it out until they wanted to reach for it, then pulling it back, away from their grasp. This ballet would go on until the customer literally lunged to take hold of the camera. If you got to that moment, that lunge, Herr Filgus would tell us, you had a sale. And he was right. I sold several cameras in the two weeks I was there, and quit with the clear sense that I didn't want to be a camera salesman for the rest of my life, let alone another week. But the lesson of how to sell is still with me. Part of my success in Hollywood was a variation on that skill, pitching script ideas to executives in such a way that made them hunger for the story I was selling. I built a career on that.

I traveled down to Los Angeles, a horrible trip that would reorient my life and send me back to New York. I spent a day together with Raymond Burr at the *Perry Mason* studios, but he no longer seemed interested in me and said he couldn't get me a job. I visited Ida Lupino and Howard Duff, movie stars whom I had befriended during my Northland Playhouse days and who told me I should visit if I ever came to town. I called them and it turned out they were having a party, so I took a bus to their home in Westwood. I had anticipated a Hollywood mansion, but their home was a traditional bungalow. Ida and Howard were kind and loving but no longer in the mainstream of Hollywood life. I think I had hoped that they might help me find work, but they had nothing to offer other than kind words. My illusions were disintegrating. I was about to walk to the bus stop on Wilshire when one of the guests offered to drive me back to my rental not far from the Hollywood Bowl. He had worked as an editor on *Spartacus* and was without any of the arrogance I expected from people with a film credit like that. I began to see that my ideas about Hollywood had been shaped entirely by the movies, when in fact for many people doing their jobs and making a living, life there wasn't in the least bit glamorous.

I went with Larry, who was visiting LA, to Disneyland, and we talked about our lives, our futures, our uncertainties. The conversation turned into a close examination of all we had known and learned up to that moment. All I knew coming away from that visit, from being in California, from seeing Larry and Mark, was that friendship was everything – the most important gift in the world. I also realized that Hollywood wasn't waiting for me with open arms and that I had a lot more to learn. I headed back to film school.

Back in the classroom, we pitched ideas for films we wanted to direct. Mine was *A Frog Croaks at Twilight*, a dark fairy tale about a witch who lives in a garbage can. Using my camera sales technique, I successfully sold the class – including Professor Manoogian – on the story and was given my first shot at directing. Scorsese had a wonderful script he had written that he wanted to make called

What's a Nice Girl Like You Doing in a Place Like This?, about a guy obsessed with a picture of a boat on a lake. There was some doubt as to whether it would make the cut in class, where only seven scripts were chosen for production. I thought Marty was worried he would be passed over, which I felt would be a horrible injustice, so one night we decided – Marty and I and a fellow classmate named Bob Siegel – to drive out to Haig Manoogian's house in New Jersey and persuade him to let Marty direct his film. Bob drove and Marty and I strategized on how to deal with our teacher, who probably had never had anyone so directly interfere with his selection process.

Manoogian was surprised to see us at his door but somehow pleased at our initiative, and invited us into his home. I sensed that Marty wasn't fully ready for the battle, but I became totally and unexpectedly impassioned. I talked lovingly about how brilliant Marty was and how he knew more about motion pictures than anybody, and if anyone could make a movie, it was Marty. He jumped in and eloquently explained his story in such a way that no one could refuse him. Manoogian, clearly impressed, smiled and relented. And with that, Marty became a film director.

I moved into a new apartment on West 12th Street with a friend of Mark's cousin Bobby, a photographer named Barry Kaplan. He was two or three years younger than me and had no interest in going to college. Barry had just moved to New York from Detroit and needed a place to live. His additional rent money made it possible for us to get a one-bedroom apartment many steps up from the one I had before. Barry was an oddball guy, but endlessly fascinating and full of colorful adventures that he'd had with Salvador Dalí and LSD gurus Timothy Leary and Richard Alpert. Having him in the city added color and excitement to my early days in New York.

That semester at NYU, I directed *A Frog Croaks at Twilight*. The story begins in a little courtyard on Great Jones Street, where a witch who is desperate for love keeps a collection of frogs. At one point she appears suicidal, as if she's going to jump off the Brooklyn Bridge, but just before she jumps, a troll comes out from underneath the bridge. He looks at her and she looks at him, and it's pure Hollywood love. They're so happy to have found each other. They have a joyous day together – going to amusement parks, riding the roller coasters. Then she brings him back to her courtyard where they have dinner, and there's a slow buildup to their first kiss. As their lips touch there's a huge puff of smoke, and we see that he has turned into a frog. She adds him to her collection and goes back into her garbage can. At that moment we sense, with some horror, the total calculation of the day's events.

I was doing what's called the A-rolls and B-rolls, where the negative is prepared for printing in a lab. I was using a segment of blank negative to practice, but suddenly discovered that I had been practicing on the actual negative, and ruined the exact moment – the smoke, the explosion – where the witch and the troll kiss. I had footage right up to where their lips touched, but the smoke and explosion were lost. I was heartbroken. If there was one moment in the film that couldn't be replaced, that was it. There was no way to re-shoot it. I thought the world had come to an end. Everything I had worked for was gone. And then an idea came to me. I had the beginning of the kiss and the aftermath of the kiss, so I filled the space in between with clear film onto which I drew a heart exploding, then a flower with petals circling around it. It lasted about two seconds, 48 frames. And that became the highlight of the film – an explosion of hearts and flowers. I saved the film by applying a new level of creativity that arose out of the depths of inexperience and suffering. Transcendent creativity sometimes emerges when you need it most.

Shooting *A Frog Croaks at Twilight* had been traumatic. The actors liked being cast in a student film, but didn't feel all that responsible about showing up for the actual shooting. My student crew was also haphazard, and though friends offered to help, they often ended up having better things to do. Every day of production was a struggle. In the middle of the shoot, I was having lunch with my friend David Moscovitz, my cameraman on the film. We were in Greenwich Village and noticed that everyone was strangely quiet. We finally asked one of the owners what was going on. He looked at us as if we were crazy not to know. "The President's been shot," he said. We were dumbfounded. We went out into the street and headed toward Sheridan Square, which was full of people milling around. A newspaper bundle was thrown out of a truck, like in a Forties movie. "KENNEDY DEAD" screamed the headline in massive bold letters. History was unfolding around us. It was the saddest Thanksgiving of my life, of our collective lives. Two days later, Barry and I sat in our apartment, glued to the TV, and watched as Lee Harvey Oswald, being escorted out of the headquarters of the Dallas Police Department, was shot dead. I had never seen a man killed in front of my eyes before. The world was spinning.

I managed to finish my *Frog* film in time for the film festival that honored student work. The audience laughed and applauded hard. I was in my element. There were two awards given out that night for best student work, and I won one of them. Scorsese got the other, the top award, for *What's a Nice Girl Like You Doing in a Place Like This?* I was glad to be in such company.

That spring Larry came to visit and stayed with me. Seeing him lifted my spirits. I had missed our nonconformist group and felt a real longing for the connection of old friends. And Larry was one of my favorite people on the planet. One evening, rather seriously, he said he needed to tell me something. I was quiet and curious. We sat down and he looked at me for a long time without speaking. "I think I'm queer!" he said. It was a breathless moment. I had never suspected and hardly knew what to say in response. After a long pause I blurted out, "Me too." We both smiled and laughed. "I thought so," he said. I had been writing him letters about my sadness and depression in New York without ever naming its source. But he knew – or at least thought he did. The courage he found to come out to me was one of the great moments of both of our lives. I finally had a soulmate, someone I could share my deepest thoughts and fears with. And so did he. From that moment on I was able to breathe in a way I had never known before. I told him everything about my sexuality, the hidden secrets. I was out of the closet (at least to one friend). The lightness and openness I felt was liberating.

That was the summer of the 1964 New York World's Fair in Flushing, Long Island. I desperately needed a paying job, and Helaine's father, who for some reason was running some of the concessions there, offered me a position selling beer at a hot dog stand in the center of the sprawling fair grounds. I was a terrible employee. Even worse, I stole money from the concession. Profits were measured by how many empty beer cups we ended up with at the end of the day, so I reused the cups and sold a lot of beer to customers out of used containers. In the end, I added up how many cups we still had and how much money that would add up to, then pocketed the rest. That, and writing answers to exam questions on the soles of my shoes, are the two biggest karmic regrets of my life.

The best part of working at the World's Fair was the Johnson Wax Pavilion, a magical building that looked like a metal egg suspended in mid-air. The bottom dropped down with seats for several hundred people and then lifted them up into the egg. Inside was a huge wall that became three movie screens, like Cinerama (a three-screen movie process developed in the 1950s). A short, twenty-minute film appeared on the central screen and then, magically, expanded to all three. It was breathtaking to watch it fill the room. The film, *To Be Alive*, co-directed by Francis Thompson and Alexander Hammid, followed families from all over the world throughout one complete day. It ends with a celebratory montage and a simple spoken statement that brought me to tears each time I saw it: "To be alive is a wonderful thing." I watched *To Be Alive* every lunch break and cried every time.

Years later I worked with Francis for a few weeks, editing a film about the Cathedral at Chartres. When I told him how much his film had affected my life and how sad I was that I would never be able to see it again, he linked up three projectors and gave me a private screening in his New York office. As usual, I cried like a baby, realizing that life had somehow brought me into that room with a filmmaker whose work I had loved and cherished. Now I was working for him. *How does the universe deliver a moment like this?* I wondered. *How is it possible that I got to be in the presence of this man whose work had affected me so deeply?* The synchronicity was beautiful. But wait – there's more. For my seventieth birthday, my son Joshua told me to pack my bags because he was taking me on a journey to some random town near Minneapolis. Mystified, as we drove through the Minnesota countryside, I saw a sign for the Johnson Wax Corporation. I was about to come full circle on one of the formative events of my life. We drove onto the Johnson Wax grounds and I learned that they still showed *To Be Alive* to occasional audiences and that I was about to have a private screening, arranged by my son. We sat in an empty theater reminiscent of the eggshell theater at the Fair. The lights went dark and I was transported back to 1964, to Francis's office years earlier. The emotional wholeness of the experience hadn't stopped resonating. All I ever wanted was to make other people feel what I felt watching that film, the simple emotional joy of just being in this world. It drove my entire Hollywood career and is why this book exists. I couldn't thank Joshua enough. Even now the tears well up.

The last film I made at NYU was *Heads Up, Feets Down, Granny's Swinging All Around*. I had heard this urban legend about a couple who go camping with one of their grandmothers, who dies. They don't know what to do, so they wrap her in a tent and tie the tent to the top of the car, but when they arrive home, there's no tent and no grandma. The story follows the journey of this tent through several people's lives, including a group of Boy Scouts. It was supposed to be funny, but somehow the whole thing fell flat. Nobody laughed. I had been kind of a rising star because of my previous film, but with this new one, my reputation plummeted. The only person who liked it, beside my parents, was Brian De Palma, who said I was the new Blake Edwards. That barely registered with me because I wanted to be the new François Truffaut. I felt like a failure at 22.

My high school girlfriend Helaine decided to move to New York that summer. After taking a look at my apartment, she moved in with our mutual high school friend Paula. Helaine and I saw each other sporadically, I'm sure much less than she expected. It finally emerged that a Detroit boy had proposed to her and offered her a mink coat, which I sensed was a major inducement. I told her that I didn't know if I would ever be able to provide her with anything like that, and that a life with me might be one of poverty and uncertainty, especially since I was gay. She got the message. By the end of her visit, we were no longer a couple. She moved back to Detroit and married the coat guy.

The Christmas before graduating NYU, Brian offered me a job working on a documentary that he and his longtime actor/collaborator Bill Finley wanted to make in England. The project was Bill's idea. His dad had died and left him some money, and he wanted to make a film about two opposing social groups in the UK, the Mods and the Rockers. The Beatles, a new music group, were the epitome of the Mods. A group called The Rolling Stones was at the core of the Rockers. I was thrilled to be invited by Brian, because for the first time in my life, I didn't go home for the Christmas holidays. We arrived in London and met a woman who would be our liaison, Midge McKenzie, a dynamic conduit to everything that was happening in town. Our first order of business was to go to Paris and buy a new handheld 16mm camera called the Éclair. We got the third one off the production line. In Paris we met up with my friend Bob Fiore, who was on a Fulbright there. He had been in film class with Brian and me, and his proximity to London made him an attractive additional crew member for the film. Bob would go on to shoot many films, including *Gimme Shelter*, which documented the Rolling Stones' infamous American tour, *Greetings*, one of Brian's earliest films, and *Pumping Iron* with Arnold Schwarzenegger. Our new film in London really bonded us. We traveled all over the UK shooting emerging singing groups like Herman's Hermits and The Who. We never did get the Beatles or the Stones, although one day Brian and I saw Mick Jagger walking about a block away and chased after him with the camera for what seemed like a mile. He was faster than us.

New Year's Eve we were in London's Trafalgar Square. I stood up on the edge of the fountain to film the hordes, and before I knew what had happened I was underwater, pushed in by the rowdy crowd screaming to welcome in 1965. Proudly, I held the camera up in the air and managed to keep it dry. I felt heroic. A day before we left, I went with Midge to buy a corduroy suit for her friend Bob Dylan. She suggested I get one for myself. It was very Mod. There would be only two in America, mine and Dylan's. When I got back to NYU, I was the most stylish guy in class, and my travels to the UK to shoot a film were helpful in re-establishing my credentials. I became friendly with a fellow student, Mike Wadleigh, and we began to talk about working together and perhaps even forming a film company. Nothing came of it, and he went on to direct the movie *Woodstock*.

I was about to graduate from NYU with no idea what to do next. All I wanted was to find a way into the world of film, but there was no clear path forward. Clearly, my NYU directing efforts weren't going to open any doors. Scorsese's mastery of the craft was clear, and my efforts seemed pedestrian in comparison. I sensed that my best path forward would be through writing. After all, it was my storytelling that gave me the green light to direct at NYU. I assumed that it could also be my entry point into a larger career. The problem was, I had nothing to write about. It was always a struggle for me to come up with ideas. I didn't know the process for finding my stories. I didn't have enough of an inner life. I was still just a kid enamored by an empty stage. I knew that without the ability to tell stories, I had no future. My destiny required that I find a voice.

Seven

Seeing – LSD

I was supposed to graduate from NYU in the spring of 1965, but my grade point average, affected by my math and French classes, was one tenth of a point too low for me to get my diploma, so I had to go to summer school, where I took a class in Russian history taught by the father of a film class friend. I was sure I would get the B grade I needed to graduate, and was fine up until the final exam, when I froze. I begged the professor to give me a B–, but he wouldn't. My C+ felt sadistic. When I told my parents why I wasn't graduating, my father, assuming a heroic role he had never assumed before, wrote to the president of NYU and explained my situation. The president intervened and my diploma arrived in Detroit weeks later. I was so grateful to my dad. It was a demonstration of love and concern that he was rarely able to display in words.

The Vietnam War was underway and there was a good chance I would be drafted right out of college. I didn't want to be a soldier and wasn't sure how to avoid military service. Larry decided to tell them he was gay, which worked for him. I asked my old therapist for a letter confirming my sexuality and he gave it to me. It worked for me, too. Being gay finally seemed to be an advantage.

Around the end of my NYU days, Brian vacated his basement apartment at 65 Bank Street and I moved in. The apartment was a dilapidated space but a large one, with two huge bedrooms, a middle windowless kitchen/workspace, and a furnace room for the whole building. My bedroom had huge pipes running along the ceiling that shook every time someone flushed the toilet. Luckily, it was fully furnished, including that carpet from the Columbia library covering the cement floor. The bathroom was small, the walls all painted white. I splattered it with glow paint so that when you turned off the light you were suddenly surrounded by a galaxy of unexpected stars. During parties, a lot of people, especially when stoned, would lock themselves inside, creating havoc for those with full bladders. The furnace room had a large laundry sink but lacked a shower. I bought a blowup swimming pool and a hose so I could clean myself, but emptying the pool led to unexpected floods, and I usually ended up walking to Midge McKenzie's apartment on Bleecker and Jones for a shower. Midge was responsible for one of the most haunting memories I have of 65 Bank. I have no idea where I went that day, but she dropped by with François Truffaut. The note she left read: "Was here with Truffaut. Wanted you to meet. Sorry you weren't home." She later told me that she wanted to show him my *Frog Croaks at Twilight* film. I wonder what direction my life might have taken had we met.

Barry Kaplan and his girlfriend Barbara Dunlap, a wide-eyed, mystical young lady, were now living in the other bedroom on Bank Street. Many people had lived there, including Scott, the young boy in *Jennifer*, my first NYU film. It was a constant parade. Barbara had a young son named Alexander who often lived with his father but occasionally visited us. We would go for long walks around the West Village, and I got my first taste of being a father. I loved it. It suited me.

Barry and Barbara were often guests at the Hitchcock Estate in Millbrook, NY, where Tim Leary was "experimenting" with LSD. The drug had had a profound effect on Barry's life, and his descriptions of his inner journey intrigued me. He encouraged me to try some. I wasn't quite willing to commit to going to Millbrook, but I was curious enough to say I would experiment with it at home, so Barry procured a tablet for me – 100 micrograms I think, a pretty heavy dose. "Keep it in your wallet," he said, "until the right moment comes." It stayed in my wallet for months, like a condom waiting for the lucky moment. In the meantime, I had smoked weed for the first time and found it fun. Cartoon characters would parade across my bedroom wall. I imagined LSD would be a stronger version of that. What did I know?

LSD was *the* drug of the moment at that time. It hadn't yet been demonized. There were a lot of influential articles talking about this chemical that was changing people's lives. When *Life* magazine ran a story about Cary Grant and his experiences with LSD, I realized that I wanted to be affected as he had been, to see the world anew. I didn't know where it might lead, but I was open to the possibilities. I wasn't a druggie, an adventurer or an experimenter. I was fearful of most things, especially change. But something was calling out to me.

Barry and Barbara gave me a copy of the Leary/Alpert/Metzner book *The Psychedelic Experience: A Manual Based on the Tibetan Book of the Dead*. Reading it set me up for a particular Buddhistic approach to the LSD experience. It was my guide for what was going to happen. I think a lot of people who did acid at that period were unprepared and had no vocabulary for what they experienced. But because of my immense fascination with that book, I had a rather elaborate understanding of what I was about to go through.

[The drug] acts as a chemical key – it opens the mind, frees the nervous system of its ordinary patterns and structures. The nature of the experience depends almost entirely on set and setting. Set denotes

the preparation of the individual, including his personality structure and his mood at the time. Setting is physical – the weather, the room's atmosphere; social – feelings of persons present towards one another; and cultural – prevailing views as to what is real. It is for this reason that guidebooks are necessary. Their purpose is to enable a person to understand the new realities of the expanded consciousness, to serve as road maps for new interior territories which modern science has made accessible.

From **The Psychedelic Experience**

The night finally came. I had a large poster of Buddha on my wall alongside my bed. I lay down staring at a large ceiling full of pipes for the building above. It was a mostly empty room with a big sofa and a large writing desk. Barry and Barbara pulled up chairs alongside me. I took the 100-microgram pill and waited for an hour. Nothing happened.

Earlier that day, a man named Michael Hollingshead, the man who brought Tim Leary his acid from Europe, had arrived in New York and showed up at my apartment with a container of LSD, about the size of an applesauce jar. He asked Barry if he could leave it in our refrigerator overnight before they all went up to Millbrook the next morning. This was *pure* Lysergic Acid Diethylamide, straight from Sandoz Laboratories in Switzerland. If someone had poured this bottle of acid into New York's water supply, we would be living in a completely different world today. When Barry realized that my LSD wasn't working, he went to the refrigerator and pulled out the container. He said he had an eyedropper and would administer a single drop to me. He filled the eyedropper and held it over my mouth. Very gently he squeezed on the tube.

Suddenly I heard him say "Oops," and the entire syringe of LSD – thousands and thousands of micrograms – went surging down my throat. Barry seemed horrified. Barbara gasped.

I said, "Well, okay." I mean, what could I do at that point? There was nothing I could do. Nowhere to run. All I could do was wait.

You must be ready to accept the possibility that there is a limitless range of awareness for which we now have no words; that awareness can expand beyond the range of your ego, your self, your familiar identity, beyond everything you have learned, beyond your notions of space and time, beyond the differences which usually separate people from each other and the world around them.

From **The Psychedelic Experience**

Everything I knew about life was instantaneously destroyed. I had no idea or concept for what was happening to me. Life as I knew it was gone. And yet in some odd way it was bizarrely familiar. My first and only thought – beyond the sensation of pure terror – was "Oh, THIS again." I knew this wasn't the first time I was experiencing this. I had been here before. The experience in the sandbox when I was five seemed to point at this, only now I had the sensation that it had happened many, many times, over endless lifetimes. It was a journey into death. It was taking me apart.

You must remember that throughout human history, millions have made this voyage. A few (whom we call mystics, saints or buddhas) have made this experience endure and have communicated it to their fellow men. You must remember, too, that the experience is safe (at the very worst, you will end up the same person who entered the experience), and that all of the dangers which you have feared are unnecessary productions of your mind. Whether you experience heaven or hell, remember that it is your mind which creates them. Avoid grasping the one or fleeing the other. Avoid imposing the ego game on the experience.

From **The Psychedelic Experience**

I remember, early in the experience, walking down a long flight of stairs – miles long, it seemed – and seeing two winged demons at my side.

"Where am I?"

They said, "You know where you are."

"Where am I going?"

They laughed and said, "You know where you're going."

And I *did* know, but I didn't want to face it. I kept trying not to think or say the word "Hell," but I could see the entrance to Hell waiting for me at the bottom of that elongated staircase. It was delineated in neon lights – very garish, very real. I tried to close my eyes and imagine that this wasn't happening, but it made no difference. They took me down the stairs. Then I entered the abyss.

The panel depicting Hell in the Hieronymus Bosch painting "The Garden of Earthly Delights" – that's exactly what it was like for me. I began a journey that was timeless but felt like billions of years of being devoured and dismantled, and there was nothing I could do to defend myself. There was no one I could call on. There was no God. Hell was the absence of God, the absence of the very thought of God.

I spent millennia fighting everything that was happening to me. I tried to resist being disassembled and brought into nothingness, being taken completely apart, cell by cell, molecule by molecule. Each molecule had a vast history of its own, so I had a lot of unraveling to do. My memories, my ideas of self and of the world – all were taken away and fed into something I couldn't see or understand.

At one point I became aware of Barry and asked him to take me outside. It was nighttime on Bank Street and there were very few people around. I was barefoot and the cement was painful. I ran into a phone booth. I wanted to call my parents because I desperately needed to know that they were real and that the world I believed in was still out there. It was beginning to occur to me that New York didn't exist beyond my immediate perception of it. As soon as I got in the phone booth, I *knew* that the world ended at the end of the street. I knew that there was nothing beyond what I could see, hear and feel at that moment. There was no reality one block away from where I was standing. It was like that Saul Steinberg drawing where America is just a vague, empty space west of the Hudson River. My parents were supposed to be in Detroit, but I realized that there was no such thing as Detroit. My parents didn't exist. Nothing existed. It was all in my head. I had invented the whole world.

I ended up back in my bed, ten hours and several billion years later. Barry, who was guiding me through this, was in a state of shock because he had never seen anybody go through what I was going through. The LSD gurus say that cultural expectations are very powerful at this moment. You see what you expect to see. If you have a Heaven and Hell sensibility, those come into play very strongly.

In the end, or something that felt like an end, I had the realization that there was nothing but me. That the entire universe was me. I felt that I was the best and the worst that life had to offer. I was everything that ever was and ever would be. And then that total sense of self dissolved.

I totally evaporated.

There was no one left.

I arrived at nothingness.

Complete stillness.

I was filled with a kind of awe inside that stillness. There was nothing I needed, nothing I wanted. I was beyond life and death. There was no "me" anymore. There was no "I." There was nothing. Simply nothing. There was *no thing* left. There was just abstract awareness, Being, Presence – but disembodied, with no reference points at all. Emptiness beyond understanding.

And yet that emptiness felt somehow very holy, very complete. Although there was no one to be comforted, it felt like comfort. Oceanic comfort. An eternity of comfort.

Whenever in doubt, turn off your mind, relax, float downstream.

From **The Psychedelic Experience**

Then, out of nowhere, I felt something drop into the vast stillness of Being, like a pebble falling into a lake. There was a "plop," and then this thing that I was – I didn't know what I was, but whatever I was – felt like a seed had entered me. I was impregnated. This Presence I was feeling began to divide into two, four, eight, sixteen, thirty-two. It happened so fast. I wasn't watching it because I had no eyes, but I was experiencing this complete reconstruction of everything. My body was reconstructed as if in mid-air. A finger emerged. An elbow. My bed. A lampshade. The entire room I had been sitting in was totally reconstructed around my emerging body. Then my eyes formed, vision arose, and I could see it all. The Buddha. The pipes on my ceiling. I could feel the city of New York forming in my mind. Then the Earth. The Sun. Chunk by chunk, the universe was being rebuilt and I found myself back where I began, in my room at 65 Bank.

People ask me how long the trip lasted. To be honest, I'm still not convinced it's over. But if there were a time frame, I would guess that it was three or four billion years long. It's hard to be accurate. Even the eight or ten hours of human time that had passed were meaningless. I remember that I started to laugh. I laughed the biggest, loudest, longest laugh of my life. It was huge. I just roared with happiness. I felt so much joy in being back, in being alive. I felt I had been reborn, that I had arrived at the beginning of a new life. I just sat there for a long time wondering and even asking out loud, *Why am I here?* "*Why did I come back?* And a Voice, a loud, penetrating but loving Voice, answered out of nowhere, *TO TELL PEOPLE WHAT YOU SAW!* That was my directive.

But there was one huge problem: I had no idea what I had seen. There was no way my mind could grasp, let alone articulate, the massiveness of what had just occurred.

And so began a lifelong quest for answers.

What is it that happened to me in those billions of invisible years?

How do I live with a source of knowledge that is beyond understanding?

What am I supposed to do now?

❖

The next morning, Barry and Barbara left for Millbrook but asked a friend, George Subkoff, to come by and look after me. I was grateful to see him. He did all he could to assure me that what I had been through was nothing new, that many people, including him, had begun this journey. I had a sudden sense that I was part of something huge – a new adventure, possibly for the entire world. When I saw Barry next, he gave me a copy of a book he had been reading, *The Bhagavad Gita*, the Hindu song of God. If he had given it to me before the acid trip, I wouldn't have understood it at all. But now I started reading and saw everything in an altered context. I realized that my journey wasn't new. There was a name for it in the history of religion and human perception. It was called a *mystical experience*.

I started reading everything I could, including Aldous Huxley's *The Perennial Philosophy*, and understood that mystical experiences are not an isolated part of the human journey but at the core of every world religion. These are ancient and primordial truths that have existed throughout the history of the human experience. I read about Teresa of Ávila, who recognized that she had to give up Christ to gain admission into Totality. I read about the fourteenth-century mystic and theologian Meister Eckhart, who said that angels and demons are the same beings, and the only difference is how we humans perceive them. He said that people who are afraid of dying see demons tearing them from their flesh. People who are open to death see angels freeing them from the Earth. They are the same Beings. I knew I had seen the demons. I sensed also that I had experienced something like an angelic or godlike presence. I read that many of those who have had mystical experiences believe they have seen Truth and God and that they understand the ultimate reality of the world we live in. I had no certainty. I had no words for what I had witnessed. I just knew that the rug had been pulled out from beneath my feet, but I was still walking, and nothing could deny the magnitude of ungraspable truth, that somehow I was still here, that I was meant to be here.

I didn't know what to do with the massive vision I had been given. I felt I might be perceived as delusional because it originated from a drug. People could always explain away my experience as a chemically induced hallucination. I had assumed that everyone who did acid saw the same thing, that we were all on this new journey together. But I discovered that many people had a simpler response: "Wow! That was cool!" Then they returned to their lives. They might have gained some insight, but they didn't have the full journey. They didn't take the voyage into death and back. I call those shorter trips "sub-orbitals." If you take the full journey, you come back a different person.

I knew I was a different person, that my body chemistry had somehow changed. My very being was been altered, and I no longer knew who I was. I found myself drawing pictures in an effort to depict what I had seen, because at that moment in my life it was easier than articulating and explaining my experiences in words.

There was another strange manifestation. For nearly a year or more after my LSD trip, I began having something called "astral projections." I would be lying in bed napping or preparing for sleep when suddenly my body would freeze. I would become totally paralyzed and terrified. There was usually a huge roaring sound that accompanied the paralysis, then suddenly I would shoot out of my body and find myself hovering perfectly still in the air above it. All was silence. It took a moment at first to realize what had happened, but I gradually got used to it. I was simply floating in the middle of the room. Slowly I learned how to maneuver, flying through the space, hovering over the floor, my desk, the couch.

The first time, I had no idea what was going on, and remember looking back at my body still on the bed. I gasped loudly and in a tenth of a second catapulted back into it. I remember shooting up in the bed, gasping, astonished that such a thing was possible. In time I learned how to fly around the apartment, and one night

I decided to fly through the bedroom window. Suddenly I was hovering over Bank Street. I could see the full Moon above me, and before I knew what was happening I was barreling toward it. New York and the Atlantic Ocean spread out below me as I kept rising faster and faster. Soon the entire globe appeared and then the Moon, like images from NASA. But I kept speeding through space. It was astounding and beautiful. The entire Milky Way appeared, galaxies rushing past. Then it dawned on me that I could no longer see Earth. It was blending into a universe of stars. At that moment I feared I would never find my way back to my home planet, to Bruce. A sudden shock of terror and, instantaneously, I was back in my body, gasping in wonder. I didn't really enjoy the strangeness of the experience, but sensed that some Overseeing Awareness respected my fears and was guiding me. After a while, the astral projections mostly fell away. I was left with a pervasive awareness that something indescribable was at work in our lives.

My experience with LSD and astral projection changed everything. I now knew there was a vast "other world" that was much more meaningful than the one I was living in, and that I had to devote the rest of my life to finding out more – everything – about it. But I also had to eat, pay rent, keep a roof over my head. I had no idea how I was going to do that, especially now that I had seen behind the cosmic curtain, now that I knew that nothing I believed was certain or true.

Eight

Searching – Journey to the East

Two weeks after I took LSD, I was at NYU in the film department and saw a sign on a bulletin board listing a job at NBC News for an assistant film editor. I tore it off the wall and applied that afternoon. To my amazement, I was hired. I was suddenly working on the NBC Nightly News with Huntley and Brinkley at 30 Rockefeller Center. It paid moderately well, and my parents were thrilled. The position had upward mobility and allowed me to take over my own finances for the first time in my life. I regularly dropped in on the Johnny Carson show, which broadcast from one floor below. Pure joy.

My job was mostly splicing news film as it arrived via motorcycle from various airports, including the newly renamed JFK (formerly Idlewild). I would run the film up to the editors on the ninth floor, help splice the negative, then run it to the elevator and bring it down to the fourth floor where projectors were waiting to share it with the world. I remember a reel of uncut film arriving from a revolutionary war zone in some South American country. There was one shot of a boy on a bike with a red flag, and no other political images on the entire reel. The producer singled out the shot of the boy and said, "We open with that." To American audiences it would look like a Communist-led battle. I suddenly understood about the control and manipulation of "the news."

Early on, I sensed there was a reason why I was working for NBC. Perhaps I could use my position to tell the world about LSD. I very much believed that it was going to save the world, that it provided a sacramental experience and that everybody needed to be taking it, and began proselytizing for it whenever I could. I managed to get myself onto the radio station on the fourth floor at 30 Rock and gave a couple of interviews about this new magical drug. The producers told me not to use my real name, so I always called myself "Barry." Then, one day, some kid killed his mother in Brooklyn and blamed it on LSD, and the curtain came down really fast. LSD was declared illegal in America, and I realized I had to shut up about what had happened to me. I sensed that it wouldn't be legal or tolerated again in my lifetime. In fact, all mind-altering drugs were immediately outlawed. The government felt threatened by all mind-altering substances, which were a threat to the status quo. A sudden surge of mind-control legislation blanketed the entire country. Life in America was changing.

65 Bank Street was still my refuge – until one day it became a war zone. A huge, gnarly friend of a friend who had come to a party at the apartment broke in the following day and threw all my belongings into the outdoor passageway. When I came home, he blocked me at the door with a warning never to come back. He said I had bad karma with him from a past life and it was time for payback. He was going to take 65 Bank Street for himself. I had never heard the word "karma" before, but the power of the concept was now inserting itself dramatically into my life. Who was this guy and what could I have done to him in a past life that would explain this moment? Or was he just crazy? I was frightened enough that I decided to vacate my apartment. My friends thought I was mad. How could I ever leave such an amazing place? George Subkoff, Bob Fiore and others stood up to defend me, and George had a friend with a gun who added some drama to the looming

confrontation. I still had a key to the apartment. The next day, while the new occupant was out, we assembled, hidden inside, waiting for his return. When he showed up and the gun came out, he barricaded himself in the boiler room. It ended with the police arriving and the gun being tossed out the back window. It was clear to everyone that he was crazy, and the police pulled him from the apartment, warning him that if he ever returned he would be thrown in jail. I had never fought for an apartment, or much of anything before, and expressing such a sense of ownership was a new experience for me. I also became curious about the Hindu law of karma, wondering if it really existed, and, if so, how much of the human story evolved from it. Karma offered a way to view plot points intersecting with our journey, aspects of past lives, past experiences, playing out in the present. These thoughts consumed me. I was on a new path.

Soon after the epic battle, I decided to leave NBC. I sensed that my path as a film editor was obstructing my search. Old friends, Liz and Jeff Carson, had a house on an island in Greece that would be empty for a year, and I thought I could go there and figure things out. I would take all my books and read about Tibetan Buddhism, Judeo-Christian theology and mysticism, and everything else. My plan was to read myself into enlightenment. When I announced to the people at NBC that I was leaving, they all thought I was crazy. No one left NBC. I was on a real career path there. My parents thought the job was the greatest thing that could ever happen to me, but I knew it wasn't. I knew I had more important things to do.

Al Wasserman, a producer at NBC, had taken a liking to me and knew of my intention to leave. He offered me a position working overtime on a documentary, *JFK Remembered*, that was almost finished. I would make a lot of money, which could either support me in New York or pay for my travels if I still decided to quit. I worked so hard that they put me up at the Hilton Hotel across the street, so I could get a few hours of sleep. Wasserman was a true gentleman and seemed to appreciate my desire to write. He was the brother-in-law of Norman Mailer and one time invited me to Mailer's home in Brooklyn Heights, where I got to walk the plank into his writing studio. Yes – a plank. It was a strangely precarious journey, over a solitary rafter, without railings, to a writing space hovering over a two-story living room below. One needed to be balanced and focused to enter Mailer's workspace.

By the time *JFK Remembered* aired, I had $1,500 dollars that Wasserman's generosity helped put in my wallet. I thought long and hard, but still decided to leave. The world of film editing had been changing before my eyes. Video film production and video editing had arrived, and job security looked shaky. To my surprise, the entire ninth floor of film editors and assistants took me out for a farewell lunch at a restaurant run by a former chef to General, later President, Eisenhower. We sat at a massive round table, and I was celebrated in ways that made no sense to me. It was only later that I realized I was doing what every one of them wanted to be doing: moving on.

Leaving NBC was my second big leap of faith after departing Detroit for New York. It was clear to me that the LSD experience was making this new risk-taking possible. I was able to let go of everything that seemed comfortable and secure and jump into the abyss, the unknown. I had never known this Bruce before. I had always been scared and shy and not prone to adventure. I also felt that it was time for me to make friends with myself. This Bruce, who was leaving for Greece, was fascinating to me. I was excited to get to know him.

Summer 1966.

Liz and Jeff had a beautiful little house that overlooked the Aegean Sea on the island of Paros. They had lived there for a couple of years but were temporarily returning to America to earn enough money to stay in Greece permanently (something they achieved – they are living on Paros to this day). I wrote to them about coming to visit and they suggested I take over their lease – $11 a month – while they were gone. I had an army knapsack full of books about Tibetan Buddhism, Teresa of Ávila, *The Doors of Perception*. I brought so many books that I couldn't get them from the boat to the house, and hired a donkey to carry them for me.

I had a great time in Greece, but it wasn't because of the books. Liz and Jeff introduced me to many of their friends before they left. Two of them, Brett and Nina Taylor, were especially kind and available. They had moved to Paros from Philadelphia to establish a school on the island called The Aegean School of the Fine Arts. It was already filling up with students, some of whom I got to know. This period became a valuable time for me not only because I was developing a new inner life, but because I was uncovering a new vision of my outer life as well. I had left behind everything familiar. I didn't have a phone. I didn't have much money. I was just there by myself, learning to live with myself. That was important. I remember thinking before I had departed that I was better friends with my friends than I was with me. Here was an opportunity to change.

Paros is in the Cyclades, about a seven-hour boat trip from Athens and the port of Piraeus. Liz and Jeff had been close to my friend David Moscovitz in New York. I always referred to them, along with Bob Fiore and Joel Freedman, as the Waverly group, since at one point they had all lived in an apartment on Waverly Place. They were mostly left-wing politicos, members of groups like SDS and CORE, and played ongoing roles in my life. Without these expanding connections I would never have made it to Greece. Liz and Jeff introduced me to many locals on the island, including two goats and several cats. I lived up the hill from a gorgeous beach and the local slaughterhouse. My water came from a well halfway

between the house and the industrial-looking building where cows went to die. I would lug full five-gallon containers past my donkey and goats, into the house, and use it as sparingly as I could. The walk into town took about twenty minutes and followed the spectacular Aegean coast, past a huge windmill, then an outdoor movie theater that showed American films. In town were cafés where old men sat outside, drinking ouzo and laughing. Many of them, I later learned, were retired from immigrant lives in New York. They had made enough money to return home, where they lounged outside playing cards, happily watching the days go by with a quiet contentment that I appreciated, maybe even longed for. I didn't really understand their passive lives, although I was trying to experience their contentment in my own way.

I loved shopping for fresh produce. I had become a vegetarian for no particular reason, but it felt spiritually right, and the vegetables I was able to buy on the island were all locally grown and absolutely delicious. After Liz and Jeff left, I inherited a life of stillness. I had a small, cozy space and no reason to get up in the morning. When I did, I often found that my new cats had left an offering – a dead mouse or dying lizard at my doorstep. It took me a while to appreciate that. When I looked up from their offering, the heavenly Aegean sparkled in front of me. At night the cats would curl up in my lap as I sat on the porch, and together we would watch the most beautiful sunsets I had ever seen. After dark I would go to the movies or read or smoke hash. I was now a bit of a druggie, although mind-altering drugs were so reminiscent of my acid trip that I needed only a couple of hits before I was revisiting the Infinite Cosmos in my head. I witnessed it from a respectable distance, but it was a definite reminder of what my journey was all about, why I had come to Greece, what my larger mission was.

Susan was a student at The Aegean School of the Fine Arts, which hosted people from all over the continent. She was an artist who took to me the moment we met. I told her I was gay, but she didn't seem to care. She came back to my house and essentially moved in with me. The sex was liberating. I had no idea I could be that satisfied by anyone. I was glad to be living with her. Her departure at the end of her semester left me profoundly alone. Brett and Nina were great friends, and we would often dine together, drink ouzo and laugh. But I felt lonely, as if my time in Greece were coming to an end. I wrote long, sad letters to my family about how much I missed everyone, but at the same I had no desire to return home. I received a letter from my dad saying that my Grandpa David had died, so I wrote a letter of condolence to my Grandma Dora. A week later I got a note saying it was Grandfather Abe who had died, not Dave. I felt so foolish and confused. I wrote another condolence note, this time to my mom, but it seemed like I was no longer part of the Detroit world. I was an afterthought.

One morning, as I was walking to the well to get water, a cow on a leash and its owner passed me by. The cow glanced at me as if it knew what was awaiting it down at the slaughterhouse. The look in its eyes was so moving, so Christ-like, I almost began to cry. It didn't put up a fight, it just moved forward with a certain acceptance and nobility. I wondered if I would have that still pointedness when the time came. I watched the cow disappear into the dark building and then went to pump my water. Nothing came out. The well was dry, or at least not pumping. I didn't know what to do. I decided to go down to the slaughterhouse and try and get water there. Just as I entered, the cow that I had seen was being hoisted upside down by a rope around its hind legs. It was a horrifying sight. It struggled and moaned for a moment before one of the men in a white apron slit its throat. Blood shot out onto the floor and poured down a drain.

I watched the cow struggle for a moment, then saw something amazing. A strange darkness floated out of its forehead and its body went limp. It was as if I had seen a soul leave a body as it died.

I had never witnessed anything like it. It was so sudden, so easy, so liberating. The cow was dead, its soul was free, and I was left with a sense that this animal had come into the world to feed me, to feed mankind. A body had grown up around its tiny soul and prospered and procreated, then, in an instant, died. It had left a carcass, a body of meat, for people to consume. Its instant death, its liberated soul, spoke to me – and I was a vegetarian no longer. That very night I had the first meat I'd had in a year, a lamb souvlaki, in a restaurant in the town I had walked past many times. They sliced off the meat and put it in Greek bread. I ate with a mix of joy and unexpected gratitude to the lamb that was making me so happy and full. This felt like such a reversal. Most meat eaters upset about seeing an animal slaughtered become vegetarians. For me it was the opposite. I rediscovered meat. But more importantly, I sensed a larger cosmology at work, a profound interaction between man and beast. The universe was simply not the way I imagined it. Encountering the unexpected became a key to the rest of my journey. I was keenly aware of how death seemed an essential part of the life cycle, that a cosmic and universal energy attaches around the soul, grows flesh, then returns to the soul again.

After four months, I accepted that I wasn't going to find what I was looking for in Greece. I would sit by myself and read and write and meditate and try to find my way into the deeper part of my being, into the mystical dimension I knew was within. But I couldn't find my way to anything. Finally I said, "I'm in the wrong place. I need to go to Tibet." I was convinced that the Tibetans had a handle on the truth, that they saw the bigger picture I had seen on LSD. So I mapped out an overland journey and sent a letter to my parents explaining the new world I was about to visit – an adventure through Turkey, Iran, Afghanistan, Pakistan, India, Nepal. It was exhilarating to write about and fearful to contemplate, but I knew I needed to go. I got rid of everything. I sent my library of books and the typewriter my grandparents had given me back to America, and began my long, mythic journey to the East.

I started in Istanbul. The city surprised me – it felt so familiar and foreign at the same time. I loved the mosques and the food and how inexpensive everything was. I felt a real sense of expansion and excitement for the journey ahead. After being told it was the Paris of the East, I took a three-day train ride to Erzurum at the eastern end of Turkey, but all I found was a barren desert town. The dirt streets were watered down to keep the sand out of the buildings. On the train I discovered that I wasn't the only one making the journey east. A fair number of hippies were also heading to Nepal. The underlying chant was "Christmas in Kathmandu." It was still nearly three thousand miles away and there was no railway past Erzurum, but apparently thousands were expected. Each person had to figure out transportation and housing on their own. It was an arduous trip, and many fell by the wayside.

Luckily, I made some friends when I arrived in Erzurum, and we ended up traveling all the way to Nepal together. Jacques Darmon, an Algerian, was a photographer for UNICEF and Julio Pizzati was an architect from Italy. Most importantly, Julio had a car that he was going to try to sell in Nepal, and he invited us to join him if we helped pay for gas. Unfortunately, the car blew a tire a few miles from Tehran, but only ten yards from the beautiful Caspian Sea. We all went for a swim and then spent two days trying to get the tire fixed. Finally, we made it to Tehran.

The city in those days was fairly modern and devoted to the Shah, whose image was everywhere – alongside JFK, who had become a worldwide saint after his assassination. I remember being approached wherever I went – surrounded by kids, invited for tea –

because I was American. People wanted to touch me. The world was very embracing, and far from frightening. That was another turning point for me. I was becoming sensitive to the blending of cultures and races. Maps and politics define us but create a false sense of the world. People and cultures appeared to me as a continuum that had been divided – artificially, politically – into territorial space. The sense of Oneness was astounding. There was a kind of rigidity that seemed to temporarily disappear as I traveled. I was invigorated by the continuity of it all, the wholeness of the human race.

We drove from Tehran to the city of Mashhad, on the way to the Afghan border. Julio's car was giving us more trouble and I was worried I would go broke helping him repair it. But we managed to cross over into Afghanistan and ended up in Herat. It was another world. Everything was impoverished, roads were in terrible condition, buildings were dilapidated, women were nowhere to be seen. The men wore turbans and carried guns. We were no longer in safe territory. Before that, I'd had this idea that the world was our oyster and we could go anywhere as long as we had open hearts. In Iran and later in Pakistan, people embraced me. But I never felt safe in Afghanistan.

Our first night there, we went to what we were told was going to be a strip club. The room was filled to the brim and the guys were excited and ready for action. An overly dressed female dancer appeared on the stage and began moving to what sounded like fiddle music. The Afghan men were going crazy watching her. We waited for her to begin to strip. She took off several veils, but we never got to see her face and her multiple dresses were untouched. You could feel the men panting, desperate for action. After a long wait she lifted her skirt and exposed her ankle. The room erupted in hysteria. Finally, some flesh! It was, we were told, the most we would see that night. Out on the street we roared with laughter and walked back to our tiny hotel room with mattresses on the floor. The next day we drove to Kandahar, where the car broke down again and where Julio abandoned it in a barely functioning repair shop. He was unhappy and ready to end his trip, but we were in the middle of nowhere.

The three of us began hitchhiking to Kabul, and a trucker drove us across an endless desert landscape. We stopped at a roadside restaurant where the head cook came over to us with a live chicken in each hand and asked what we wanted for dinner. Our driver pointed to one of them and the cook swung it by the neck, killing it on the spot. The other, which he dropped to the floor, fluttered back to the kitchen. In twenty minutes, the chosen chicken was plucked, boiled and served. Later, the driver, who slept in the cab of his truck, motioned for us to spend the night in the remains of a small house that had three mud walls and no roof. I remember lying there on the ground in my warm and cozy sleeping bag, looking up at the stars, the wind howling around us.

We made it to Kabul, which looked a little bit like a modest American city. It had mostly paved streets, a few buildings over two stories tall, and an occasional electric sign. This was as close to civilization as we would get in Afghanistan. One restaurant, the Khyber, was in a relatively upscale hotel and offered the best meals and a sense of comfort I hadn't experienced in a while. We stayed in a nearby cheap hotel that had no bedding and no heat, and on the last night of our stay were so cold that we broke up a wooden chair and burned it in the middle of the room for warmth. The smoke floated out the broken windows. Julio went back to Kandahar to deal with the car. I wouldn't see him again until he found me in the US a decade later. He had eventually returned to Italy, where he began an architectural career.

I got very sick when we first arrived in Kabul, and remember having to stop the car to vomit all over the dusty road. I lay on a mattress on the floor of our hotel room for two days, unable to get up. I had no idea what to do or how to find help. And then two angels appeared, a beautiful young couple from the Netherlands, part of the Kathmandu for Christmas brigade who must have been staying in the hotel. They had heard about me and came to the room with a bag stuffed full of vitamins. They insisted that I take them and handed me a bottle of water and a barrage of medications they said would bring me back to full health. Then they wished me well and left. I never saw them again, but two days later I was as good as new. I never knew how they found me or why they seemed so primed to help, but their appearance was a taste of care from the great beyond, of angelic kindness. I wanted nothing more than to repay it, and feel that to this day.

While we were in Afghanistan, Jacques was hired to shoot a photographic spread about life in an Afghan village. He asked if I wanted to go along, and I hesitantly said yes. I had heard a story about a couple traveling through the country on a motorcycle who approached a village and were stoned to death by the villagers. Because Jacques worked for UNICEF, an advance team was sent to the village to make sure it was safe for us to be there. When we arrived, the villagers had chained up their dogs, which were trained to attack outsiders. I have never seen more vicious animals. I sensed savagery in the world.

A couple of days later, I was wandering around central Kabul and heard great cheers in the distance. As I got closer, I came upon a game of buzkashi, the national sport of Afghanistan. On a field about the size of a football stadium, teams of horsemen decapitate a calf and try to deposit its dead carcass in the opposite team's goal. Public observers routinely get trampled by horses that gallop out of bounds – sometimes trampled to death. The King of Afghanistan happened to be at that game, watching from a raised royal platform. I didn't want to stand on the sidelines and get trampled, and it seemed clear to me that the safest place was on the King's platform, so I ambled toward it. I've always had a kind of strange chutzpah, and on this particular day it carried me up those steps. I don't think the King's guards knew what to make of me, but they let me stay there, and I found myself watching this game while standing next to the King. He glanced at me for a moment and sort of smiled. I smiled back.

I'm intrigued by the idea that innocence can allow a person access to a world that would otherwise be completely forbidden. There is real value in that kind of simple audacity, instead of what we so often do, which is to construct mental barriers to other possibilities. If you believe you can actually go into the universe and explore places that the mind tells you are inaccessible, you will find a way in. The alternative is closing doors to the world around you. The world doesn't close doors – we do that ourselves. As soon as you think, "I can't go there," you're *definitely* not getting in. Know the boundaries, but know, too, that innocence often obscures barriers and allows more access to the wonders of the world than you would imagine.

Pakistan was a very different experience. As we drove through the beauty of the Khyber Pass, color returned. Jacques and I caught a ride on the back of a truck, our new form of transportation, and made our way across Pakistan to the border city of Lahore, just on the edge of India. We went to the crossing and presented our passports, but were told we weren't allowed into India. There had been a war in the past year and they weren't letting people leave Pakistan without exit visas, which we didn't have. The border guards suggested that we go to Karachi and try to get exit visas there. It was seven hundred miles south and about a fifteen-hour truck ride. We talked to some people who had already tried it. "It won't work," they told us. "They'll just send you back to the border."

"In America," I said to Jacques, "we have this thing called 'sit-ins.' If you want to get something done and there's no path forward, you just say, 'Okay, I'm just going to sit here until something happens.'" We got the name of the governmental agent in charge of giving exit visas, went to his house, and staged a sit-in on his front lawn. Right away one of the servants came out and said, "You can't stay here." I told him, "We'd be happy to leave. We just need visas." The man just stood there staring at us. He had never heard of anything like this. Others came out. No one knew what to do with us. They brought us some tea. They were very polite.

After a while the government agent himself came out. "I can't give you visas tonight," he said. "I don't have the paperwork. But if you come to my office in the morning, I will give you visas and you can leave." We said, "Okay, but if we go to the office tomorrow and we don't get the visas, we'll be back again." The next morning, we got our visas. We had to be out of the country before sunset or begin the whole visa journey again. I remember the drama of trying to find a truck and get to the border on time. As the sun dipped below the horizon, we arrived in India.

I loved India from the moment we got there. It felt totally familiar to my psyche. The colors that filled Pakistan were even more enhanced. Beauty was everywhere – and so was poverty. But I sensed no unhappiness. It was there, of course, but never announced itself. Children played lovingly in the street. Cows and dogs wandered everywhere. There was a freedom and spirituality in the air that pervaded the entire space. Jacques and I, along with a small group of other guys we met soon after arriving, became instant tourists. We all stayed at local Sikh Gurdwaras, temples that let spiritual seekers spend the night and then fed them breakfast in the morning. It felt too good to be true. We spent time in New Delhi, a contemporary city full of government buildings and old Mogul forts, then made our way to Agra and visited the Taj Mahal. It was as thrilling, beautiful and memorable as the photos had led me to believe. I felt the magnitude of my journey and its mythic elements.

We visited two holy sites. The first was the city of Benares, now called Varanasi, on the banks of the Ganges, where for centuries Hindus have gone to die. It has long been held that a death and cremation in Benares lead to a higher birth in the next lifetime. There was an ancient vibrancy about the place, including the holy burning ghats, the platforms along the river where the bodies were cremated. That mesmerized me. I sensed that my ashes may have been tossed into the Ganges many times, for many lifetimes. The other holy spot was Sarnath, a deer park near Benares where Buddha gave his very first lecture, where he first taught the Dhamma. It felt different than any worldly space I had ever known – elevated, like it was floating, hovering outside of time and space. It was the same kind of mystical power I felt at Bodhgaya, where Buddha had his enlightenment. The only place in the Western world that has this energy, at least in my experience, is Glastonbury Tor and the Chalice Well in the UK, a mystical site in South West England connected to Arthurian myths. The energy was unexplainable, but astoundingly present.

Christmas in Kathmandu was approaching. I remembered the prediction that thousands of hippie spiritual seekers would arrive by then and we would all celebrate together, but I kept hearing about people getting waylaid and turning back. It was a long journey to Kathmandu – through Turkey, Iran, Pakistan, India. When our tiny group did finally arrive, there were less than a hundred Westerners there, and everyone seemed dog-tired and a bit sick.

On Christmas Eve, our small group, maybe ten of us, went out on a mountainside with a couple of baby goats we had bought. The idea was to slaughter them and have a banquet with a big hunk of Swiss cheese we had purchased in the only cheese store in Nepal. But none of us had ever slaughtered a goat before. Someone had a

Searching – Journey to the East 107

big knife, so we chased after one of them. Killing the animal was gruesome beyond belief. Some Nepalese guys came around the bend and were horrified by what we were doing. They said they would slaughter the other goat for us if they could take the head, which for them was a delicacy.

They cut off the head, the body fell to the side, and the head rolled forward. The body shook and the eyes in the decapitated head started darting around, panicked and desperate, searching for its body. Suddenly, the eyes grew wide as if they were seeing something far off, something amazing. At that very second the eyes rolled up into the head and its body stopped shaking. There was no physical connection between head and body, but the body still responded instantaneously to whatever the head saw. How did that happen?

The Nepalese guys took the head and we ate the body. I threw up everything that night and slept terribly. Christmas in Kathmandu.

Nine

Exploring – Lord of the Universe

After a week in Nepal, I moved into a Tibetan monastery near the stupa at Boudhanath, a small town about ten miles from Kathmandu. The stupa, a Tibetan domed shrine housing Buddhist relics, was one of the largest in the world, with a diameter exceeding 330 feet and a wall-to-wall circumference nearly the size of a football field. The surrounding walls housed about a hundred one-foot-high cylindrical prayer wheels built into its side. Monks, Tibetans and even Nepalese paraded around the stupa, spinning the wheels day and night, sending their prayers and blessings outward to the whole world. The village surrounding the stupa was full of restaurants, shops that sold ritual implements and Tibetan paintings called thangkas, and tea shops selling hot buttered yak tea, which I grew to love. The monastery was near the center of town, steps away from the stupa, filled with a small group of monks, all of them recent escapees from Tibet after the Chinese takeover in 1950 and the Dalai Lama's escape in 1959. A young monk named Lobsang Chonjor welcomed me in and gave up his room so I could sleep there. The monks said that if I would teach them English, they would let me live in the monastery and teach me about Tibetan Buddhism.

The first thing I asked about was the *Tibetan Book of the Dead*, which had guided me through my LSD trip, but they didn't know what I was talking about, so I said, "Bardo Thodol," which is the Tibetan name for it. And they said, "Oh – heretic work!" That's when I realized there were many sects of Tibetan Buddhists, and that these monks didn't believe in the mystical teachings that had informed my travels and driven my search. Regardless, I felt lucky to be welcomed into their world.

Our monastic lives weren't very structured. We had long morning prayers punctuated with tea and a sweet grain called *tsampa* for breakfast. Horns were blown and after a couple of hours, prayers ended. Tibetan refugees would gather at the monastery, prostrating themselves on the ground outside the doorway. Their purity of love and devotion was like nothing I had ever experienced. Just seeing a Tibetan anywhere in the world was, for me, a kind of blessing and a sign of good fortune. I had a lot of free time after morning prayers and spent it wandering the countryside and occasionally giving classes. But I didn't sense that I was on the road to Enlightenment. I knew that LSD had opened a door, although I didn't know where I was headed or exactly what I was supposed to find. I had hoped that hidden secrets would be unveiled in the monastery, that the universe would speak to me, teach me, and share its wisdom. But I wasn't feeling it. I felt unguided, lost.

One day I was walking down a long road near the monastery. I saw two young Nepalese guys walking toward me in the distance. They kept getting closer and closer until we were standing right in front of each other. They were grinning widely as they reached out and hugged me. We embraced for about a minute, then continued walking our separate ways without saying a word to each other. I thought, *Well, maybe this is the answer. Maybe this is what life is.* It was so beautiful, so immediate and complete. We just acknowledged each other with love, appreciated the fact that we were making a connection, and walked on.

One afternoon I took some of the monks into Kathmandu. I had arranged for them to watch some films at the United States Information Agency. They had never heard of World War II or the Vietnam War, and knew nothing about things like television. I thought I could fill in some gaps. They were fascinated by the films. I had opened their eyes to a world they didn't know, but immediately questioned what I had done because this information didn't seem especially helpful to them. In retrospect, I wondered whether knowledge of world historical events had as much value as spiritual insight and awareness. In some ways the journey I was embarking on came to be a reckoning with the balance between the physical and historical world we see and the unseen mystical world that underlies it all.

I stayed in Nepal for about two months, until one day I went to get my visa renewed and was told, basically, "We don't know what you are doing in Nepal and we don't think you should be here anymore." I think they thought I was CIA. The monks went with me to explain that I was teaching them English, but nobody wanted to hear it. I was told I had two days to get out of the country. That was it. In the blink of an eye, I was on a truck heading back to India.

I discovered that I had acquired a sense of unexpected safety in the world. I had become an innocent, no longer in need of a hotel or any special comfort. I was able to sleep wherever I found myself. One night I woke up in a field surrounded by a pack of growling wild dogs. I didn't have an ounce of fear. I just sat up and said, "Okay, guys, I don't have to be here. I'm on my way." I just kept talking to them. "I'm leaving, so don't bother me. I'm not going to be around to bother you." I saw some buildings in the distance. One had a couch-bed on the front porch, so I lay down in my sleeping bag. The following morning, I awoke to see an entire family gathered around, staring at me. "Good morning," I said. I had to go to the bathroom, and asked if they had one. They gave me a pot full of water and pointed me toward a path where a group of people were walking. I followed them to a nearby hillside, where everybody was pissing and shitting. I realized, *Oh, the hillside is the bathroom, and the water is for cleaning up.* When I went back, the family gave me breakfast. They were the sweetest people. Then I said goodbye and went on my way. That kind of thing happened again and again. The world embraced me.

One night, in a dream, a voice came to me. "Rajpur" is all it said. I had no idea what that meant. The next day I was on a bus. I don't remember where I was going, but I saw a sign for a city called Rajpur. Something in me said, "I'm supposed to get off here." I jumped up, pulled the cord, and got off the bus. Then I wondered, *Why am I here?* I asked someone on the street if there were any yogis or saints in town, and was told there was a woman, a great Indian saint who had many ashrams throughout the country, named Anandamayi Ma, who happened to be in Rajpur that day.

I went to the ashram and learned that she was giving Satsang, or spiritual teaching, that afternoon. I was led right up to the front of the temple, where I sat down just feet away from her. She was old but lovely. Pictures of her as a young woman hung in the entryway and showed a stirring beauty. I wondered why someone so beautiful would step away from the world. I felt her presence immediately and sensed that she was a real teacher. At some point, she asked, "Does anyone have any questions?" And I thought, *I have finally found someone who can answer my questions.* But when I opened my mouth, every question I ever had just flew out of my head. I had nothing to ask this woman. I also had a sense that nothing she could say would really answer anything because the truth I was seeking wasn't intellectual. It wasn't about *knowing*, it was about *being*.

I had a feeling that this falling away of questions was the true beginning of my spiritual life, that somehow, something had changed in me when I could find nothing to ask. I felt no reason to stay and left hours later. She was my first teacher.

I was in Rishikesh, sitting on the banks of the Ganges. And I was digging. Just digging with my hands into the sand. Suddenly I had this memory of my mother telling me, when I was a kid sitting in the sandbox, that if I dug deep enough, I would end up in China. And here I was – not in China, but in India. I thought, *I'm digging back to myself.* That was the feeling. *I'm digging back to America, back to my childhood.* Then some guy appeared, standing over me, and asked if I wanted to come and meet a great teacher.

We walked up a long hill to a beautiful ashram. Inside was the Maharishi Mahesh Yogi, a funny little bearded guy with a squeaky voice. He asked what I was doing, and I said I was looking for a teacher. He asked where I came from. I told him New York. He seemed suddenly uninterested in me and said I couldn't stay. "But I've traveled ten thousand miles to find a teacher," I said. "Why are you rejecting me?" He told me to go back home.

"I have many groups in America. You can study there."

"But I'm sitting here, now."

"No, no, no," he said. "You're not ready."

I thought, *What is wrong with me? What is my failing?* There were Americans all over the place. They had all come there to study with him. *Why did he reject me?*

He gave me some newspaper articles about himself – reviews from his travels in Finland. I kept waiting to read something about his teaching, but there was no teaching to be had, just a lot of self-promotion. I kept sitting, hoping he would change his mind, but he was focused on another guy who was creating cover art for one of his books. "Peacocks," he said. "More peacocks. Because Americans love peacocks." Then he got up and left the room. About six months later, after the Beatles discovered him, I wanted to tell them he was a fraud. I had a sudden sense of the coming corruption of spiritual teaching heading to the West.

Then I heard about a teacher named Ma Yoga Shakti, who had supposedly become enlightened. I went to find her but ended up befriending her family instead – four boys who took me in and were very kind to me. They told me that she had abandoned them years before, and they were still bereft over her absence. They couldn't understand how somebody claiming to have a spiritual life could leave their family behind. Neither could I.

Some monks came to see me while I was there and said they could take me to a *real* guru called the Lord of the Universe. I should have seen that as a red flag, but like many Westerners on a spiritual journey, I was a babe in the woods. We set out first thing in the morning, riding in an ox cart, and ended up at a large ashram in Dehradun, in the Himalayan hill station of India, where I was introduced to a pudgy eight-year-old kid. His father, a holy man, had died the year before and supposedly reincarnated into his son. His many thousands of followers were all trying to invest the father's energy in this eight-year-old boy, who seemed to relish power and attention. The group was called the Divine Light Mission. The son was called Guru Maharaj, and he was the most obnoxious kid I had ever met. He liked to pour water on the ground just so that people would run over and lick it up. Repeatedly. It was dislike at first sight.

While I was there, I reconnected with Charles, a friend I had made in Kathmandu. He was French and spoke only a little English, but with my limited French we were able to communicate. Charles announced to me immediately, with absolute certainty, that the kid was the real thing. I was perplexed. What was I missing? Maybe there was more for me to learn. I had to admit that our accommodation was exceedingly comfortable. We both had huge private suites and a big connecting balcony where we could watch hosts of birds flying over the roof. It took me a while to realize that the birds were actually bats, which seemed like a symbolic misunderstanding. They filled the sky. Everywhere I looked I thought I was seeing birds, then realized they were something else, something more sinister. Guru Maharaj was like that, covered in dazzling robes and gold chains, but nothing about him felt right to me. Charles was smitten, but I felt he hadn't seen beneath the trappings.

It turns out that the guru's family wanted us to become promoters of their son beyond India. They thought I was the guy who was going to bring him to America, which explained the luxury, the car and chauffeur. Charles would take him to Europe. We became important celebrities.

The Divine Light Mission held a big annual festival, where over fifty thousand people gathered for four days in a makeshift city to celebrate their guru. It was taking place the following week, and we were asked to go onstage and speak to the crowds. I felt strangely trapped, but it was also extraordinary to experience being so celebrated, so loved and adored. I stood on the stage with a translator and a bank of microphones before tens of thousands of people, but I had no idea what to say. I didn't have the spiritual language down, so I talked about the wonders of LSD. I don't think anyone understood. Then they asked me and Charles to dance, to show our love for the guru and express our joy. I said I didn't dance, but it was clear they didn't care. Certain things were expected of

Exploring – Lord of the Universe 117

me. I smiled and danced hard. The huge gathering cheered. It was like being on the stage at Radio City Music Hall. Later, when I walked through the crowd, garlands were draped around my neck and people bowed down to kiss my feet. Everyone was applauding. I was being treated like royalty, but felt oddly seduced and abused. They were programming me to be something I had no desire to be. I sensed that India was full of gurus and teachers waiting for their moment. How could *I* be the best opportunity that they had? After spending a few more weeks with The Divine Light Mission sharing luxurious quarters with Charles, I had a nagging urge to move on.

I read that the Dalai Lama wanted to go to New York, to the General Assembly of the United Nations, and decided somehow that I should be the one to tell him what he needed to know about America before he made his trip. I figured he knew as much about world history as the monks I had lived with. It also worried me that Americans had a distorted view of Tibet, if they had a view at all, and probably thought of it as some kind of Shangri-La, as envisioned in Frank Capra's *Lost Horizon*. To my knowledge, few Westerners had any idea of the depth and breadth of Tibetan Buddhist wisdom and the horrifying story that was playing out with the Chinese takeover. Someone needed to tell the Dalai Lama what to expect.

I told the leaders of the Divine Light Mission that I had to see the Dalai Lama. "The Dalai Lama is nothing," they told me. "You're with the Lord of the Universe now. Why would you waste your time with the Dalai Lama?" "I don't think it's a waste," I said. "I think it's important." Charles was beginning to share my doubts about the Lord of the Universe, so he and I began the trek to Dharamsala. It should be said that this eight-year-old guru grew up, broke with his family, and developed a massive following with millions of seekers around the world. *Life* magazine covered his arrival in America, where he held sold-out rallies in huge stadiums and bamboozled many Westerners searching for easy enlightenment.

Somewhere, just before beginning this journey, I heard the phrase "Give up everything and follow me." It made me think that my problem was that I was still attached, still holding on to material things I thought I needed. I had a knapsack, a sleeping bag, and a little blanket with a mosquito net in it. I gave away everything except the clothes I was wearing and a small shoulder bag with a single change of underwear and socks. I wanted to see the Dalai Lama, and I wanted to be worthy of a real teacher, so I surrendered everything I had.

Dharamsala, a small town in the foothills of the Himalayas where the Dalai Lama was living along with the Tibetan government in exile, was very cold. When the people at the tiny hotel where Charles and I stayed gave us some blankets, I realized that life had provided. I was taken care of. I know the world doesn't always work that way, but in that moment, real innocence and a trust of the universe had a strange power. It was palpable.

Charles and I knocked on the gate of the Dalai Lama's palace, which turned out to be a spacious, suburban-type bungalow surrounded by a metal fence. The guards at the gate looked at us suspiciously. I explained that I needed to talk to His Holiness. "Sorry," they said. "You can't just show up and talk to the Dalai Lama." I explained how I needed to prepare him for his visit to America, but was unable to persuade them. Charles tried to convince me that it was a fool's mission and that we should leave, but I wouldn't take no for an answer. I had learned that the Dalai Lama's sister ran an orphanage in a place called Happy Valley, a few hours away, so I decided to go see her. Unlike her brother, she was unprotected and available, and after an emotional talk she said she would arrange a meeting. Four days later Charles and I had an appointment to meet with His Holiness. I was told it would be a half-hour meeting.

As we strolled through the "palace" gates and approached the bungalow that housed him, I was surprised to see the Dalai Lama himself walking toward me along the front porch. We had silk Tibetan scarves to offer him, a traditional Tibetan greeting. He smiled warmly as we presented them to him. With casual grace, he blessed the scarves and placed them around our necks.

The moment I saw him and felt the intelligence and warmth radiating through his eyes, I understood that he knew more about the world than I ever would. It was instantly clear that I had nothing to teach him about America's perception of Tibet. We sat in a casual and comfortable Western-style living room. His Secretary of State served as our translator, but His Holiness often spoke in English. Charles, who spoke mostly French, struggled with the talk but seemed happy just to be there. The Dalai Lama's eyes were laser-like in their focus. He seemed excited to share with us the teachings of Tibetan Buddhism and was grateful to be with people who wanted to talk about something other than Tibetan refugee problems or other governmental issues. It was a beautiful exchange. By the end of our meeting, three hours later, His Holiness reached out to us and offered to be our teacher. I'm not sure Charles understood what was being proposed, but I was taken aback. The truth is that while His Holiness was clearly an exceptional being, responsible for a people and a nation that had been overrun by Chinese invaders, I didn't sense a doorway to the mystical, life-shattering insights I was searching for. I sat dumbfounded for a minute, not sure what to say or do. Words seemed to rise out of my mouth.

"Forgive me, but I don't think you're my teacher. I'm profoundly grateful for the invitation, but I sense that I need to continue my journey. If I don't find a teacher, will you still be here for me? Will you let me come back?" He was unbelievably gracious. "Of course," he said.

I met him again, years later in Los Angeles. Richard Gere threw a party for him at his home, where I reminded His Holiness about our first encounter. He didn't remember me, of course, but touched my balding head and said, "You must have had more hair then." We both laughed. Decades later I came to understand that, even without sitting with him, his teachings had filled my life. His sense of human goodness and kindness embodied a much larger truth than I was capable of understanding at the time. I had been his student all along.

Charles and I started hitchhiking again. We didn't get far before a police captain picked us up. There weren't many hitchhikers in India, and he was curious about us, especially after we told him we were on a spiritual quest. He drove us to his office, offered us tea and bananas, and gave one of the most beautiful spiritual talks I've ever heard. It was a karma yoga talk, about how you have to integrate your spiritual life into everyday life. I thought, *This is incredible. He's not a teacher. He's just a policeman.* He reminded me of Siddhartha in Herman Hesse's novel, who worked as a ferry boat operator, casually teaching anyone who crossed the river with him. I was inspired and felt that this was the kind of teacher I would like to become someday. Then he drove us back to the main road. Charles and I went our separate ways. I don't remember why we parted, but I wanted to go to Varanasi and he had other destinations in mind. It was a sad goodbye, but we both sensed we would see each other again, which did in fact happen. Charles became a tour guide in Martinique with his wife Monique on their boat, the Celimene, which he captained lovingly until his death in 2021.

I left the Dalai Lama and ended up living in Varanasi. I can never figure out how long I was there. It seemed like a timeless place.

I lived on a houseboat on the banks of the Ganges that had been rented out to several hippies. We were all smoking opium, which was being sold by the government in a store not far away. It was very cheap, just a few rupees. I had no bed on the boat, so I slept on the hardwood floor. As I inhaled the opium, I could feel the floor getting softer and softer until it was like a cloud enveloping me. Around 4am the cloud got harder and harder as the opium wore off. That's how I knew it was time to get up.

I would go up on deck and see the mass of people surrounding the boat, stretching up and down the banks of the Ganges for miles, bathing in the healing waters. People came to Varanasi from all over India to die there, to have their bodies cremated at the edge of the river. It was said that if their ashes were tossed into the holy water, they would be reborn into a higher incarnation. Every day I walked up the steps into the town and saw people waiting in the streets to die. Sometimes I would offer them food, and they would say, "No, no – cigarette." Tobacco was all they wanted, because they thought it might help keep their pain at bay. They were just waiting to die so they could be burned in the ghats and have their remains thrown into the sacred river. The whole town smelled like roasted chicken. The river was filled with fish that ate the organs that didn't burn – mostly stomachs and hearts, I think. People were bathing in it all.

I heard about a woman called the Priestess of the Burning Ghats. She was a wrinkled but ageless woman with no teeth and her hair tied up in a tall knot. She was probably in her forties, but she looked as if she were in her seventies. She lived in a cave-like structure under a building above the burning ghats, and would preside over them – stirring the ashes, tossing bones and unburned organs into the flowing waters.

She loved opium, so one day I brought her some. She laughed and indicated that the store-bought stuff was horrible. She pulled out some real opium and we smoked together. Then she covered me in ash – the remains of bodies burning on the funeral pyres about a hundred yards away – and drew cryptic marks on my forehead. Suddenly I entered another psychedelic universe. I lost all sense of my personal story and had no idea where I was, who I was, or what I was doing there. The cave-like environment felt like an ancient spiritual space, as if I had been dwelling there forever, as far from Western culture as anybody could get. Curiously, this initiation seemed preordained, as if waiting for me to arrive and partake of its blessings. No part of it seemed odd. Mostly it felt like a reminder: "Wake up and know who you are."

I lay on the boat that night and heard a voice coming out of the ether. "You must create a masterpiece," it said very distinctly. It was like a commandment, and I took it very seriously. I understood that my spiritual liberation would be aided by my creating an enduring work. I had no idea if I would ever achieve such a thing, or how I would even know if I had, but it was clear that those were my marching orders.

It was time for me to leave India. There was no grand announcement. I just knew that I hadn't found my teacher and it was time to move on. I was drawn to Southeast Asia and headed in that direction.

In a train, traveling from Delhi to Calcutta, I read a book by George Gurdjieff called *Beelzebub's Tales to His Grandson*. There was only one other person in the compartment, a young man. Suddenly he leaned over and said, "That book was written for me. I am his grandson. I am Gurdjieff's grandson." I didn't know what to make of that. How was it that I could be sitting on a train reading a book by a major world philosopher that was titled for his grandson, and that this very grandson would be on the same train as me, in the same compartment, sitting across the aisle, traveling from Delhi to

Calcutta? *What were the chances? In a world full of people...* I was struck by the synchronicity. I actually saw him again and even met his mother in London, a very sweet woman with many stories to tell about her famous father. He became a New York art dealer with little in common with his grandfather. Coincidence was an ongoing wake-up call for me, a series of taps on the shoulder, reminders that something bigger than I could possibly understand was going on.

I flew from Calcutta to Bangkok and lived for a week in a huge Buddhist temple in the center of town, which was filled with boys who were fulfilling their two-year commitment as monks. They all had portable radios, were into weightlifting, and begged for food from local residents, who provided all the meals served at the temple. The old monks ate first. The young ones, and me, ate last. The joys of Western materialism had recently been discovered, and the monks were exulting in it. There was nothing remotely spiritual about the place. They were headed 180 degrees away from traditional Buddhist teachings, and the West was embracing them in a stranglehold. I found it profoundly disheartening.

I decided to hitchhike to Saigon. The war in Vietnam was in progress and I thought that I could be the guy who would spread peace and love throughout the embattled country. The embassy workers in Bangkok thought I was crazy and wouldn't give me a visa, which was fortunate, as I'm sure I would have been killed in Vietnam. I ended up going through Laos and heading to Cambodia instead. I got on a boat that went down the Mekong River, then hopped on the back of a truck that was driving through the Laotian jungle. After a while, the truck was ambushed by a group of soldiers with guns. They were members of the revolutionary group Pathet Lao, which was closely associated with Vietnamese communists. They were surprised to see an American, and there was a moment when it seemed like a cosmic joke. Instead of being killed by the Viet Cong, I thought I might be shot by the Pathet Lao. Suddenly the soldiers jumped into the back of the truck and the driver took off. One of the guys reached into his knapsack and pulled out some ganga and we started smoking together. I'm looking at them, they're looking at me – then we all start laughing. There was no more fear. I knew they weren't going to kidnap me or kill me. We were just a bunch of guys on the back of a truck, getting high.

I spent a week at the long-abandoned city of Angkor Wat, which was still being excavated from the surrounding jungle. The ancient Buddhist statues had trees growing out of them, their faces and bodies entwined by roots, carved heads strangled by dense foliage. A lesson in impermanence. We all return to nature in the end, even Buddhas. I slept in the temples, on hard marble floors, and knew I had mastered the art of the journey when I was able to sleep on those rock-hard surfaces without a mattress. All I had was a mosquito net.

After that I returned to Thailand and made my way south to Malaysia and Singapore. The border between Thailand and Malaysia was open and unattended. I simply walked into a tiny building, found an official stamp, stamped my own passport, and moved on. I kept thinking that this was how the world should work – easy passage from one country to another, one culture to the next.

While living in a Sikh temple in Singapore, I became very sick and so weak that I couldn't eat. Luckily a young man took me into an empty apartment that his family owned and gave me a bed. He brought me food and occasionally looked in on me. I don't know how or why he appeared in my life, but it was as if another angel had arrived. There was a record player in the apartment and a Bob Dylan album, *Highway 61 Revisited*. I played the first side of the record endlessly because I didn't have the energy to get out of bed to turn it over or even turn it off. I heard "Like a Rolling Stone" so many times that it became the anthem of my entire trip.

How does it feel, how does it feel?
To be on your own, with no direction home
A complete unknown, like a rolling stone

To this day, when I hear that song, I'm transported half a century back in time and simultaneously uprooted from time altogether. I remember total homelessness, aloneness, my childhood fears of abandonment encompassing me. And yet, those fears were turned into beautiful music. My journey suddenly felt mythic, heroic, liberating.

When I met Dylan years later at Whoopi Goldberg's house, I wanted to share with him my story about listening to his song over and over and how anthemic it had become in my life. I also wanted to tell him we both had the same corduroy suit that Midge McKenzie had found for us in London many years before. We had a bond. But he wasn't interested in talking. He sat on a big couch looking strangely imperious, and everyone left him alone. Clearly some stories are not meant to be shared.

Slowly my health and energy returned. I thanked the young man for his generosity and bought a ticket on a French ship sailing for Japan. It turned out I had to wait a week longer than expected. War had broken out between Israel and Egypt, and no one was sure the ship would make it through the Suez Canal. I went back to the Sikh temple where I had stayed and befriended two Israeli guys who had been planning on going to Japan but now sensed an obligation to go back to Israel and fight. The war lasted only six days. Our ship, the Messageries Maritimes, was the very last one to make it through the canal before it was closed.

Life aboard was amazing. The French food, even in steerage, was excellent and there were movies screened every night. We passed between the Islands of Corregidor and Bataan, the scene of major battles between America and Japan only twenty years before. There I was, standing on the deck with a group of Japanese kids, hugging and laughing, as though nothing had ever happened, as though our countries had never been at war. It felt like a momentous realization – how quickly animosities evaporate, how little of wartime experience passes from one generation to the next. It gave me great hope for humanity. Life goes on. The human spirit endures.

When we stopped in Manila for an afternoon, I quickly got the sense that it was a city that rambled. It had no center, and I was happy to leave. We docked in Hong Kong for a day and I managed to get myself to the top of Victoria Peak, overlooking the entire city. I sat there for a long time, alone, watching airplanes land on the huge runway extending dramatically out into the bay. I had a sense, sitting there, that I had finally accomplished what I had been trying to accomplish for many lifetimes. I had circumnavigated the globe. It was as if I had completed some kind of circuit, a major karmic cycle. For many incarnations, it seemed, I had wanted to do this – and now it was done. The sense I had was that there are many key moments in the spiritual/cosmic journey, and I had completed one. It was the end of a great adventure and the beginning of another.

I spent a month in Japan. I arrived with twenty dollars in my pocket and left with ten. I was proud of that. I had learned how to travel. The Japanese were fascinated by me, a bearded American hitchhiker. They hadn't met many people like me before.

I loved Tokyo, especially the statue of the Kamakura Buddha – two stories high with its hands folded in a meditative pose. I wanted to be embraced by those hands. The park where the statue was situated was closing and I decided to hide until everyone was gone, then climbed up onto the Buddha and tried to nestle in its folded palms. The welcoming hands were filled with uncomfortable tiny metal girders from an abundance of soldering. I ended up sleeping on a picnic table instead and being bitten by mosquitoes all night. The next night I stayed with a lovely couple who ran a Christian church. They were very welcoming, and in the morning even made a tuna sandwich for me, the first I'd had in over a year.

I set out alongside a roadway with a long traffic jam. Everyone in their cars stared out of their windows, shouting, "Hitchhiker, American!" They were applauding as I walked past. People invited me into their cars, but they were going nowhere fast, so I kept walking and enjoying the cheers. Hours later, when traffic started moving, I hitched a ride part of the way to Hiroshima. The driver turned off onto a small road and left me sitting in an empty field. It was lunchtime, so I pulled out my tuna sandwich. I sat there, thinking that this was a moment of perfection, and that the only thing that could make it more perfect would be a cold can of Coca-Cola. At that very second a huge semi-truck stopped on the highway and the driver leaned out the window. He was holding a can of Coke. He called out to see if I wanted it. "American! American! Coke? Coke!" It had never tasted better.

The truck driver took me to Hiroshima, a city of such historical power and horror that I was almost afraid to enter it. I had nowhere to spend the night, but was invited to sleep on a table in a school gymnasium. When I woke up in the morning, I was surrounded by hundreds of young kids screaming and dancing around me. The entire space was exploding with life.

In Nagasaki I met a young girl who claimed to be Miss Butterfly, a reference to *Madama Butterfly* I suppose, who invited me into her home, where I met her family. Her dad dressed me in local costume, and we all went out for a Japanese dinner. I spent the night in their house, feeling nestled in the heart of Japan.

The next morning I made my way to Kyoto, my favorite of all Japanese cities, full of the aura of Buddhist teaching and hospitality. At nightfall I knocked on the door of a temple and asked the priest if I could sleep there for a night. He said no. I told him about my world travels and how a Christian couple had housed me. He seemed pained by the comparison and relented, even offering me a meal. While I was eating, a group of local reporters arrived to document my being there and I was asked to pose with the priest for the Kyoto newspapers. His hospitality had turned into an act of self-promotion.

After a month of traveling around Japan, I found myself in a Tokyo record store, where I discovered two albums that had been released in the year and a half that I was gone. One was The Beatles' *Sgt. Pepper's Lonely Hearts Club Band*. The track "With a Little Help from My Friends" meant a lot to me. Then I heard Grace Slick singing "Somebody to Love," from Jefferson Airplane's *Surrealistic Pillow*.

> Don't you want somebody to love?
> Don't you need somebody to love?
> Wouldn't you love somebody to love?
> You better find somebody to love."

Those words popped out at me louder than anything I had heard on the entire trip. And something inside of me said "yes." I took those lyrics as new instructions: "Please, bring me somebody to love."

It was time to go home. I considered teaching English in Japan to make enough for an airplane ticket, but I really didn't want to stay. I called my dad in Detroit and begged him to fly me home. I knew he didn't have much money, but he didn't hesitate. The next day I had a ticket to San Francisco, then Detroit.

I spent a few days in Berkeley, visiting Mark and his sister Carol, who was staying with him. It was San Francisco's Summer of Love.

Mark, Carol, Larry and our friend Gayle all went to a big outdoor concert where we heard Mussorgsky's *Pictures at an Exhibition*. The joy of that symphony enveloped me. I was with friends again. I was back in America. I was home.

A few days later I flew to Detroit, where the embrace of family was overwhelming. I had fallen even more in love with them during my travels. They were the very essence of me. We were woven of the same fabric. It's hard to describe the completeness, the fullness I felt in their presence. But I was a man of the world now. Detroit was no longer home for me. I knew that New York was calling. And that I needed to find someone to love.

Ten

Finding – Blanche-Rudi-Joshua

I had tried everything. I had gone on a pilgrimage. I had spent a year and a half hitchhiking around the world. I had visited ashrams and met with holy teachers. I tried everything I could think of, made every effort I could make, to find a teacher. But I had failed. And so, I gave up. I didn't know what else to do. None of it worked. So I surrendered.

And that's when everything began.

The word "surrender" as it is used in relation to spiritual development does not have the negative connotation it often has in ordinary speech. The action of surrender, as the term is used here, is the voluntary casting off of the thoughts and emotions that interfere with the realization of the spirit within.

Rudi, **Spiritual Cannibalism**

Fall 1967.

My wife Blanche has a hard time with me telling the story of how we met because she doesn't think it's romantic. But for me,

it's extraordinary. I told Blanche that I had petitioned God to bring me somebody to love. "If you bring someone into my life," I told God, "I will love them. Whoever you bring through that door, I will devote myself to them." On one of my first nights back in New York, my friends George and Cheryl said, "Do you want to meet a girl?" I smiled and said, "Yes." I suppose I would have been happy to meet a guy, but I wasn't putting any conditions on my request. That evening Blanche walked into the room. Nothing jumped out at me. She seemed nice, open and very warm. I nodded to the universe in approval. George and Cheryl's apartment was on East 10th Street. Blanche's was on East 2nd, a storefront near the Bowery on the Lower East Side.

I walked her home that night. Her place was what was called a railroad apartment, with a long storefront entry, a kitchen about fifty feet further in, and a bedroom and toilet in the back. The walls were covered with huge bold, bright paintings, some totally abstract, some with figures. One particularly insistent image stared at me. It was an abstracted naked woman with huge thighs poised next to a huge rock. It was a demanding presence, boldly painted in vivid orange and purple. It had so much force, determination, big-heartedness. The moment I looked at it, I knew I had really met Blanche – the artist, the inner being. That painting has been in every home we've ever had, front and center, a constant reminder of the moment when I first knew who this person was. There was a swing hanging from the ceiling in the middle of her kitchen, a round cozy cup of blue fabric. I asked if I could sit in it. She said sure. She sat beside me in a chair.

It was a very quiet moment, pregnant with possibility. She told me a little bit about herself. She was from West Hempstead, Long Island, coincidentally, perhaps cosmically, only fifteen minutes from Mineola, where my dad was born. And I wouldn't know it until after our wedding, but she babysat for cousins of mine who lived just around the corner from her house. She told me that her

mom Fanny, or Fann as everyone called her, sang in the choir at their temple, that Fann had lost two children, both sons, one at the age of four, one in childbirth, something she had never gotten over, and that Blanche had an older sister, Rhoda, seven years her senior. Her dad, Arnold, owned a home improvement store at 1010 Sunrise Highway and later lived off proceeds from the land he rented to the Sunrise Motel next door. Her mom worked for him as a bookkeeper. I tried to absorb all this information. Then it was my turn.

"I'd like to tell you a story," I said. She smiled. I began by painting the full picture, my life in Detroit, my film aspirations, the LSD trip, my travels around the world and the moment in the record store in Tokyo. I told her how I had asked God to bring me someone to love and how I had agreed to accept whoever God chose. I remember looking at her very intently. I told her that I had made a deal that whoever walked through that door would be the person I would give myself to in this lifetime. "And you walked through the door," I said. She looked at me strangely. This clearly wasn't expected. I could feel her curiosity and her discomfort. Then I said, "I want to tell you everything about me. Everything. And if at the end you want to pursue this, if you'd like to try and be together for this lifetime, we could see if maybe we could make it work." I said that if she wasn't interested, I would be on my way. I continued talking for probably another hour, leaving nothing unsaid. Instead of slowly unpeeling the onion, I just chopped right to the core. I told her all my secrets – including all the stuff that I had spent much of my life trying to hide. I told her I was gay but that I'd had pleasurable sex with women (one to be exact). At the end of this long-winded monologue, as she later confessed, she thought I was a madman, even certifiably crazy. But to my ongoing amazement, and I suspect her own, she eventually said yes. We married two years later and are still together after more than fifty years. I call it an arranged marriage. It was arranged by God.

There are plenty of additional elements to this story and many that Blanche and I disagree on. I had been offered a job in England with Midge McKenzie and her new husband Frank to make a movie about the Beatles, and was due to leave for London in a month. I had also found a job when I arrived in New York about ten days earlier, helping edit a film called *Astarte* for the Robert Joffrey Ballet Company. I was working with Gar Compton and his companion Emile Ardolino (who later directed *Dirty Dancing* and *Sister Act*). I told Blanche that I would be working day and night and couldn't promise that I would have much time to see her. Today she insists that I never called her at all, although I definitely did take her to the premiere of *Astarte*, which was a big success and made the cover of *Time* magazine. But the real celebration was time together in Blanche's apartment. We sensed immediately that we belonged together. We had wonderful sex on the mattress on her bedroom floor. It was joyous. We explored the Lower East Side and found restaurants we loved. We felt like a couple. Then, after about ten days, she drove me to the airport and I flew to London. She was in tears as I promised to return, although I had no idea what my future held.

My time in London wasn't pleasant. I was supposed to live in an apartment provided by Midge and Frank, but it wasn't ready. I tried living in their apartment for a week, but Midge had just had a baby and discovered the little boy had serious health issues. It was clear I didn't belong in their home at that time. To add to that, the movie about the Beatles seemed suddenly less certain and was being delayed. My friend Barry Kaplan was living in London and offered me a spare bed, but that was all he could offer. He had no food, and we ran out of people to beg from. I remember one night eating nothing but green peppers for dinner.

That same day I received a beautiful, hand-colored letter from Blanche, in which she included a list of everything that she remembered I loved from our brief time together: bagels, lox, truth, God, Detroit, *Citizen Kane*. It was as though she knew every button to push. I could sense that she knew me better than I knew myself, but more importantly, that she loved me. I realized what a mistake I had made traveling to London and how unsupported I felt. It was as if the universe were showing me what happens when you make the wrong decision, when you make choices through your mind instead of your heart. I knew I had to leave London right away and get back to Blanche.

I called my dad for the second time in a year and begged for a plane ticket back. He agreed, but I needed to come to Detroit first. The next day I was on my way. I had a brief stay in Detroit, once again embraced by everyone and feeling lucky to be so loved. As soon as I got there, I called Blanche. We talked and talked, and it was clear to me how desperate I was to get back to see her. Within a week I had moved into her apartment. We haven't been apart since.

Around the same time that I met Blanche at George and Cheryl's – it may have been the very same day – I went to an Asian art store in Greenwich Village called Rudi's Antiques. It was on Seventh Avenue next to the Village Vanguard, the famous jazz club. I had actually been there a few years earlier. Before I went on my journey to the East, I went in looking for a Buddha figurine. I was drawn to one in particular, about two inches high, but chipped at the base, so I dismissed it. I went to the owner – this heavy-set, very business-like character named Rudi – and said, "I'm looking for a Buddha." He said, "How much do you want to spend?" "Three dollars," I said. He didn't even blink. He went over and pulled out the chipped Buddha. I said, "Yeah, I was looking at that one... but it's broken." He said, "Search for perfection in yourself, not in external objects."

I told him that was the best sales pitch I had ever heard – and bought it. That little Buddha traveled around the world with me and is still in the center of my meditation altar at home. He reminds me daily that the perfection I seek can't be found in the material world.

When I came home from my travels, I went back to Rudi's store with some Tibetan carpets I was trying to sell for the monks I had lived with in Kathmandu. He wasn't interested in the carpets, but he asked me why I had been in Nepal. I told him I was looking for a teacher. He asked if I had found one. I said no. Then he told me, "Well, I can teach you everything you want to know." I stared at him oddly. I wondered how this strange, portly guy in this overcrowded antique store could be a spiritual teacher. Partly it felt like a come-on, like a set-up of some kind. But something inside me responded. I sensed it was true. I don't know how I sensed it, but I did.

The old adage is that the teacher appears when you're ready. It seemed odd that I had to hitchhike around the world to find the proprietor of an Asian art store in downtown New York claiming to be the guru I had been searching for. I didn't know what to make of it. Did I really have to travel twenty thousand miles – sleep in a crumbling hut in Afghanistan, live on the bank of the Ganges, sit on Victoria Peak – in order to walk into his store four blocks from where I used to live? But it was dawning on me, even as we spoke, that I would never have recognized him any other way.

Rudi was born Albert Rudolph in 1928 in Brooklyn, the youngest of three boys. He was an overweight, gay Jewish man, not very different from me I suppose (though after India I was barely 130 pounds). Maybe finding someone similar to me was appropriate and comforting. There was certainly no question that I felt a strange familiarity in his presence. His divorced mother, Rae, who had raised her three sons, was a one-of-a-kind personality, and I was told that at one point she had worked as a stripper. A couple of years after I met Rudi, he hired his mom to work for him, saying

she was the most difficult person he knew and that she needed "the most work." For Rudi "work" was a daily gift, requiring him to transcend all judgment and hostility. I know very little about Rudi's life, or even how Albert Rudolph became Rudi. Nothing about him announced his extraordinary being. Outwardly he was cherubic, articulate and soft-spoken, given to joyous laughter and very playful. But when he grew silent or just looked at you, everything stood still. He saw you. He embraced you. You could tell that he knew who you were.

I was told that around the age of eight he had fallen or was pushed down a flight of stairs and required a series of operations. When first told he would need a second operation, he ran out of the hospital into an empty field where he was approached by a group of Tibetan monks, real or imagined. They told him that he was going to be a great teacher one day, and that he would affect many lives. The operations he was having were preparing him for that role. Whether or not that's true, he went back to the hospital a changed person.

Years later, after getting out of the navy, he began a spiritual pursuit that included studying something called Pak Subud, which introduced him to a concept central to his later teaching called "the art of surrender" and then the writings of Gurdjieff. (He was very pleased when, one day, I introduced him to Gurdjieff's grandson). At one point he decided to go to India, where he happened upon the man who would change everything, Swami Nityananda. He met him in a small town outside of Bombay called Ganeshpuri, where he had an ashram and many disciples, including Swami Muktananda, who later became his successor and Rudi's teacher. His meeting with Nityananda only lasted a day, but Rudi was completely transformed by the encounter. Nityananda told him to stop his search, give up his travels, and return to America – which he did. He opened an Asian art store, instead of the fancy telephones he used to sell, and began teaching whatever it was that Nityanada imparted to him.

Rudi's store was tiny, maybe six hundred square feet, filled with art and photos of Nityananda, almost always naked. It was hard to take your eyes off the images. I could feel some kind of energy radiating from the photographs, especially because of their profound strangeness. The store's front window was dominated by an eight-foot-long reposing Buddha that caught the eye of anyone walking past on Seventh Avenue. When parents and kids came into the store, Rudi always had candy for the children. He knew many customers by name. Being in Rudi's presence didn't feel like being anywhere else on earth. Maybe it was because the store was overflowing with Buddhist and Hindu art. Maybe it was Rudi. But I knew I was where I was supposed to be in ways that can't be easily explained. It was full-bodied, full-souled knowing.

Rudi's store had no space for teaching, so he took two folding chairs outside and put them on the subway grating on Seventh Avenue. Then he sat down opposite me, looked into my eyes, and said, "Okay. Take a breath, draw it into your heart, hold it there and ask for help to surrender…"

I did.

We were on a crowded street and people were walking around us, but I felt there was nobody else in the world but Rudi. Everything else fell away. He was looking straight at me, really accepting and loving me. I had an inexplicable sense of coming home.

Rudi described a simple system of energy centers called "chakras," openings into the inner workings of a human being. In the West we refer to things like open minds, open hearts, fire in the belly, knowing things with your gut. Rudi provided a map to those centers and said they had a vast oceanic depth that few human beings ever explore. Westerners, he said, live in the outer manifested world, an impermanent space that will not last and with little idea of access to their inner being, which he and mystics before him said was infinite and eternal. His practice, or "work" as he called it, could lead you there. It felt like he was articulating many of the insights from my LSD trip, that he was offering me a passport to the universe I had witnessed inside myself.

Rudi said that open-eyed meditation is a transmission. Two people looking at each other have a kind of connectivity that is built into human experience. Gazing at one another – without fear, allowing oneself to be seen, allowing oneself to experience that moment of connection – is a simple and very real human experience. Lovers staring at one another feel it. He said he was sending me that energy. I could feel things stirring inside me as he looked into my eyes. I wondered at first if I was being hypnotized, if there was some kind of mind control going on. I had heard stories of guru-disciple mind manipulation and spiritual cults. But mostly, I just felt loved. At that moment, I sensed I had somehow become a disciple.

The true cementing experience was going to Rudi's meditation class, which he taught in a converted funeral parlor on Hudson, just off Christopher Street in the West Village. He lived upstairs and the class was taught downstairs in the small, chapel-like environment where the dead used to be laid out in caskets for final viewing and goodbyes. There were meditation pillows for people who wanted to sit on the floor closer to Rudi and chairs for the rest of us toward the back. In the beginning I would sit on a chair, but my very first class in that space made me question that choice. Rudi entered the room and sat down on a small platform on something like a stage. He grabbed his shirt, pulled it off, and sat half naked before us. I was surprised by the sudden sense of such raw, unprotected presence. I didn't know what to make of him or what to expect. I questioned whether I should even be there. As he looked at people in the room, their bodies jerked up or shook as he made contact. It was odd to witness. My mind was spinning. Then he looked at me. I felt a surge of energy much stronger than what I had experienced sitting with him on Seventh Avenue. It was like nothing I had ever felt before. Energy shot up my spine and my body jerked upward with a furious blast, like a rocket taking off, and I found myself lying on the floor. This, I later learned, was an uprising energy called kundalini, often described as serpent power in Hindu teachings. I wasn't the only person to have this experience. Many people were now jerking violently as the energy that I had called love, and Rudi called shaktipat, went surging into their chakra system.

Until my LSD trip, I knew nothing about the inner life other than experiences of emotion, fear, hope, love, hate. Most of these were superficial and experienced through the mind. The mind blocked the entrance to the stillness of our deeper self that Rudi, like others, often called the soul. Rudi said that the mind was the slayer of the soul. It took me years to appreciate that.

The talks that Rudi gave after his meditation sessions clarified his teaching and were powerfully directive. He didn't believe in the kinds of ascetic practices that were preached in India, and didn't advise us to abandon the world and join an ashram and give up meat and sex and dancing. "*This* is your spiritual life," he said. "This day-to-day reality is your spiritual life. It begins with making your bed in the morning. Get that in order. Make this life function as part of your spiritual practice, because that's what it is." I wanted a life. I wanted a career. I wanted to get married. I wanted children. Many teachings promote letting go of the world, but as Rudi explained, "You can't let go of what you haven't had." I didn't want to renounce my dreams in hopes of becoming spiritual. To me, spirituality shouldn't involve the loss of the things that made life wonderful. Rudi's practice didn't run from life – it brought us deeper into it. It taught us to have and then to detach, often at the same time. It was liberating. I began sitting in Rudi's class three times a week. It was my salvation. It was a constant teaching.

After I started studying with Rudi, whenever I walked into his store I felt like I was passing through the looking glass. It was like entering Wonderland. Sometimes I had to walk around the block a few times before I could go into the store. It was frightening at first, because I knew that when I went in there I was going to be *seen*. I was coming in with all my anxieties and tension, and didn't want to bring that exposed craziness to Rudi. I was embarrassed to walk into his space feeling so completely dominated by the tensions of the world, the drama of my job. I didn't want him to see that in me.

He did, of course. There was no way for me to hide it. And he loved me in spite of what he saw. He knew it was there, but looked past it. He told me as much. He said, "You're really crazy." It wasn't clinical or derogatory, just a simple observation. He didn't care because he knew that if you look into any human being, you see the same thing in everyone. Under the surface you see the Self. You see God. He kept staring at me until all my tension, all my craziness, melted away.

Sometimes I would cry. He would just smile at me, give me a hug, and maybe make some tea. Then I was back in the world again – but I was back in the world with a sense of the depth of my own being. I felt that I was one with something greater. And then I would think, *Why was I so nervous about coming here? It's so simple.*

The thing we basically suffer from is a lack of awareness of what we are involved in, which is life. Life has a quantity, a quality, and a density. Our lack of awareness, our unconsciousness of it, allows us to use it improperly.

Rudi, **Spiritual Cannibalism**

"You have to do this every day for the rest of your life" was one of the first things Rudi said when he was teaching meditation practice. I found that off-putting. I didn't know how I could possibly make a lifelong commitment to something I was just hearing about for the first time. But I said, "Okay." And I started meditating every day.

For a long time, I could never explain to anybody why I would sit and meditate every morning. People said I was wasting my time. I couldn't explain it to them, but every time I meditated, I knew where and what I was. I knew I was where I belonged. And over the years I've watched what that experience – day after day – has meant for my life. It's a little bit like a sailor's awareness of the North Star. It's something that guides you and keeps you on course. If you haven't discovered the North Star or something equivalent in your life, and you aren't constantly checking in to see where you're headed, it's easy to get lost.

I studied with Rudi for about a month before I asked Blanche if she was interested in coming to class. She was curious, and when Rudi finally met her, he told me that she was a deep well. I was impressed by that. I wanted to be a deep well too. He immediately embraced her, and she embraced him back. It was the final building block in our relationship. We were clearly on the same path.

Rudi's advice was simple: "Get your life in order." He recognized that if your life is disordered, you want to escape. If you try to turn a disordered, dysfunctional life into a spiritual life, what you'll end up with is a disordered and dysfunctional spiritual life. "You need structure," said Rudi.

But he didn't leave it at that. He took action and bought four buildings on East 10th Street that needed to be fixed up. One would be his new home with the classroom downstairs. He also bought a new antique store around the corner on Fourth Avenue. And who did he ask to do the work? His students. He asked that we come as often as we could to help tear down ceilings, repair the walls, throw out the garbage. He made us understand that by taking out his garbage, we were, in a sense, removing our own garbage. It was a commitment to learn and grow.

At one point, my mom and dad said, "He's just using you. He's taking advantage of you. It's a scam. You're getting nothing in return for all this free labor." But I knew that wasn't true. I was getting plenty out of it. The more I worked, the more I sat with Rudi, the more I grew. For the first time in my life, I felt worthy. I felt worthy of being in Rudi's presence and receiving the energy he gave – because Rudi was asking for great effort, and I was responding with great effort. I was committed to the work.

One other thing about Rudi was that he was openly gay and not above sleeping with some of his students – me included. He certainly wasn't my type, but his energy transmission during sex was massive and unmistakable. I slept with him and afterwards he told me that I wasn't really gay. I had no idea what he meant. I knew men aroused me. But I think he saw something more complex in me and understood the transformative power of my relationship with Blanche.

His use of sex as a spiritual transmission was clearly fraught with the potential for damage and misunderstanding, and in later years I wasn't surprised to see other teachers misuse their sexual power. When I asked Rudi about the sexual side of his teaching, he said: "If you go to a cow for milk, you pull at its tit and drink. If you put your hand up its ass, you get what you deserve." I found that somewhat self-serving, but at the time I discounted it all. Rudi's honesty and openness seemed courageous, even essential, to me, and it helped that we shared a sexual path that remained for me an ongoing source of secrecy and shame.

The commitment that Blanche and I made to Rudi's practice became the foundation of our spiritual and material lives. At our wedding, we vowed that the only reason we would ever leave each other would be if one of us stopped growing. For over half a century we have sustained that commitment. Rudi taught us how to work in every aspect our lives. We took those skills and built a life.

Arriving at the wedding wasn't as easy a ride as I had imagined. Two people getting to know one another is a challenge, and having had our marriage "arranged" didn't change the amount of work required to learn who we were, individually and together. We had no idea how to be a couple. We lived in Blanche's showerless storefront apartment and bathed at friends' nearby apartments. On the occasions that Blanche's parents came to visit, I would remove all my clothes from our closet and hide them in the trunk of Blanche's car. There could be no indication that we were living together, for fear of her parents rejecting us both.

I was surprised that our sex life was so good, and that Blanche was such a caring and comforting companion. I would have gay longings and fantasies the rest of my life, but the reality of our sex life together was surprisingly satisfying. Mostly I was self-absorbed and career-focused, and Blanche supported that while trying to teach me what it meant to be in a relationship. We shared household duties, but it was clear that she was the chief cook and bottle washer. I helped where I could, but was inept in so many ways. She had inherited many skills from her mom and dad. She could do carpentry and balance a check book as well as make beautiful art. I could do none of that. She'd had boyfriends before me and could see how I measured or didn't measure up. At various times Blanche would find me irritating and even insufferable. I wouldn't dispute that. I was this guy living in a storefront who wanted to work in Hollywood, but was mostly unable to support her. She taught art at a school in Pearl River and worked at a summer camp in upstate New York. I took whatever jobs I could, but wanted only work that served a future Hollywood career, and there wasn't much of that around.

Occasionally I could sense Blanche was frustrated with me. At one point I know that she even went to Rudi and talked about breaking up with me. Rudi saved our relationship with a brilliant line. "If you break up with Bruce," he told her, "you'll only end up with another schmuck just like him." She knew that was true. But I had begun to have my doubts too. I worried if I had made the right choice. I was afraid of denying my sexuality, even though I had made no effort to pursue it. I knew I wanted family and children and was willing to sacrifice a gay life to have it, but how did I know if Blanche was the right person? I was growing increasingly insecure and fearful. It felt like it was happening too fast. I began to question everything. Then, while we were on a trip to Canada, I decided that I was making a mistake, that it was wrong to move forward. I'm sure she could feel my discomfort. We were sitting on a rowboat in the middle of a lake in the Laurentian Mountains. Blanche was facing me. I was about to tell her that it was over, and I could feel she was braced for that, but something unexpected came over me. My heart broke open and all I could say was that I totally and profoundly loved her. I don't know where that revelation came from – the words poured out on their own – but I knew it was true. I told her that I wanted to spend the rest of my life with her, that I wanted to get married and have children with her. The look on her face was something between total astonishment and profound relief. Her smile announced with heart-breaking clarity that she was in love with me too. I think we were both overwhelmed by what had happened. The sense of impending dread disappeared and the trip back to shore was one of the most joyous moments we have ever shared.

I never really proposed to Blanche. I just told her that while I was having dinner with my mom and aunts, Pearl and Esther, I had announced to them that we were getting married. Blanche stared at me with a *We are? We're getting married?* look. But by that point she knew me. I rarely followed protocols. "Um, can I tell my parents?" she asked. And that was it. No kneeling down, no asking. If I were to write it as a scene in a movie, I wouldn't change a thing. It just worked. Our love, our connection, was blooming. We didn't need formalities. I bought a portable radio for her (the one in the car was broken) so she could listen to it on her drive to Pearl River, where she was teaching. It was like an engagement gift. It never crossed my mind to get a ring.

When we told Rudi we were going to get married and wondered where to do it, he offered the classroom on the first floor, which fit a hundred people. When we talked about catering, he said he would take care of everything. Fann, my mother-in-law, was flummoxed. In her mind it was her job to organize the wedding, yet here was Rudi taking over and not even telling us his plans. Two weeks before the big day he went around the room and said, "Chicken, roast beef, fish, pudding, dessert..." pointing at the good cooks in the room. Everyone just nodded, and on the day we were provided with one of the greatest feasts any of us have ever had.

I worried about our extended Jewish families coming to a wedding in a space overflowing with Asian art, full of Buddhas and Shivas, and I told Rudi I was concerned that my family would see it all as idolatry. "Not to worry," he laughed. "All they'll see is money." And, as guests arrived in the elaborate, museum-like temple where Rudi now taught, everyone said, almost to a person, "Oh my God, this stuff must cost a fortune!" Rudi's home on East 10th Street was indeed museum-like, yet very warm. Blanche and I had been among the many students who helped it become a sumptuous spiritual enclave. Our unforgettable wedding, conducted by a Rabbi, his cantor and a sitar player, was a combined Jewish, Buddhist and Hindu ceremony. My family talked about it for years. Marrying Blanche was one of the great gifts of my life. Why she ever decided to give herself over to me, to try to make a life with me, was beyond understanding. And yet we were suited for one another. Her artful being astounded me. Her openness, her sweetness and goodness, her courage, her unalloyed availability were, and still are, remarkable. Having Blanche walk down the aisle in Rudi's ashram filled me with indescribable energy. It felt like a sacred space separated from the world outside. A massive ten-foot-tall standing Buddha hovered above the Rabbi and the cantor, and huge circular Shivas stood on either side of the Jewish chuppah. Rudi was glowing as we walked back down the aisle as husband and wife. It was the final benediction in a night full of joy and blessings.

Right after our wedding we went to the Berkshires and stayed at the Red Lion Inn. In a different world, this would have been our honeymoon, but I had gotten a job I couldn't afford to turn down, doing sound recording on a movie about Arthur Penn, who had directed *Bonnie and Clyde* and just finished *Alice's Restaurant*. It was a great opportunity, financially and professionally. My friend Bob Fiore was the cameraman and had asked me to join the crew. Blanche didn't mind me spending our honeymoon with Arthur Penn, even though it meant that she was stuck in a hotel room writing thank-you notes while I was at Arthur's home recording his life story. The truth is, my career exists because of Blanche's selflessness and her support of my work from day one. Luckily, she enjoyed Stockbridge on her own that week. We made love every night and visited it often after that. In fact, our son Joshua was conceived at that very hotel two years later.

Right after Stockbridge, we went home to our new loft that we had rented just blocks from Blanche's old apartment. It was a huge, light-filled space at 2 East 2nd Street, just across from the Bouwerie

Lane Theatre and the Amato Opera House, which needed a lot of work. We used what we had learned working on Rudi's building and spent weeks tearing down a rusting metal ceiling, exposing dramatic ceiling beams, putting up wallboard and adding a kitchen (of sorts – we never finished building the cabinets). We slept in a tiny, wood-paneled bedroom with a fireplace. The building had once been a sewing factory, and when we tore down the ceiling, needles rained through the floorboards above us. We could never walk barefoot at 2E2. There was a theater downstairs, the New York Theater Ensemble, which rented us the space. It was strange but oddly pleasurable having audiences applauding just below our bedroom at night, especially after sex.

Just over a year and a half of living at 2E2, and a month or so after a sentimental visit to the Stockbridge Red Lion Inn, Blanche discovered she was pregnant. I had wanted a family more than almost anything in the world. I had given up a gay life to have it and Blanche had now made it possible. As a way of celebrating, we decided to take a long-delayed real honeymoon – without Arthur Penn – first to Europe and then Paros, my favorite island in Greece. It would be our last chance to travel, just the two of us, as a couple. Within days of our decision to make the trip, we were told, quite unceremoniously, that we were being evicted from our apartment, that our space was needed for the theater. We were given two months to find a new apartment. It was a painful moment. Not that I loved living on the Bowery. It was the skid row of New York at the time, which made it affordable. But it had its dangers. Right after our wedding, a man knocked on our door, supposedly looking for the auditorium. He rushed into the apartment, pulled out a huge knife, and tied me up. I feared for my life as he ransacked the apartment, but I was more upset about all the wedding gifts he might steal. In the end, all he took was a MixMaster. On another occasion, as Blanche and I came into our apartment and piled our winter garb on a sofa near the entryway, I heard her sneeze. "Bless you," I said. "I didn't sneeze," she said. A moment later I heard a cough and saw the pile of coats heave. There were two feet sticking out from underneath them. A homeless drunk was sleeping there. I escorted him out of the building and he went back to sleep on the front doorstep. As naïve hippies, we had never locked our doors. Within minutes we became full-fledged adults and never left our doors unlocked again. We knew it was time to move. We talked to Rudi about our need to cancel our European "honeymoon" so we could find a new apartment. He said that was absurd, and told us to go on our trip and that he would help us get an apartment when we came home. There was something angelic about his assurance, and we decided to go.

Blanche was excited to be traveling to Europe and even more thrilled to be having a baby. Other than the tension about not knowing where we would live when we returned, we had a spectacular time. This was Blanche's first time in Europe, and she was in love. We flew to London and Paris, then took a train through Switzerland to Florence and finally a boat from the tip of Italy to Piraeus and Athens. Days later we were on Paros, where Liz and Jeff were now living full time. Our friends Joel and Debbie were visiting there as well. We ended up staying in a shed without a bathroom, but it had a small stove and some pots and pans, and Blanche's inventiveness as a cook took over. We were close to the house I had inherited from Liz and Jeff years before, and the Aegean was just outside the front door. It was great to have Blanche connect with that part of my life and to share it together with our unborn child.

When no one picked us up at the airport in New York, we quickly discovered that it was because Arnold, Blanche's dad, had been diagnosed with cancer and was in the hospital. Fann, my mother-in-law, was devastated and had completely forgotten we were arriving that day. It was a traumatic return. We went to visit Arnold, then went to our apartment at 2E2, knowing we only had less than a week before being evicted. I was fearful about how little time we had to find an apartment and no idea how to do it. We spent our first day home looking, but found nothing suitable, then went to see Rudi, whose first words to us were that he had a place for us, a 1,200-square-foot studio apartment on the corner of Greenwich and 12th. It was a three-story walk-up with a view of the World Trade Center, as it was being constructed before our eyes. One of Rudi's students lived on the seventh floor and had told him about it. They had arranged for us to buy it even before we got back from Greece. Among its many virtues was that it was an artist's co-op set up by the Kaplan Fund, which also ran a much larger co-op called Westbeth, at the far west end of Bank Street. Blanche, as a painter, qualified to live there. The building's most famous artist, Robert Smithson, known for his Spiral Jetty, lived across the hall. This was a true gift, although the purchase price, $5,000, was beyond us. Rudi said not to worry. He would give us the money and we could pay him back over time. I never knew a man as generous and caring. His antique business grew dramatically over the years we knew him, and he became very wealthy. Several of the pieces from his living room are now in New York's Museum of Natural History. I remember wanting to buy a large white marble buddha (actually a Jain Svetambara Tirthankara) that had been displayed in the classroom. It really spoke to me, and I sat beside it for every class. He sold it to us at cost, far less money than if we had purchased it in his store. He said he wanted all his students to have at least one major piece and made them affordable for us. We paid everything off over time, as our incomes grew.

The skills Blanche and I had learned while working on Rudi's building were again put to good use at our new apartment. The previous owners had painted the entire space – floors, walls, ceilings, even the tub – black. It all needed to be redone. All by ourselves, working day and night, we constructed a full kitchen, bookcases, platforms with sunken beds and sliding Japanese-style shoji panels. We had to work fast because our baby was due in early February of 1972. Luckily, he was late. Then even later. We hoped for Valentine's Day. Come March we began to worry. On the eve of March 4th, we went to see the movie *Cabaret* at the Music Hall Theater. I found the film an unexpected turn-on, and even though Blanche was ten months pregnant I wanted to make love. We did. Five hours later she was in labor, and I was running up and down Hudson Street trying to find a cab.

Joshua's birth was a Caesarean, which Blanche wasn't happy about, as she wanted natural childbirth. I was removed from the delivery room as she was wheeled into surgery, and began imagining everything that could go wrong. I finally surrendered to whatever arose. Suddenly a nurse came into my solitary room and said, "Come meet your son." I never imagined such words being spoken to me. Tears began to flow down my face. I was a dad. I ran into the hall and met Joshua, who was lying in a wheeled basket. He was the color of a brilliant pink rose and beautiful beyond belief. I never felt so proud. We hadn't yet chosen his name and were debating between Joshua and Noah. I had problems with the name Noah, since I couldn't stop imagining its opposite, Yesah. But it didn't matter. One look at him and he was Joshua. We had a Jewish bris for him in the hospital. Trying to create a minion of thirteen men wasn't easy, but as usual, Rudi took care of it. The room was crowded, and Rudi was among the first to hold our new baby. We decided to give Joshua Rudi's Sanskrit Swami name as his middle name, Rudrananda. It was a lot to saddle a newborn with, but it has served him his entire life. Joshua Rudrananda Rubin. He was uniquely himself, but has had Rudi's massive heart and spirit since the moment he was born.

The doctors kept Blanche in the hospital because of an infection, which gave me time to do all the finishing touches on the loft, so that when she and Joshua came home and walked in the door she started crying. It was so beautiful. We had created a home.

Joshua's arrival was one of the most magical moments in our lives. Sacrificing the gay direction of my life, at least in those restrictive times, allowed me to experience my greatest joy in the world. Meeting Joshua was an ultimate fulfillment. And raising him in New York was also a dream for me, one I was denied when the stork dropped me off in Detroit twenty-eight years earlier.

Life with a newborn was wonderful, even though we lived across the street from a paper-packing factory that began making noises at 3am, and near a fire engine station. The sound was something I fought with nightly, but Joshua and Blanche slept through it all. Joshua was nothing but a sleep-through-the-night delight, a skill he has retained to this day. We loved the West Village. We were close to my old apartment at 65 Bank Street, and everything was familial and familiar. Our families came to visit. I would kiss Joshua and Blanche good morning and head out across town to meditation classes at Rudi's home on East 10th and from there to work. At night Blanche made great dinners and we played with Joshua until we put him to sleep. Pure heaven. What could go wrong?

Eleven

Doing – The Screen Trade

When I took LSD in my twenties, it blew my world apart. From that point forward, my life went down two parallel tracks. I began a spiritual practice with Rudi, but I still wanted to make movies.

Some people go live in an ashram, and that becomes their story. Some people abandon the spiritual journey, and their professional life becomes their story. Luckily for me, these two things came together. I was eventually able to write movies about what I was learning in my spiritual practice.

First, I had to figure out how to get into the movie business. People in Hollywood don't generally open the door and invite you in. I came to learn that the way through the door is the crack at the bottom. Prostrate yourself, lower and lower... then crawl.

My first feature film credit was on *Dionysus in 69*, based on Euripides' *The Bacchae*. We shot it in the summer of 1968 and it was released in 1970. Brian De Palma was close to The Performance Group, a celebrated avant-garde theater troupe in New York, and arranged with Richard Schechner, its director, for us to shoot two performances of their play. Bob Fiore, Brian and I made the movie together, and documented a powerful theatrical experience.

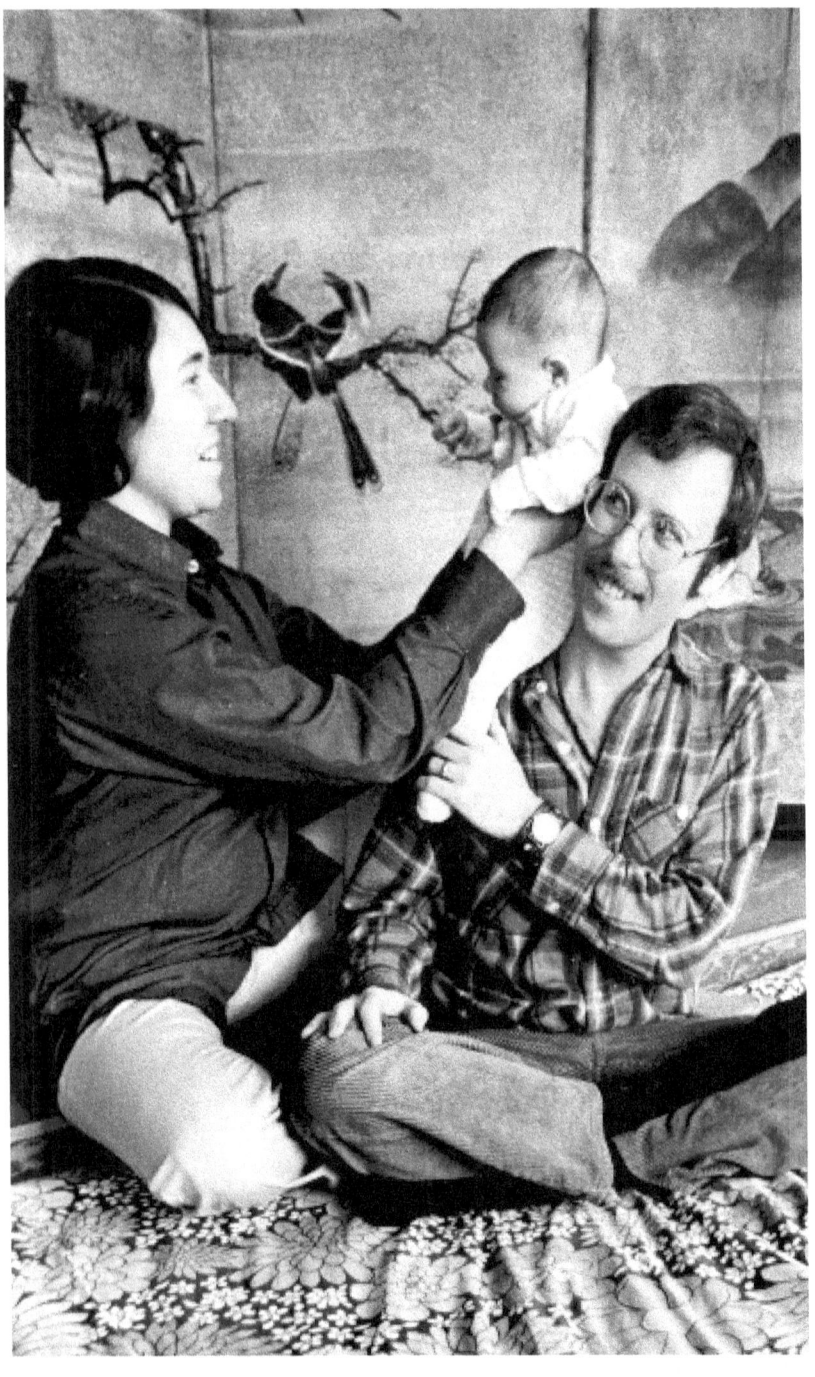

There was no stage, no separation between actors and audience. The action takes place in the city of Thebes, the audience became its citizens. At one point King Theseus needs to seduce an audience member and force her to sleep with him in order to save the city. Every night the actors went into the audience determined to seduce someone and make love right there. It never went that far – at least, not to my knowledge – but there was a lot of nudity and cast members making out with audience members. It went way beyond any traditional theater experience. Blanche got so into the mood the night we were filming that she took off her blouse and her beautiful breasts filled the screen on both cameras we were shooting with. I knew at that moment I would never be able to show *Dionysus in 69* to any of my relatives.

Brian, who is nothing if not a voyeur, loved having two cameras rolling at all times. The film was edited for two screens, to capture the POV of both audience and performers simultaneously. It was thrilling theater and made for footage that was great to edit. Fiore and Brian shot it, I edited the split-screen movie and did the sound. When it was released, Roger Greenspan of *The New York Times* published a rave review, but he called it "A film by Brian De Palma," even though the credits on the film specifically say, "A Film by Brian De Palma, Robert Fiore and Bruce Rubin," in alphabetical order.

"Although rough in a few technical details," wrote Greenspan, "it is a film of extraordinary grace and power. With exceptional imagination and intelligence, De Palma has managed both to preserve the complex immediacies of Schechner's dramatic event (based on *The Bacchae* of Euripides) and to work those immediacies into the passionate and formal properties of his own creation... It is exciting as a movie, approaching its material with great brilliance and ingenuity, but never trying to supersede the material... De Palma, a witty, elegant, understated young director (for example,

Greetings) seems to have found new ease and vigor and a taste for risks in meeting the challenge of this film."

The only problem with the review is that it doesn't mention that Bob and I were equally responsible for the film, for its "grace and power." We were disappointed with the focus on Brian, so we wrote a letter to Roger Greenspan to correct that misunderstanding. "This is a film by three people," we explained, "not by one, as the credits indicate." We both signed it, then gave the letter to Brian for his signature. But he wouldn't sign it. As far as he was concerned, it was his film. That was an upsetting moment for Bob and me, a kind of betrayal, but it was also an important lesson about the nature of ego.

For the record, it *was* Brian's idea to use two cameras and wed them together with split-screen editing, a technique that later became a signature of his work. The three of us remained friends despite this. I guess we realized that this was business as usual in the film industry.

After *Dionysus in 69*, I worked on a movie in Florida called *Adventures of the Lamp*. I never understood the significance of the title. The director was a very wealthy guy named François de Menil, whose grandfather had invented a process that became a key component of the oil-producing business worldwide. He had a quarter of a million dollars – a big sum in those days – to make this film. A mutual friend recommended me as his assistant director. I got my friend Mark to join us as a crew member. I told him it would be fun.

It wasn't until we got to Florida that we realized that François had no script, just a title. He had a cameraman and actors, and this idea that we were going to shoot the whole movie in nine takes of ten minutes each. We went to a place called the Rod & Gun Club, somewhere in the Everglades between Naples and Miami. There was nothing for eighty miles in any direction – just this club where they served dinners of lobster, steak and key lime pie. Good food, but it got very old after two weeks.

The first day we shot a scene on a boat. We mounted the camera behind François, who I realized wasn't just directing the film, he was starring in it too. He stood on the stern with a parrot on his shoulder. We were sailing toward his character's girlfriend, who was waiting for him on an island about eight minutes away. Nobody knew what the scene was about. We were told where to put the camera. François called "action," then began to disrobe. He took off every shred of clothing and stood there in front of us, stark naked, as the boat moved toward this tiny island in the distance.

Thunderclouds rolled in. I remember thinking, *Maybe we shouldn't be out here on the water...* Suddenly thunder roared and lightning shot through the sky – an unbelievable storm that came up out of nowhere. None of us had brought umbrellas or anything waterproof because nobody knew in advance what we were going to be doing that day, so our equipment was getting ruined. François just stood there. The bird on his shoulder was so freaked out by the thunder that it dove into the water and killed itself. We approached the shore. The girl was sitting there on the beach, soaking wet, waiting for us. François said, "Cut!" He wanted to do another take but the equipment had stopped working.

François and the cameraman were both in love with the lead actress, and after a while all three of them disappeared into a hotel room for three days. The crew just hung out by the pool at the Rod and Gun Club. We were told that they were working on the script... but we could hear through the walls that they definitely weren't working on the script. When they did finally emerge, François told me I needed to hire a tribe of Seminole Indians for the next scene.

I found a tribe living in the Everglades and somehow convinced them it would be financially worth their while to be in the film. We hired a bus to bring them all in. Then we laid down camera track in the middle of the Everglades for a scene where an Indian kid gets in the water and the camera tracks with him through the swamps. When the time came for the child to step into the water, his parents insisted that there were alligators in the swamp and wouldn't let him. Everything came to a halt. There was no way to convince them, so François decided he would go in the water instead. Of course, that made no story sense. But by this time, very little was making sense. He was about to get into the water when he started fighting with the cameraman – they were having major battles over how this scene should play out. Eventually they decided that François would run the camera and the cameraman would play François's part. "But François," I asked, "how is that going to work in terms of continuity?" "We're going to make it work," he said. "My character is going to be played by many people."

The sun went down before we could shoot anything, so we had to bring in lights and a generator. We were in the middle of nowhere, so that took a couple of hours. Finally, the cameraman, who was playing François, jumped into the water. François called "action," but then realized that he didn't know how to operate the camera. He yelled, "Shit! Cut!" though the camera had never rolled. That was a wrap. Not one foot of film was shot and we had a whole Seminole tribe that had to be paid and taken home. I was reading Kurt Vonnegut's *Slaughterhouse-Five* at the time and felt like I was living a chapter of that mind-bending book. I didn't know what the hell was happening. I was just eating a lot of lobster and key lime pie. Days later we returned to New York. To the best of my knowledge, the film was never finished.

I worked as the assistant director on Brian De Palma's film *Hi, Mom!*, which starred a young Robert De Niro and Jennifer Salt, who had been in my first NYU film. Brian had already had a success with a film called *Greetings*, also staring De Niro and shot by Bob Fiore. We were a ragtag operation, but it was fun. De Niro was just another young actor back then and we were all early in the game. There was no pretense to greatness. The film ends with people attending a theater performance called *Be Black, Baby*, in which white audience members are covered in black face paint and black actors in white face paint. It was meant to be degrading for the white audience, a way of teaching them about the black experience. Predictably they all leave the theater uniformly transformed, saying it was the most revealing and uplifting experience of their theater-going lives. Critics seemed to agree with the play's audience. They found *Hi, Mom!* funny and audacious, and Brian was on his way.

He was asked to document the opening of an exhibit at the Museum of Modern Art called "The Responsive Eye." Curated by William Seitz, it included seminal works by major and emerging artists like Larry Rivers, Marisol, Josef Albers and David Hockney. I was the second unit director and assembled a crew of old friends – Bob Fiore, David Moskovitz, Gardner Compton and Emile Ardolino – to shoot opening night. I remember wondering, *Is this really what I wanted to do with my life?* Yes, I was working on a movie in the Museum of Modern Art, but where was Hollywood in all this? It was the same old question yet again.

The idea of writing kept cropping up for me, but I wasn't doing anything about it. Rudi, who was forever encouraging, told me about an idea he had for a Broadway musical called *The Big Black Rainbow*. He wanted me to write the book for the show, although he didn't really have a story. It was about a well-endowed street kid who breaks into Hollywood through porn, and with the unexpected hard-earned wisdom of Big Mama, the owner of a black whore house in Watts, he becomes a movie star. A strange story for a meditation teacher, but, then again, so was the very idea of Rudi creating a musical. He had a collection of about twenty song lyrics he had written. They weren't all that great, but they did have a strange kind of spiritual uplift. "The black rainbow glows between the pain. Color and darkness together again." My job was to string them together into a cohesive and bankable script. Reading the lyrics, I kept thinking, *Why exactly did Rudi write this?* I knew he loved theater and musicals – he had been a huge fan of *Hair* in its first Off-Broadway production – but I didn't know he had aspirations to be part of that world. And if he did, he was connected to a lot of New York celebrities who might have helped him. Bayard Rustin was a close friend of his. So was Milton Glazer, the illustrator and co-founder of *New York* magazine, and Bob Benton, the writer of *Bonnie and Clyde*. It's hard to imagine I was the only person he knew that could possibly write a musical.

I wrote quickly, and the end result was surprisingly good for a pornographic musical. Rudi, at least, seemed to like it, and he asked Walter, another classmate and aspiring composer, to write the music. We even had a sing-through in Rudi's apartment with an invited audience. Musical theater wasn't on my agenda, and that night was as close as I ever imagined I would get to writing a Broadway musical in this lifetime. The music certainly wasn't Rodgers and Hammerstein, but we had a finished work and I managed to get the script to Joseph Papp's Public Theater which, a week later, politely rejected it. Rudi didn't seem in the least bit upset – he was just grateful that I had done the work, and it was never spoken of again. Years later I had a strong sense that Rudi had never really pursued this project for himself. In many ways he was doing it for me and Walter. He knew I wanted to be a writer but that I wasn't actually doing any writing. He knew Walter wanted to compose and needed a nudge. When he gave us those lyrics, he was pushing us to begin our creative lives. He was pushing us to overcome our resistance, our fear of facing the task. When I hesitated at first, he told me to just *do it*. And because I loved Rudi, I did. That was an enormous gift. It was my first script.

Around that time, Bob Fiore's girlfriend, Marcia Tucker, an art curator at the Whitney Museum, hired a friend of mine, David Bienstock, to run their new film department. Film was increasingly being recognized as a genuine art form, and the Whitney wanted to bring to light work that the public might otherwise never see. David established a celebrated program called The New American Filmmaker Series and became the Curator of Film. He hired me as his projectionist, but I was terrible at the job, so he promoted me to Assistant Curator.

I had met David during my days as a member of the Waverly group. He was a graduate film student at NYU, a gifted filmmaker whose most important work was a short film called *Nothing Much Happened This Morning*. It starts in black and white, following a young man through a mundane morning preparing to leave his house to go to work, then switches to color to revisit the experience through the vibrancy of the objects all around him. An entire inert world comes brilliantly and colorfully alive, a world without people, totally vibrant and animated. I was knocked out by it, and David and I bonded over his film. His decision to hire me at the Whitney was another huge gift. Together we programmed a weekly series of screenings by independent American filmmakers who had little exposure in the larger culture and whose work reflected the trend toward personal cinema. Amos Vogel described David's work as some kind of continuation of his own programming at Cinema 16.

The New York press, including Archer Winsten in *The New York Times* and Jonathan Rosenbaum in *The Village Voice*, reviewed some of the films we screened and helped create a following for a new branch of American cinema. The series was a big success, even though, as the *Times* pointed out, the Whitney didn't have a plush auditorium, only "a large, undistinguished room containing 125 folding chairs."

The showcase began in 1970 with my friend Joel Freedman's film *Skezag* (co-directed by Phil Messina) and included James Whitney's *Yantra*, Jordan Belson's *Cosmos*, and films funded by the American Film Institute, including Mike Kuchar's *Variations* and Hollis Frampton's *Manual of Arms*. Later seasons included *Imagine* by John Lennon and Yoko Ono, Robert Nelson's *The Great Blondino*, and films by Mike Gray, Ed Emshwiller, James Broughton, Saul Landau and Haskell Wexler. We focused on women filmmakers like Maya Deren and Shirley Clarke, animators Standish Lawder and Robert Breer, and new video work by Stan Vanderbeek and Nam June Paik. We also showcased documentaries like Yolande du Luart's *Angela Davis: Portrait of a Revolutionary* and Peter Bogdanovich's *Directed by John Ford*, and tried documenting the "spiritual revolution" that was taking place with a program called "Steps Toward a New Consciousness," which included John Whitney's *Matrix*, Gunvor Nelson's *Kirsa Nicholina* and Jud Yalkut's Kusama's *Self-Obliteration*.

Other outlets for independent films existed, including those created by Jonas Mekas – Anthology Film Archives and the Film-Makers' Cooperative – but David wanted to celebrate avant-garde work more broadly and bring it into the mainstream. There was always an unfortunate tension between David and Jonas, who seemed to feel that screening underground cinema in a museum space and having it reviewed by the New York press was unseemly. He felt that David was usurping him, but David believed there

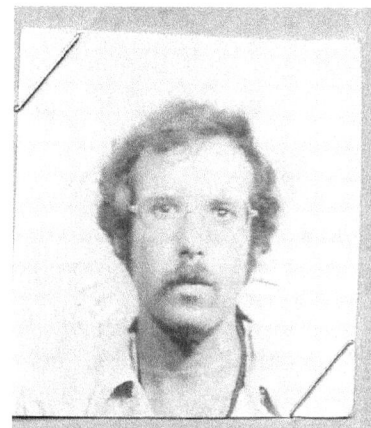

was room for everyone at the table and that bringing independent cinema to a larger audience was doing everyone a favor. I agreed.

Blanche and I, along with David and his girlfriend Emily, went camping on Monhegan Island off the coast of Maine. David and I wanted to write a movie together, and we stayed up late one night hashing out story ideas. I had come up with a story about an astronomer who discovers what he thinks is a giant quasar, but it turns out to be something else, something that erupts into a spiritual dimension and potentially affects all life on planet Earth. What he has discovered is perhaps the source of all creation, the very beginning of everything. David and I talked about it through the night and the story, which we called *Quasar*, began to appear. It was a breakthrough moment. For the first time I sensed how I could merge my spiritual journey with a filmic narrative. It was the story I had been searching for. With David's help, I was finding my voice.

Quasars were a new scientific discovery in those days and nobody understood exactly what they were, so we had an opportunity to imagine what they might be. What if the quasar our hero sees is actually the Big Bang, the moment of creation itself? Like my experience with LSD, this realization jolts him into an ultimate reality and alters his sense of day-to-day life. It's now impossible for him to live life as he had known it before. He moves beyond ego-centered striving and begins to experience the profound oneness of all living things. The story was a kind of celebration of a higher mystical energy arriving in the world, as told through the eyes of the first man to experience it. We watch as a growing group of people begins to see how this new mystical awareness might transform civilization. It was a utopian story, very optimistic about what the future could be.

In a way, I've been telling the same story in different ways ever since – or trying to. In almost all of my stories, somebody has an initiation into that underlying reality, then gives voice to that reality. Unfortunately, in the first draft of *Quasar* I gave too much voice to that initiation experience. The final few pages were a lengthy monologue about the nature of reality, followed by several dialogue-free pages. David, who was a good storyteller, reminded me that this was a movie, not a sermon, and helped guide me through the unfolding of the plot. He also began meditating and became a student of Rudi's.

I loved the script, which I gave to Brian De Palma, who gave it to Marvin Minoff, an agent at William Morris. Marvin sent it to Ingo Preminger, who had just produced *M*A*S*H*, and who offered $25,000 for a two-year option – a huge amount of money in those days. I said no, because I didn't want the script to be tied up for so long, but we agreed to let him option it for three months for $10,000. Ingo sent it to producers Richard Zanuck and David Brown, who said they didn't understand the ending. I remember telling Ingo, "Well, we'll fix it." He said, "No, no, they didn't understand it. They're not doing it, Bruce." That was painful, because I thought we had a real shot. David was annoyed that we hadn't taken the $25,000 and given Ingo a full two years to shop it around, which is probably what we should have done. Some careers don't survive the often excruciating lessons that Hollywood teaches. For me, the takeaway from *Quasar* was that a movie doesn't get made unless the studio power brokers really love it. Liking it isn't enough. Respecting it isn't enough. Not understanding the ending is a death blow.

One afternoon, while I was taking a nap at Blanche's parents' home, I had an astral projection, my first in years. I felt like my floating body was being filled with energy, like I was being prepared for something. Almost as soon as I re-entered my body, Blanche came into the room. Her dad was ailing. "We're going to the hospital," she said.

We stayed at the hospital all day. It was getting late, and Blanche and her mother left the room to have dinner. I stayed with her dad, who was unable to speak. He was in great pain and having a terrible time with his catheter. He was moaning and his whole body was trembling. I was just sitting there. I felt guided by the astral energy that was still percolating inside me, and suddenly felt that I should try to talk to him.

My father-in-law used to love sailing with his family on Long Island Sound, so I got close to him and said, quietly, "Imagine you're on your boat. It's a beautiful, sunny day and the water is smooth and inviting. We're sailing away from the shore. There's another shore visible in the distance, and we're making our way toward it. The wind is gentle and soothing. The sunlight is bouncing off the water." I took him on this imaginary ride. As I was talking, he gripped my hand. If I stopped for even a moment, he would grip my hand tighter, so I kept talking, and as I did, his legs stopped shaking.

Something's happening, I thought. Then the stillness started moving up his legs. I started telling him to head toward a brilliant sunlit shore in the distance, saying, "We can go there, we can cross over, we're nearly there." I told him how beautiful it was. When a nurse came in to check on him, I nodded for her to leave, and then – I don't know why – began reciting the 23rd Psalm. "The Lord is my shepherd. I shall not want. He leadeth me beside the still waters…" As I spoke, I saw his entire body becoming very quiet, motionless. I thought, *He's leaving. He's crossing over, to the other shore.* Then I heard his breath changing. He was having much shorter inhalations and much longer exhalations – really long. I whispered in his ear, "God loves you. Go with God. God bless." When I said, "God bless," his breath just kept going out and out. It never returned. He was gone.

That was my first experience of both watching and assisting in a soul's departure. What I did that day might have been the best thing I had *ever* done. On one level, I worried that I was intruding on a holy moment. On another, I didn't feel like "I" had done anything at all. I was simply a conduit. I felt well used. Something had used me in order to give him a peaceful release. All I could imagine was that the astral experience had prepared me to serve something greater. It seemed to lead the way. About ten minutes later Blanche and her mother came back. "He's gone," I said. My first thought when they began crying was that I had helped Arnold avoid all that emotionality.

Blanche's sister Rhoda had a five-year old daughter, my niece Laurie, who had been diagnosed with leukemia. Three years before Arnold's passing, I had been in the hospital room when Laurie died. She was struggling and I didn't know what to do. The nurse came in and said she had to change Laurie's bed sheets. I told her not to because Laurie was in so much pain, but the nurse insisted, saying it was her job, and ignored me. I was horrified, and so was Laurie. I looked at her face as the nurse shoved her aside to extract the sheet. I had never seen a look as frightened as that. At that moment, Laurie gave out a tiny shriek and died. The nurse stepped back. I could have strangled her on the spot. I knew at that moment I would never again let anyone ever die like that. When the nurses came in to check on Arnold, as he was dying, I asked them to leave. I wasn't going to let anyone in. Years later, as I revisited that moment in my mind, I re-imagined the nurse as a kind of angel of death. It helped dispel my ongoing anger.

174   It's Only a Movie

Twelve

Hoping – Big Indian

In 1970, shortly after Blanche and I married, Rudi decided to create a spiritual center in the mountains of the Hudson Valley because his teacher Swami Muktananda was coming to America for the first time. Muktananda was one of Nityananda's chief disciples in India and now headed the ashram that Nityananda left behind. Rudi, out of respect for Nityananda, wanted Muktananda to have a place to teach in America, so he bought an old hotel in the Catskills in a place called Big Indian, where large gatherings and classes could be held. Blanche and I were part of a small caravan of cars that went with Rudi to go see the land and hotel for the first time. It took us nearly three hours to get there from Manhattan. We finally pulled onto Lost Clove Road and saw a dilapidated old hotel with an empty swimming pool and a large vacant theater space. The buildings hadn't been occupied for years and the paint in the pool was cracked and peeling. Inside the hotel there were old mattresses everywhere. The window sills were covered with an inch of dead flies.

Rudi was really excited. Where I only saw a lot of work, he saw endless potential and what that work could mean for us, how much we could learn and grow while developing the space. Rudi handed me a small paint scraper and told me to clean the pool. I couldn't imagine a worse job. If I was able to remove two feet of paint in a day, I felt I had accomplished something. Then I would look at the rest of the pool, which seemed to go on forever. There was so much more to be done. It was bigger than any job I had ever tackled in my life.

A number of us spent much of the summer, our vacation time and weekends, getting the place together. Blanche and I got up every morning and worked and worked. We did plastering and drywall and swept and cleaned. We watched the transformation of this decrepit space into something beautiful. As we worked, we felt enormous personal expansion. Every day we were growing.

Rudi's talks in those days were all about growth. Growing meant overcoming resistance, breaking down the ego-mind that says, "I want this, I want that, I don't want this, I don't want that, give me, give me, give me, me, me, me…" Growing meant tapping into a "we" force, a "thy will be done" force. Most of us had a strong resistance to doing all that work, but we knew that nobody else was going to do it. It was just us, so we jumped in with a kind of fervor. It was thrilling.

It seemed to me that this was the right path: *Get your life together. Do the work. Don't be lazy.* Rudi hated laziness. He hated inertia and resistance. He pushed us to become who we could be. It was an extraordinary thing to watch all these people, including me, work harder than we had ever worked in our lives. When I was a kid in Detroit, my dad would tell me to mow the lawn. I would say, "Oh, I'm too tired." Then he would go out and mow the lawn himself. Rudi *made* me mow the lawn. He made me want to mow more lawns than I had ever imagined. He said I was paying the price for not mowing the lawn for my dad. At one point or another, in this lifetime, you have to do the work.

One day I decided to cook dinner for everyone. God knows why. I was no cook. But Rudi inspired me to move beyond my comfort zone. Mostly I remember deciding to make a Béchamel sauce to go with the vegetables I was grilling. Although I had a recipe book, I didn't really read it properly, and put all the ingredients into the pot at the same time instead of slowly adding them bit by bit. I ended up with a solid lump of food. Rudi walked in as I was struggling and saw the fear and tension I was experiencing. He criticized me for not following directions and pointed out that this wasn't the first time. It was, he said, a pattern in my life. He added that I was filling the dinner with my tension, and that if I didn't turn it around and add love instead, it would be a disaster. Then he walked away. I have never worked harder to turn tension into love, but the effort paid off. The solid lump of sauce floating in the pan began to dissolve and the sauce turned out to be delicious. Who knew that love was an ingredient in good food? So many lessons in one cooking experience. Rudi was a master of that. I remember walking with him and watching him stoop down to pick up some trash on the sidewalk and put it into a wastebasket. "If it's in front of you," he said, smiling, "it's yours." I was learning to take responsibility for anything that appeared before me. Years later that line would morph into "If it's in front of you, it's sacred." That has been an ongoing directive in my life.

We are separated from our spiritual life by layers and layers of tension. Laziness and dreams do not make for evolvement. Work, hard work, is the essential ingredient.

Rudi, **Spiritual Cannibalism**

The only break from physical work at Big Indian was meditation. We had class in the morning and late afternoon. The late afternoon class was exhilarating because I had no energy to resist what was happening. The day's work completely broke me down. I was so tired and worn out that I just sat there. I sat – and I was suddenly filled with energy.

Rudi, always practical in his approach to energy work, described the process in mechanistic terms. We weren't connecting to the energy flow that belonged to us and that had a universal source. If we turned on the tap and very little water came through, we had to work harder. Rudi saw himself as a kind of spiritual Roto-Rooter. He was a roaring, whirling mechanism that cleared the pathway for energy. We were clogged pipes and he was the plumber. We just had to ask for and be open to his help.

For me, that became the fundamental idea behind spiritual practice: open yourself to the flow of energy from a teacher. It cleans you out and makes you a vessel for the flow of greater energy. Over time you become a pipeline, channeling this energy to whomever you're with – your friends, your family, your students. You facilitate the flow of energy through the world. Once enough people are flowing, the world will be a different place. Everybody will be connected. There will be constant exchanges of energy. We'll all be sharing in the same ancient force. At least, that's the idea, the dream.

Rudi kept his message simple. "Change yourself. Don't worry about changing the world, just change yourself." When I first began studying with him, I was actively protesting the war in Vietnam. I remember being in front of the Hilton Hotel on Sixth Avenue where I had stayed when working on the *JFK Remembered* documentary at NBC, only this time I was helping a group of protesters overturn a police car. Dean Rusk, Secretary of State under Kennedy and Johnson, was speaking there. Policemen on horseback came charging at us. I moved my hand from the car just in time to avoid being crushed by a swinging billy club. "What the fuck am I doing?" I said to myself. After that I began meditating more committedly. "If I can't change the world," I said, "I'll change myself." Rudi agreed when I told him what had happened. He was opposed to turning energy outward if you hadn't yet taken care of what's inside. Decades later I went on a peace march to protest the war in Iraq. There was no peace to be had, only angry people. That was the last public protest I ever did.

A guest came to speak to our class. Pir Vilayat Inayat Khan was a prominent Sufi teacher in the Muslim world. His arrival in New York attracted the attention of the Black Muslim movement, possibly because they questioned his mystical interpretation of Islam. A group of them huddled in the back of the classroom as Pir spoke. They were clearly an unexpected presence, and it didn't feel like a kindly reception. They seemed agitated by his words. As the talk ended and Pir was invited upstairs to Rudi's living room, Rudi could feel the potential for confrontation. He asked me and a few others to form a protective phalanx as he and Pir headed to the stairwell. Suddenly we were surrounded by Black Muslims and prevented from going upstairs. They were intimidating. I was frightened. I wanted desperately to transcend this moment.

I figured the best approach was to overcome my fear and reach for some inner guidance. As soon as I closed my eyes, I felt calm come over me. Suddenly my peace was shattered by Rudi yelling at the top of his lungs, "Bruce, you stupid idiot! There could be an assassination here and you're meditating? What kind of imbecile are you?" He quickly ushered Pir upstairs, and us "bodyguards" hurried after them. There are times for meditation and times for action. It's essential to know the difference. My ignorance had served a purpose and Rudi's yelling saved the day. He hugged me when I walked into the living room.

When we eat fruit, the skin provides roughage essential to our growth. In human relationships, too, roughage is essential. The total person must be consumed to support life in its depth – to allow for creative interchange between one human being and another, and eventually between a human being and God. We cannot limit our intake to the qualities that are "easy to take" – we must welcome those that force us to change the patterns we have been able to deal with in the past. We must come to understand that everything is part of perfection and must be taken in, in a state of surrender; it must be digested and transcended. Life must be consumed whole – with all its tensions, pain, and joy.

Rudi, **Spiritual Cannibalism**

The buildup to the arrival of Muktananda was a big deal for us. A few months before, we had a puja, a Hindu fire ceremony, for Guru Purnima, an annual holiday in India and Nepal. We created a fire pit about thirty feet in diameter, pulled down dead trees all over the property, and built a huge bonfire.

As we walked around the fire chanting, it began to rain. I thought, *This is horrible.* But the rain came and went. It didn't put the fire out, so we kept walking and chanting, although now I was wet and uncomfortable. Then it rained again. After a while, some of the men started taking off their shirts and throwing them into the fire. I felt insecure about joining them, so I took off a pair of socks that I really loved and tried to throw them in the flames. They didn't make it and landed in the dirt. I felt rejected. Then it rained again, and the puja was over.

I remember walking to my room, thinking about what a horrible experience that was. On the way, I passed a woman named Draupadi, a student of Muktananda's. She was standing there, sobbing. I asked her why she was sobbing. "In India, when a puja fire is truly blessed," she said, "it rains three times. Usually what they do is sprinkle water on the fire three times to simulate the rain. But here it actually rained three times." She said that the Big Indian property had been properly blessed. I felt foolish, like I had misunderstood the whole event. It was as if everyone had been blessed except me, because I was unwilling to throw my shirt in the fire. And I missed my socks.

September 1970.

Muktananda's visit was dramatically hyped by Rudi. My suspicions about gurus were amplified by my time in India. The stories I heard about Muktananda didn't help.

When Muktananda arrived, one of Rudi's students named Patty Pardini offered to give me $500 to make a movie about his visit. I asked Rudi if it would be all right, and he said sure, so I rented a 16mm Éclair camera and, with the help of Beau Buchanan, another aspiring filmmaker and student of Rudi's, we documented Muktananda's arrival and the four weeks he was in New York.

Our first shots were of him getting off the plane. A group of us, along with Muktananda's American followers, greeted him at the airport and Draupadi led us in chanting, something we never did in Rudi's classes. As Muktananda emerged in the terminal, Rudi and many of the followers bowed down to greet him and touch his feet. I was instantly uncomfortable with that. Luckily, as a cameraman, I didn't have to bow. A limo covered with bouquets of flowers spirited him away and we raced to Rudi's house on 10th Street to film his arrival. The room was full and there was a procession of students offering flowers. Muktananda took Rudi's seat and Rudi sat on the stage beside him. Muktananda placed his hand on Rudi's head and Rudi shook violently. Clearly something was going on.

That week Muktananda gave classes every morning. Blanche and I attended. I was embarrassed that I didn't feel any connection to him. Everyone seemed so enthralled, but he left me dry. He seemed like a pretender and had none of Rudi's energy or authenticity. I couldn't understand Rudi's connection or devotion to him, except that he was Nityananda's successor. On weekends we would go to Big Indian and sit for hours in huge classes punctuated with trips to local sites and volleyball games. At one point Baba Ram Das came to visit for a day. Muktananda seemed to embrace him and push Rudi aside. I hated seeing that, but I kept the camera rolling. I filmed it all.

After a while, I realized that perhaps I wasn't having a genuine experience of Muktananda because I was always seeing him from behind the camera, so I hired a cameraman from CBS to come and do some of the shooting. But my experience didn't change. I could find no love, and I could tell that Rudi also had unspoken issues. One morning I was in class, meditating, without a teacher. A devoted student of Muktananda's had been sitting in the front of the classroom for two days without moving or eating. I was curious about him and thought I would never be as accomplished a student as he was. Then, unexpectedly, Rudi charged into the room, went directly for this young man, and began shaking him violently. "Stop it!" he yelled. "That's not meditation. You're in a trance. Stop it now!" The young man stood up and stumbled from the room. Rudi left too. I sat there confused by what had happened. I had been awed by the young man's capacity to sit so deeply, but Rudi saw it as something else – a disappearance. It wasn't evolving consciousness, but *un*consciousness. That was another important lesson for me.

There is a profound balance between the inner and outer worlds. The idea is not to get lost in one or the other. You can be as caught in a meditative space as in the material world around you. Both are imprisoning in their own way. The dance is between the two.

During one class I was looking at Rudi while Muktananda was sitting with him and I had a "krya," or a moment of sudden shaking and falling over. Shortly afterward, as Muktananda was leaving, he walked past me and through his translator told me to stop shaking during the meditation, as if I was initiating the experience myself. More than a critique, what I mostly felt was that he didn't approve of my connection to Rudi. There was a power struggle going on. I knew where my loyalties lay. I was clearly not his student.

Toward the end of the second week, we were back in the city and Muktananda asked to see some of the footage I had shot in Big Indian. I was excited about something we had filmed the previous weekend on the front lawn, when Rudi began working with people in a new way. He had started placing his hands on people's foreheads, on their third eye. His touch had a powerful effect. People were crying and shaking and passing out. The ground was littered with bodies in some kind of bliss. It was a strange scene, a massive expression of spiritual, or shakti, energy. None of us had ever seen anything like this hands-on approach before and I was excited that we had caught it on film, so when Muktananda asked to see some of our material, I thought, *I'll show him this great footage of Rudi.*

Muktananda and about a hundred people gathered in the classroom, and we projected the footage onto a large screen. After about ten minutes, I heard a rumbling in the room. I didn't know what was going on, but suddenly Muktananda got up and stormed out of the screening. His translator came over to me and said, "He'll never forgive you for what you have done." Then everyone went upstairs, leaving me alone with Blanche. I had no idea what had happened. It was distressing.

I went to Rudi's store early the next morning and asked him what I had done wrong. "Don't worry about it," he said. "You gave me a gift." I said, "Well that's wonderful for you. What about me?" "Go to the classroom right now," he said. "Muktananda is in there. Go in, walk onto the stage, bow down, kiss his foot, and ask for forgiveness." He said that would take care of everything. I grimaced. Part of me wanted nothing to do with this spiritual charade, and Blanche agreed, but it seemed I had been swept up in some kind of drama and that it would be best to see it to its conclusion.

I walked around the corner to the ashram and went into the classroom, where a lot of people were singing and chanting. Everybody was looking at me as I walked up onto the stage and bowed as slowly and carefully as I could, ready to kiss Muktananda's foot. Just as my lips were about to plant the kiss, he yanked his foot away. I heard gasps throughout the room. I had been very publicly rejected. Shaking, I slowly backed away and walked out the door, went down the stairs, out of the building, and back to Rudi's store. I said, "He wouldn't let me kiss his foot." Rudi looked at me and said, "Bruce, you can't let Muktananda go back to India without kissing his foot and getting his forgiveness." Thus began a week-long process of trying to get into Muktananda's presence, let alone his good graces.

Back in Big Indian, I sat outside the door to Muktananda's room for forty hours straight. I was determined to sit there until he let me kiss his foot. He came and went but wouldn't even acknowledge me. Then, late one night, one of his people said, "Okay, come in. He will see you now." I went in, but he had just fallen asleep. I couldn't kiss his foot while he was asleep, so I went back out and sat by the door again. I knew I had to try something else.

Muktananda loved hats – weird, knitted hats that covered his entire skull. I bought one at a department store and brought it to

his room. He took it, tried it on, found it was too small, and threw it on the floor. I was dismissed. The drama heightened. The next weekend at Big Indian, I bought a big bottle of kid's bubble solution. I got Muktananda to go with me out onto the front lawn and we started blowing bubbles together like two playful children. We had the best time ever. I ran up to Rudi and asked, "Rudi, does blowing bubbles with Muktananda mean that he accepts me? Am I saved now?" Rudi said no. I smiled. It was now a game Muktananda and I were playing. And it was clear that many students were jealous of all the attention I was getting. I had become an odd focus of Muktananda's visit.

Then I got the offer to go make *Adventures of the Lamp* in Florida. I had to leave in five days. Finally, on the last possible night, I'm sitting outside the door of Muktananda's room. He invites me in. I think, *Okay, I've got to make this thing happen. It's now or never.* Muktananda is sitting on the edge of his bed, one bare foot dangling over the edge. I go over to his bed. I lean down. And I move my lips, inch by inch, closer and closer to his big toe. I'm hoping I don't get kicked in the mouth. *Smoooooooch.* He lets me kiss his foot, then rubs my head and laughs. And I was done. I went to Rudi and asked, "Rudi, why did I have to go through all that? What did it mean?"

"Muktananda just gave you your career."

"What?"

"You just got your career."

That made no sense at the time. But when I got to Hollywood, I finally understood.

I had shown Muktananda a movie about Rudi, not Muktananda. Hollywood, it turns out, is full of assholes who only want to see what they're asking for, not what you want to show them. It's not about you, it's about *them*. That's a lesson I never forgot. And it really did give me my career.

Rudi joined Muktananda for a month-long trip around the U.S., and when he returned to New York everything seemed to have changed. On Muktananda's directive, Rudi stopped doing the open-eye meditation. The classes were filled with chanting instead and had become very Indian, very devotional. Blanche and I felt alienated. Many of Rudi's students, including many of our friends, became Muktananda acolytes. Some even moved to India with him. It was a devastating transformation. Shortly after Muktananda returned to Ganeshpuri he offered to make Rudi a Swami, a certified teacher/guru in the Nityananda lineage. I was uncomfortable with Rudi's need for a title, but when Rudi returned from India after his installation, Blanche and I sensed little had changed in him. Although he had a new name, Swami Rudrananda, he was still Rudi. The chanting and eyes-closed meditation continued, but at one point, a month or so later, Rudi began tapping some of us on the shoulder as he left the classroom and signaled for us to come upstairs after the formal class. The Muktananda devotees would head home. Those of us who went with Rudi were offered open-eye meditation again, and the sessions were more transformative than ever. The division in the class felt unsustainable, but for Blanche and me it meant life as we knew and loved it had returned. Somehow there had been a hidden blessing in all the upheaval surrounding Muktananda's visit. A new level of teaching and practice had arrived.

Thirteen

Witnessing – Death and Rebirth

My writing career during the Whitney years, post *Quasar*, happened because I wrote at night. I asked David Bienstock if he wanted to collaborate on another script, but he didn't seem interested, so I would come home from my curating job each evening and try to build a second career. I told myself I would write one scene every night. *That's nothing*, I thought – one scene a night. Sometimes it took me half an hour, sometimes it took the whole night. Blanche took care of Joshua while I was writing. Every night after dinner I wrote one scene, and at the end of three months I had 120 pages – a full script. That turned out to be the very first script of mine to get produced. It was many years before it was made, but it never would have happened without that initial three-month nightly effort.

The original idea for that script, *The George Dunlap Tape* (later titled *Brainstorm*), was a multi-part question: What if you could live in someone else's experiential space – if you could know their memories, share their thoughts and feelings, and live in their head? If you could do that, who would you be? If all these things are transferable, what is the thing that's doing the living? And what if all our thoughts and memories could be stored on tape and preserved in a machine? What if those memories could be played and replayed as if living or imagining our lives? What if we were just tapes?

❖

At one point during that year, Rudi traveled to India with a caravan of his teachers to visit Muktananda in Ganeshpuri. I was out of town when they were gone but flew back to New York when I heard that he and his group had returned and that Rudi wanted everybody to attend an especially important class. That night he told us that he had broken up with Muktananda. I was instantly grateful. Although Muktananda had initiated Rudi into the ranks of Swami, Rudi clearly felt no sustained allegiance to him or his teaching. Every photo of Muktananda disappeared from the ashram. Soon afterward they disappeared from our homes as well. It was like a Stalinist purge, as if Muktananda had never existed for us. I was relieved. He always seemed too much like a magician to me.

Toward the end of his time with us in New York, Muktananda had started talking about a metaphysical blue pearl. He said you couldn't attain a certain spiritual level until you encountered the blue pearl and he made it very clear that Rudi had not seen the blue pearl, and that he had. I intuitively thought it was a ploy to keep Muktananda in a position of power and make everyone else feel inadequate. I was angry. Everyone was trying to envision the blue pearl. No one did. Luckily, when Rudi went to India and broke with Muktananda, that was the end of the blue pearl and all the deception that surrounded it.

I was happy to have Rudi back. During his talk on the night of his return, Rudi looked out at me and announced publicly that I was a true yogi. I don't know why he said it, but I was touched and warmed by his words. They were among the few outright compliments he ever offered me. The only other thing that came close was when Rudi said to me, "You know Bruce, when you first came to me you were like diarrhea. Now you are a solid turd."

After Rudi left Muktananda behind, he became his true self. Perhaps we all need to go through something similar, something that leads us into disillusionment, so we can say, "I don't buy it." After that we're free to find and pursue our own path, a path that doesn't lead to someone else's destination. Only yours. Around this time Rudi wrote a series of books. His first, *Spiritual Cannibalism*, was oddly titled, but very Rudi. I loved the book until an editor cleaned it up for publication, erasing his voice and, oddly, his power. Two later books, *Entering Infinity* and *Rudi in His Own Words*, did successfully capture him and his teaching. Today, I'm grateful that we have those works and the film that Rudi's student, Bob Sink, finished from all the raw material we had assembled during Muktananda's visit. We shot so much footage that Bob was able to edit it into an honest living experience of Rudi. It turned out that the books and the film were a true lifeline to his work. I had no idea at the time how essential they would become.

Early 1973.

Rudi started doing meditation classes at his place at seven o'clock in the morning. Our apartment was across town. "I have to go," I told Blanche. "I have to do this." It was a big effort because Joshua was still a baby and our lives were focused on child-rearing, and I had a demanding job at the Whitney, which was growing into a prestigious position. But, with Blanche's blessing, I got up every morning at six o'clock and took the local bus across town. The driver and I were often the only ones on the bus, so he and I chatted and became friends. I got off at 14th Street and walked over to Rudi's house and waited outside until someone came downstairs to open the classroom. I would sit with all these people whom Rudi had made teachers. I wasn't one of them. I had asked Rudi once if I could start teaching, but he said I wasn't ready. I accepted that. Nothing in me felt ready.

After class, we would have breakfast up in Rudi's apartment. Usually I had already eaten, so I would just sit there and look at him. He was, over time, somehow becoming something other than the Rudi I knew. One night, as I sat across from him at a party, I just kept staring at him. When the party was over, he came up to me and said, "Bruce, what were you looking at?" I said, "I was looking at you, Rudi." "That's not possible," he said. "I wasn't there." He had recently gone to Texas to visit one of his other ashrams that were now sprouting up across the country. He looked at me and spoke quietly. "Rudi," he announced, "never returned from Texas." I was taken aback. I couldn't figure out what he meant at the time, but decades later I experienced a version of it myself, a kind of disappearance of Bruce. Much of advanced meditative practice is called non-dualism, where you are freed from your story and your drama and everything that has defined you – your whole life. It's said that the loss of the personal self reveals something greater, a larger self, no longer defined by name or personality. It's akin to enlightenment or samadhi. Watching that arise in Rudi suggested that it can really happen. Although I wasn't able to grasp it myself, I felt lucky that I got to bear witness to his transformation. It gave me hope.

God cast me in a very hot fire. I was molded in great pain and allowed to cool very slowly for forty-four years. It is only in the last year that I can accept what people always offered me but which previously would have caused an internal condition that would not have let me set in the proper mold.

Rudi, January 1973

It's understood in spiritual seeking that when the teacher is needed, the teacher will arrive. But at some point, ready or not, the teacher will disappear. There comes a day when the student realizes they're on their own.

One day I went to class at six in the morning. Rudi wasn't there, and there was some vague concern about where he was. Nobody had heard from him. All we knew was that the day before, he had taken a plane to give a talk to a group upstate and never showed up. That was all the information anyone had. I left class, concerned. I took the subway uptown and had a long day at work, which included lunch with Brian De Palma, where I talked nonstop about Rudi. Then I got on the train to go back downtown and teach a hatha yoga exercise class at the ashram. I sat down on the subway and said to no one in particular, "Rudi's dead."

I had no reason to think that, but I knew it was true. I got off the subway and walked from 14th Street to 10th Street. On the ground level of Rudi's building was an art store called Quintessence, run by Bob Hamlin, one of his students. As I walked toward it, I saw a group of people gathered. I knew why they were there. I walked inside and saw my friend Jason Lew. He just looked at me and I looked at him. "Rudi's dead," he said.

I walked upstairs, and someone – I don't remember who – said, "Don't tell anyone yet." So I taught the hatha yoga exercise class without saying a word about what had happened. When the class was over, people started coming into the room for meditation. The instructor that evening told everybody that Rudi had died, then continued to teach in silence.

I later learned that a few days before, Rudi had called several of his teachers together and told them he was going to die in an airplane crash. He was supposed to go to Europe soon, and I'm sure he thought that was the flight that was going to kill him. But then he was asked to give a last-minute talk in upstate New York, and his student Beau Buchanan, a pilot (who had helped me make the film about Rudi), agreed to fly him there in a small plane. Rudi always said that when he died, his heart would explode into a billion pieces and scatter across the universe. The airplane crashed into a mountain and Rudi's chest was crushed. His heart exploded just the way he said it would. None of the other three people on the plane were even injured. I can't imagine Rudi getting on a plane after such a strong sense of what was coming. His premonition and acceptance, his assembling of all his teachers, is a mystery and a lesson to me still. He had just turned 45. His business was booming, he had written two books, and classes were expanding across the U.S. and into Europe. It was hardly time to leave. But his departure was the beginning of a new journey for me. He freed me to move on.

We gathered upstairs in Rudi's living room and were in near silence when the doorbell rang. I was closest to the exit and went down to greet whoever was there. It was Beau. He stared at me with the most frightened yet beautiful gaze, waiting for me to dismiss him as the man who killed our teacher or to welcome him unconditionally into Rudi's home. I reached out and hugged him.

Shortly after we went upstairs the doorbell rang again and I hurried down to answer it. It was Rae, Rudi's mom. She in tears, barely able to walk. She wanted to go upstairs, and I tried to help her. Halfway up she tried to throw herself backward over the banister. I held on to her for dear life. I had never witnessed such despair. I was starting to feel it rising in me as well.

If you really love somebody who has lost their physical life, the only thing to do is to sit and love that person. His or her seed is going to another dimension and should be surrounded by love and nourishment, not by crying and holding on. Allow this seed to leave full of positive feelings and energy. Otherwise, you are using the person to satisfy your own limitations and inability to live. People go because we wear them out. They have fulfilled their purpose and the only thing we can do is send them a box of cookies and a bouquet of flowers from our hearts. The nourishment they require now is on another level.

Rudi, January 1973

When Rudi died, my whole world changed. I was immediately struck by the absence of a fundamental force in my life. In my mind, Rudi seemed infinite and eternal. How could my teacher be gone? It was a powerful time, because on the one hand I had Blanche and Joshua, a glorious gift of marriage and a new life. And then, in an instant, came the loss of the very core of my spiritual being.

After the meditation class everyone went quietly upstairs, but I stayed behind for a while by myself. I kept thinking about something Rudi had taught us a few weeks earlier about what to do when people die. "If you send love into the space they left behind," he said, "that will become fuel for their transformation." I was bowing down literally to the space that Rudi left behind.

Suddenly I felt someone goose me, as if jokingly tapping my butt. I turned – but there was no one in the room. It was typical Rudi behavior. It was exactly what he would have done. As serious as this moment was, I sensed him playing with me, and I broke into laughter. From that moment on I never once cried over Rudi's death because I knew he hadn't really gone anywhere. Rudi was still there. My journey with him was far from over. All I had to do was find a way to immerse myself deeper in his work. I had to keep growing.

When Rudi died, I fully understood. *This is about me and my work.* Until then, I thought it was Rudi's energy that was making me grow. I never thought that Rudi's energy was also *my* energy. Once he was gone, I realized that nobody else can do it for you. *You* are one hundred percent responsible. That's when my real practice started. Two weeks later I turned thirty, and we had a party at our apartment. It was surprisingly joyous. Many people from class came, and amidst the community, the sharing, I could feel the sadness lifting.

Around this same time, David Bienstock was experiencing emotional problems, some of them centered around something that Jonas Mekas had written about him and the Whitney New American Filmmakers Series in *The Village Voice*. David couldn't let go of it. He had a harder and harder time functioning as head of the department, and more responsibilities fell on my shoulders.

David had shared with me a past memory that as an Egyptian, centuries before, he had committed suicide. He spoke of the many lifetimes it had taken him to get free of that karma. Now he was talking about killing himself again, in this incarnation. I had never been around anyone who was openly suicidal. I did all I could do to share with him why I thought that was a bad choice. I really loved David and his ongoing obsession was debilitating for all of us. Thankfully he seemed to come out of it and was acting like a normal guy again. Days later, Marcia Tucker, the Whitney's Curator of Painting and later founder of the New Museum, called and told me that David was dead.

Three months after Rudi died, David committed suicide. He put a gun in his mouth. I never fully understood what caused him to do it. He'd had a difficult childhood and a complex relationship with his mother. There was also the Jonas Mekas article that undermined him and sent him into a downward spiral. It was painful to watch. I had to identify the body. The horror frozen on his face was unforgettable. After David's suicide, he came to his then girlfriend Adrienne in a vision/dream and told her, "I never knew that in killing myself I was going to die." Those words impact me to this day.

I spoke at the funeral. It was hard to talk about the death of someone who had killed himself, but I tried to take it as an opportunity to look at the struggle we all share – the pain of being alive, the desire for love and to celebrate all that David had achieved, especially his film *Nothing Happened This Morning*, which was such a beautiful celebration of life. I said that David was too sensitive for this world, and that I would miss him. Haig Manoogian was there. He came up to me afterward and hugged me. "You did good," he said.

I inherited David's position as Curator of Film at the Whitney, as well as programmer of the New American Filmmaker series. It was a busy time, but mostly what I was thinking about was that I needed to continue my spiritual studies. That, to me, was more important than my career.

A group of Rudi's students was trying to build a new residential ashram in New York, so Blanche and I decided to give up our beautiful loft on Greenwich Street and move into the fifth-floor studio on Broadway and 13th Street with five other families. Somehow, we were going to build small family spaces and share toilets. It wasn't very practical, but it was going to be a demonstration of our commitment to something greater than our comfort. We told the people in our co-op building – the artists' space that Rudi had found for us with a mortgage of $80 a month – that we were leaving. They weren't happy because we had only been there for two years, and they thought we were unappreciative of what we had. It was hard to explain to them our commitment to the ashram. Then, when the new ashram failed to materialize, we tried to get our loft back, but the artists in the co-op didn't want us back. We had rejected them and now they were rejecting us. We had no place to go.

Michael Shoemaker, one of Rudi's students, invited us to his ashram in Bloomington, Indiana, for Christmas. "If you really want a spiritual life," he said, "this is where you should settle." Blanche and I had known Michael for years. He was from Indiana and discovered Rudi during the Muktananda cross-country trip. He often stayed at our apartment when he came to New York and spent a lot of time living upstairs from Rudi with a group of other emerging teachers. It was an expansive time as people spread across the country opening ashrams, with Rudi's blessing. Michael was uniquely gifted, very adept at teaching Rudi's work. He was the primary speaker at Rudi's funeral and exhibited great maturity for someone still in their early twenties. When we visited him in Bloomington, he had already opened satellite ashrams in Indianapolis, Ann Arbor and Cincinnati, and more were in the works. He was charming, seductive and convincing, and Blanche and I believed he was right – that Bloomington should be our new family home. We flew back to New York and I told John Baur, head of the Whitney Museum, that I was leaving. He thought I was crazy because I really did have the kind of job – the curator of a program at a major American museum – that you don't walk away from. "I have to do this," I told him.

It was spiritual romanticism at its best and worst. I lost a great deal. I lost prestige, I lost money, I lost a beautiful loft in New York. I ended up living with my wife and son in a tiny little room in an ashram in the middle of Indiana – with no job, no prospects, no money. And I thought, *What have I done? This is absolute insanity. I've given up everything... for what?* I was depressed because I thought I had made a huge mistake. Years later, I realized it wasn't a mistake simply because it announced to the universe in a big way how serious I was about my spiritual practice. It wasn't a casual interest. It was like the moment in India where I heard the voice saying, "Give up everything and follow me." And now I had done it. I had given up every ounce of security in my life and was following IT. I prayed that I was right.

Bloomington was a lovely town, with a university campus and great shops and restaurants. Blanche, Joshua and I ultimately found ourselves happy living there. We moved into what had been a bedroom in a nice house in the middle of town, but because it was now a yoga ashram the place was crammed with forty people living in every nook and cranny. We were lucky to have our own quiet space. Being there was mostly a joy, although we were now the oldest people in the group and one of the few with children. That quickly changed as more people arrived and the ashram grew. We eventually moved into an apartment building converted into an ashram space even closer to the center of town. We had a lovely spacious room and Joshua had his own alcove and a bunk. Meditation classes were held every morning and evening in a huge hall on the main floor. Meals were served to about seventy of us in a dining/living space. The kids, about ten of them now, had a communal kibbutz experience, sharing dinner meals every night in a basement clubhouse. Joshua loved it. Blanche and I fell in love with everyone there. It turns out that communal living suited my extroverted personality.

But there were drawbacks. Early in our move to Bloomington, Blanche and I couldn't find Joshua anywhere. We asked everyone if they had seen our two-year-old. A small group sitting on the front porch said yes, they had seen him wandering off across the street and out of sight. I couldn't imagine that they would let a little child head off on his own, but I had no time to express the depth of my shock and fury. Their lack of consciousness sent a signal that I found instructive. Devoting yourself to a spiritual life in no way guarantees a practical, conscious worldly life. Blanche and I went searching for Joshua in a state of terror. Four blocks later, after running across busy streets and dashing into every backyard, I saw a couple walking toward us with Joshua on their shoulders. They said he had been wandering across streets as if they were meadows, so they decided to carry him back in the opposite direction. I was profoundly grateful to them, to their angelic intercession, but awakened to the new world we were living in. In New York, when I took Joshua to the sandbox near our Greenwich Street apartment, I would find him picking up broken liquor bottles and cigarette butts, and felt it might not be the best place to raise a child. It had been a signal to move on. Now I worried about Bloomington – a big, unknown landscape. But Joshua couldn't be restrained. By the time he was six he would still wander off, but our trust in the world had grown. We knew to look for him three blocks away in the kids' section at Howard's Bookstore in downtown Bloomington, or at the local library, where they all knew him by name. He was a born wanderer (and reader), and has remained so to this day.

In 1974, I decided I wanted to become a Rudi meditation teacher, not just a hatha yoga instructor. Rudi had told me that when a teacher dies, his students have the right to take up his teaching, which I was hungry to do. I really didn't know how to teach, but I did feel that it was my purpose and destiny. One day I told this to Michael Shoemaker. I was expecting him to give me all the reasons why it wasn't a good idea. I was also hoping that his insight into my spiritual development, or lack of it, would help me improve and expand my effort in that direction. Instead, he said, "Great!

Start tonight!" I hadn't expected that. I asked him if he would show me how to teach, what to do. "No," he said. "Just sit there. You'll figure it out." And that was how it happened.

I sat down that night in front of a room full of seventy students – and it did happen. As I got quieter inside, a higher energy began to express itself. I looked at every person in the room and felt a real connection to them. I could see where they were afraid, hesitant, closed, uncertain, doubtful – and as I sat with them, this higher energy, this shaktipat, moved effortlessly through my body, my chakra system, and became available to them. I sensed they could feel it. There was the same symbiotic exchange that I always felt with Rudi and other teachers, but this time I was a conduit, not a recipient. Mostly, I didn't have to do anything but get out of the way. The less there was of Bruce, the more the energy flowed. I could feel it shooting out of my eyes and sometimes my hands. I was awed by it. It spoke to me. It directed me, and I could see that it was dissolving students' inner obstacles. They were falling over as sudden bolts of energy hit them. I didn't really have anything to do with it. All I did was be present and love them. I was in a state of awe and profound gratitude.

I didn't find it hard to get out of the way, although at the same time I could see how easily one might be tempted to own the power of this moment. I sensed that ownership would terminate the true power and gift of this inner flow. I felt I was on my way to becoming *nothing*. The emptier I became, the more the energy flow increased. I didn't know, in that first sitting, that any kind of mastery would take a lifetime.

Fourteen

Teaching – *Brainstorm* – Ari

My script, *The George Dunlap Tape*, nearly got made in Indiana. I had approached a guy named Bob Leckie, who worked for the Eli Lilly Foundation, about raising money for a film series that I ended up curating at the Indianapolis Museum. At some point in our discussions, I mentioned the script I had written. He had some friends who were building malls across the Midwest and wanted to get into the film business. "I can get this movie going," he told me, and started raising funds. We were going to shoot it for $400,000.

With a small amount of seed money, we rented a building just outside Bloomington, scouted filming locations, and began building sets. The university was constructing a cyclotron, a highly futuristic particle accelerator that included the most sensational industrial spaces I had ever seen. It hadn't yet opened, and we got permission from the science department to film in this unbelievable space. Indiana University was ideal for the movie and had everything we needed – except actors. For that, I went to Chicago.

We didn't have much money at that point, so for casting I found an inexpensive room in a fancy hotel where I could meet with actors. I was embarrassed since the room contained nothing more than a chair and a bed, which was all we could afford. But it turned out that a door in this room opened directly into a beautifully furnished five-room suite. It was a gift. I stood at the door to the suite when the actors were arriving and would intercept them in the hallway before they arrived at my tiny and inappropriate casting bedroom door. I felt like a Hollywood mogul leading them into my lavish living space. That made a big impression, especially on me. It was like I had arrived even before I started.

Everything was going smoothly until the mall guys, the financiers, pulled out. No explanation given. It was over as suddenly as it had begun, and our crew of ashram members and Bloomington locals were all suddenly out of work.

I took my crushed ego back to the ashram bakery, where I sold cookies, cakes and pies. We were poor. Blanche, whom I had wanted to edit the film, now had to reconsider her life and our future. Our friend, Per Johansen, who had been working toward a doctorate at Indiana University in Art Education, convinced Blanche to follow in his footsteps and she enrolled in the program that fall. I couldn't make anything happen, and was panicky. The film program I curated at the Indianapolis Museum of Art, similar to what we had done at the Whitney, lasted only six screenings. I thought about becoming a lawyer and tried convincing myself that the law was about justice and discovering truth. But as I started looking into taking the LSATs, I realized I wasn't a lawyer.

Like Blanche, I decided to go back to school. We took our final and very limited savings, and enrolled. There was only one master's degree program at the university involving film or media: Instructional Systems Technology. Mostly the program was centered on how to teach disadvantaged kids, and included making educational slides for developing nations. The old technological tools we were using in the program became obsolete very fast and much of those two years felt like a waste of time, but I was beginning to find a renewed focus on how writing could inform and uplift people. One of my professors said, "You know, you don't really want to teach about instructional movies. You want to make movies that instruct." He was right. I took a playwriting class and wrote a one-acter called *The Separation*, about a group of actors performing a play about the Holocaust who suddenly wake up to the truths behind the historical narratives they are enacting. It spoke to the power of theater to shake people up, even those performing the play. I got an A+. In fact, I got all As in the Master's Program, both years, something I had failed to do even once as an undergraduate.

My time in school and evolving sensitivity to underserved populations of Indiana led me to create The Ashram Foundation after I graduated. Our intention was to do public work and serve the Bloomington community. We formed a board of directors that included the Dalai Lama's brother, Norbu, a professor at Indiana University. The Foundation sponsored forums where invited guests spoke, and conducted a government-sponsored employment program called CETA, established by the Carter administration to assist the underprivileged and underemployed. When we taught meditation at Terre Haute State Penitentiary, I was astounded by how committed and open the prisoners were to the practice. I had never been in a prison before and sensed how the journey inward was a lifesaving experience, since there was little outer world left to explore. Prisoners thanked me regularly for the practice. Together with Bloomington Hospital and local doctors, we helped initiate the Hospice of Bloomington, something I had wanted to do after witnessing the death of my niece and father-in-law. It became a place where the experience of dying was respected and ill-informed healthcare practitioners could be kept at bay. We were one of the first hospices in the nation and continue to operate to this day. Working with dying patients beyond my own family introduced me to an underlying human connection that only enhanced my desire to serve people. One idea seems to have percolated deeper than any other:

"Trust the journey." I don't know why that's so resonant, but every dying person I have shared it with has expressed real gratitude.

Providing public service and having the ashram as a helping hand in the community was extremely important to me. But, to be honest, the pull to do bigger work – to serve a larger audience – was always there. I couldn't free myself of Hollywood. I needed to write more. I needed to create my masterpiece.

Twice during my years in Bloomington, I went to the nearby Poplars Hotel and said, "I'm not coming out of my room until I have a finished screenplay." I emptied the room of all distractions – I put the TV in the closet, took the photos off the wall – and sat down with no idea of what I was going to write. I just started typing, trying to prove to myself that I could write a script fast. This was the only way it was ever going to happen, because I simply had no time to write. I needed total immersion. I was writing for my life. That's how I looked at it. I barely had enough money to pay for the room, but I knew that if I didn't write something producible, I was never going to have a career as a screenwriter. Both times I did this, I came out with a finished screenplay. Both times Blanche and Joshua brought me dinner every night.

The Persian Diaries of Jeremy Benton, written in eight days, was my first hotel script. The story was based on a producer I knew at NBC News who was friends with Soviet Premier Nikita Khrushchev and other world leaders. In my version, her son hitchhikes around the world, is caught smuggling drugs in Iran, and ends up in one of the Shah's prisons. (This was a year before *Midnight Express.* I based the details on my own travels through Iran and Afghanistan.) If the authorities find out who his mother is, there will be an international incident. Before anyone discovers the son's identity, his mother asks the Shah for permission to shoot a film in Iran. One of the filming locations is the prison where he is being held. The mother's film company pretend to shoot the movie but are actually on a rescue mission. Interestingly, this is almost exactly what the Canadians did in real life a few years later, a story that became the basis of the movie *Argo*. I liked my finished script but didn't know how to sell it. I felt stymied.

Later I used the same lock-myself-in-a-hotel-room process to write *Teratoma*. That one took eleven days. Teratomas are tumors that grow inside the human body and take on certain aspects of human anatomy. Sometimes they grow teeth and whiskers. After people suddenly begin developing teratomas, a researcher discovers that when they are removed, the people who harbored them undergo transformations of character. They become different people – much better people. It's as if something horrible has been removed from their characters. Toward the end of the story, the excised tissues become luminescent. They glow. Humanity eventually realizes that some kind of alien life form has been experimenting on human beings. Aliens have learned how to grow a real human body. A young woman eventually becomes pregnant with one of these teratomas. She gives birth to an angel with glowing wings, and we realize that the supernatural has found its way into our world. I considered it a horror story and gave it an unsettling ending. The angel was killed. If I were to write it today, the angel would live.

Neither of those screenplays went anywhere, but the effort of writing them gave me a sense of empowerment. I knew that, given a week or two, I could write a complete script. I felt I was beginning to take charge of my life and career.

Rubin's original script opens with a nebulous image which gradually reveals itself to be cells developing into an embryo, while a caption below reads The George Dunlap Tape. *The embryo forms into a fetus, rapidly growing to term and about to emerge from the womb.*

Just as birth begins, the camera zooms into the image and we see the life of George Dunlap, rushing by at an accelerated pace. Suddenly, we are in a laboratory and into the story as it is presented in Brainstorm. *The Dunlap character was renamed Michael Brace, played by Christopher Walken in the film.*

Dunlap dies at the end of Rubin's script. The camera pulls back to reveal that the screen is really a video monitor. As the life of George Dunlap ends, a caption flashes "End of tape. Rewind." The entire movie of Dunlap's life has been a replay of a tape. The camera dollies back further and thousands of tapes are visible on thousands of monitors. They are all "life tapes" that were made and stored millions of years before, thanks to the invention of the Dunlap machine. There are no physical beings left, only lives recorded on full sensory tapes.

Kyle Counts and Charlotte Wolter
Cinefantastique, December 1983

In 1976, producer Joel Freedman, my old friend from my NYU and Whitney days, optioned *The George Dunlap Tape* for Douglas Trumbull to direct. In a way it was a Hail Mary moment for Joel, whose own career wasn't going anywhere. He had a company named Cinnamon Productions and somehow knew Trumbull, the special effects genius behind *2001: A Space Odyssey*. With nothing to lose, I felt grateful for the interest. Joel and Doug felt I had written the best version of the movie I could, but it wasn't enough for them, so with my consent they hired a mutual friend of ours, Phil Messina, a screenwriting teacher at NYU, to do a rewrite. I wasn't comfortable with being replaced, but desperately wanted the movie to move forward and wasn't sure I knew how to take the material to the next level. I flew to New York and met with all three of them in Joel's office. I had heard that Doug wanted some major changes to the script, and I hoped I could persuade him to keep the opening and closing scenes intact. They were essential to my vision. But Doug had already expressed a desire to lose those scenes. I remember pouring my heart out to him over why I had written the script in the first place and why those scenes were essential.

My conception of the story was that human life had long since disappeared from Earth and that all of us had become full-life video tapes in a massive underground cavern of video machines, playing endlessly. Today we would all be VR and AI digitized lives stored on massive banks of computers. It was a cosmic idea that I hoped would lead people to look at their own lives from a different perspective by begging the question, *Who are we and what is this world we're in?* I wasn't willing to let go of the script unless I could persuade Doug to shoot that vision. At the end of the meeting, he agreed. I was naïve enough to believe that I had persuaded him. The minute I signed the contract, of course, those scenes were gone.

Phil wrote two strong drafts and brought what remained of my script into tighter focus. Paramount Pictures expressed interest and it looked like I was about to get a paycheck as the film headed into production. Then Paramount told Doug they would only make the film if he did the special effects for *Star Trek: The Motion Picture* first. That was excruciating for me. My whole life was based on Doug Trumbull making my movie, and now I had to wait nine months while he did *Star Trek* instead. I had little money. I had no prospects.

When Doug finished *Star Trek*, the studio reneged on their promise and put the script into turnaround, meaning that any other studio could have it if they paid off Paramount's investment. I couldn't believe it. I could barely handle the endless string of disappointments, reversals and betrayals that my barely breathing film career kept delivering. Luckily, MGM – like some deus ex machina – expressed interest in the project and it was set up there.

Doug said he wanted to make the movie in a new hyper-real format he had invented called Showscan, which used 70mm, much larger than the usual 35mm, and was projected at 60 frames per second. He invited me out to Los Angeles, where he screened a test of the process for me, a first-person ride on a roller coaster, at the National Theatre in Westwood. I was terrified of roller coasters and had never been on one, but the ride transcended every film experience I'd ever had. Doug said he had done galvanic skin response tests on people taking a real roller coaster ride, then again as they watched a 35mm version of the same ride, and finally the Showscan film. Their response to the Showscan footage was more resonant than an actual ride. I sensed this new cinematic form would fundamentally and permanently alter viewers' experience of movies. This was especially relevant, since the story we were telling was about entering other people's minds. Ideally, when the characters put on the *Brainstorm* helmet, the Showscan effect would transport the viewing audience into a true mind-altering experience. In the end, no studio would make it that way because it was too costly to retrofit all the theaters in America to accommodate the process. Decades later Doug called me about remaking the film and I had a sudden glimmer of hope that he could still offer Showscan to the world, but he died shortly after our conversation, and Showscan died with him.

While Doug was working on *Star Trek*, I got a rewrite job from Bob Shaye, who had just created New Line Cinema. Bob and I had both gone to Mumford High School in Detroit. We didn't really know each other (he was four years ahead of me), but he had reached out after I sold *The George Dunlap Tape*. He wanted me to do a rewrite of a movie for New Line called *Ivy Lane*, about plants trying to rid the planet of humanity because pollution is destroying their natural habitats.

I had fun but didn't really know thematically what it was about. I wrote the script in eight days, and on the eighth day still didn't have an ending. Back then, you had to send your script through the mail, and I had only an hour to come up with a big finish before the post office closed. At the very last minute, the entire story revealed itself to me. The planet is the Garden of Eden, where two surviving characters, versions of Adam and Eve, live. Nature has ridden our world of all the dark, corrupt human forces, and now these two people are going to recreate the human race. I had been writing on faith, and along the way *discovered* the story as much as I was creating it. What *Ivy Lane* taught me was that if you do your portion of the work, the various pieces of the universe will do theirs. It's a partnership. This has been an essential understanding in my writing and spiritual practice. I do my part as best I can, often with great uncertainty. Then something happens. *Ivy Lane* was never made, but it became a great lesson in writing.

Blanche and I wanted a second child. We had been trying seriously for three years, but my sperm count was low and, as the doctors told us, most people in such a situation couldn't conceive. "At least you have one child," they said. "Be happy." And we were happy. But we felt that a second child would be a gift. It was getting late in the game. We were getting older, both in our mid-thirties, so we kept trying, with no success.

One weekend the entire Bloomington ashram visited a satellite group in Ann Arbor which worked cleaning dorms at the University of Michigan. One day, when we were done, we went back to the classroom to meditate. As I sat there, I felt strangely alert, considering how tired I was. Suddenly, I felt like something from a billion miles away was speeding toward me. Like a comet, or a bullet, it was coming and coming and coming. All of a sudden it went straight into the uppermost chakra at the top of my head, passed down through each chakra in my body, and settled in my sex chakra. Then a voice inside my head said, "Give this to your wife tonight."

Blanche and I were staying at my parents' house in Detroit, not far from Ann Arbor, so we went back there and I told her what had happened. "You're not going to believe this…" I described the strange experience I'd had during meditation that reminded me of Superman as an infant being placed in a capsule by his dad, Marlon Brando, and blasted off Krypton, a dying planet. I told her how it had landed in my genitals and that a voice told me to give it to her that night. She looked at me with crossed eyes, smiled, and said, "Why not?" So we made love in my parent's guest room and two weeks later she was pregnant with our son Ari. I sensed we had been given a great cosmic gift.

Blanche had always felt somehow incomplete as a woman because Joshua was born by caesarean, and she wanted a natural childbirth. There were very few doctors in Indiana who would allow for a natural birth for a second child after a caesarean, but we found one doctor in Beech Grove, a town close to Indianapolis, who agreed. The morning Blanche went into labor we undramatically got into our car, put in a cassette of Aaron Copland's *Fanfare for the Common Man* and his elegiac *Appalachian Spring*, and drove to the hospital. *Fanfare* felt totally appropriate to the magic of this conception, and the theme from *Appalachian Spring* – "'Tis the gift to be simple, 'tis the gift to be free, 'tis the gift to come down where we ought to be" – seemed to be a blessing. I was in the delivery room the entire time and was even able to take hold of my new son as he entered our lives. From the moment Ari appeared as a manifested being, my life, our lives, our family, felt complete.

Fifteen

Fearing – Writing My Way Out of Hell

We spent six years in Indiana. During our final months there, we moved into a new apartment across from the ashram. The script for *Brainstorm* sold to MGM for $65,000. That was the most money I had ever seen. I even took photos of the check to prove to myself that I was a real writer. Blanche now had a Doctorate of Education and was offered a job teaching art education at Northern Illinois University in DeKalb, Illinois. It was time for us to move on.

Leaving Bloomington wasn't hard. Michael, the head teacher at the ashram, had decided to become a swami in India about a year before we left. He asked me what I thought about his decision. I told him not to do it. He was already a great teacher and the title would be meaningless. But it wasn't meaningless to him. The day he returned from India, I welcomed him as Michael. He told me never to call him that again. From then on, he was Swami Chetanananda. It was the beginning of a new moment in the life of the ashram and our lives together with him.

I long suspected that Michael had bigger ambitions in the world than being a teacher in Bloomington. As he began opening new centers across the Midwest, I could feel an emerging pomposity or even the seeds of megalomania that I found inappropriate, even frightening, in the spiritual world. I had seen it in Muktananda and other gurus I visited in India. There was also a growing sense of financial and sexual misbehavior that was hard to avoid. We knew that Michael was having affairs with many women in the ashram, some of them married. We also sensed that he was taking advantage of people financially and that most of the people working in ashram businesses were supporting him. My parents had worried that Rudi was doing the same thing, but Rudi had a highly successful antique business and had become very wealthy from his efforts. He didn't need his students to provide for him financially. On the other hand, Rudi did continue to sleep with some of his male students. It always seemed consensual, perhaps spiritually energizing, but I knew it was compromising and perhaps simply wrong. I wasn't critical enough of his behavior at the time, but I was beginning to see its consequences. It sent a signal and led to ongoing misconduct in other ashrams, which became a stain on the practice of his work. Blanche and I devoted many years to the Bloomington ashram, learned many lessons, and participated in fulfilling public service, but we weren't unhappy to leave, which was made possible by the sale of *Brainstorm*. Michael made it impossible to stay.

With the money from *Brainstorm*, Blanche and I bought our first home, a new car and a house full of furniture, and said goodbye to Bloomington. It was an amicable departure. A group of Rudi's students, people I loved and would miss deeply, drove us to DeKalb and helped unpack the truck. Within an hour, the whole house was set up.

The four years we spent in DeKalb proved to be exceedingly difficult. I look back on it as my time in the desert, although we were surrounded by cornfields. I was approaching forty, and felt that I had blown it. My career wasn't happening. I was making no money and nobody wanted to hire me. My life was turning into a wasteland on so many levels. It was also a hard transition for my family, as well as for me. Joshua had left behind the joy of communal living, growing up with a dozen other kids as practical brothers and sisters, running around the halls and playing together, eating dinner together every night. It was an idyllic childhood. Now, suddenly, he was in a nuclear family in a suburban house and having to make friends all over again at the age of eight. Blanche had her own difficulties, being a new mother and a full-time teacher at the university, nursing a child, making dinner, managing the house. There was a lot of juggling to do.

Ari was only two months old and because Blanche was breastfeeding, she had to drive home from the university twice a day to nurse him. It was a demanding routine. I became a full-time parent, getting Joshua to and from school and being with Ari during most of his waking hours. That part of my life was an unexpected pleasure. I bonded with Ari in ways I hadn't with Joshua, since I was with him nearly every minute. Joshua was a very independent child who thrived in the ashram community and the larger world. Ari was happy close to home. We loved playing together, going to the park, strolling through DeKalb. Having him around was perfection for me – simple joy.

Unfortunately, we found it difficult to engage with much of the local community, and from the start I sensed that we didn't belong. Blanche and I imagined that being only ninety minutes from Chicago we would have continual access to the big city. Her best friend Joan from childhood lived there with her husband Gary, and so did my cousin Wendy. We figured we would see them regularly. In the end, we were lucky to go in once or twice a year. The isolation was numbing. Ari, on the other hand, seemed content. His happiness was a gift to us all. Another saving grace was our neighbors. We lived next door to a church, where the pastor's family lived. Norman, the priest, and his wife Roberta, mother of four, embraced us. They were our primary emotional support and helped smooth our transition.

I didn't expect to find an ashram-style community in DeKalb, so I decided to build one. I asked the university if I could offer a hatha yoga class at the student center, and they said yes. I had taught hatha yoga for years in Rudi's ashram and found that I still had it in me. I ended every class with a meditation session. At the end of the six-week class, I said, "If anybody wants to take this meditation further, I'm going to hold classes at my house once a week. The class is free and you are all welcome to come." Ten people came to the first class. Then more people, and then more. Somehow, I managed to form a community around me. That's how, for the next four years, I sustained and expanded my spiritual life.

I wrote several industrial films while I was in DeKalb – one for the local library, one for Mutual of Wausau, another for Morton Thiokol, the parent company of Morton Salt, which also made munitions. It was a challenge to put the full spectrum of that company's identity into one film – the iconic image of a girl with an umbrella under a soft rain of salt, and all those bombs falling as well. I made a little bit of money, maybe enough to live on for a month. When I approached the university in DeKalb and offered to instruct a class in screenwriting, I dropped a few anecdotes about *Brainstorm*, thinking they didn't get many "Hollywood" writers out this way, but that didn't impress them one bit. Several days later I got a call saying that they needed someone to teach four sections of Public Speaking 101, a required course for all university students, meaning no one actually wanted to take it. I told them I'd have to think about it. An hour later I said yes. Preparing for the classes took so much effort that I had no time to write. My students' primary interests were getting married or going to business school. I told them all to drop out of school, have meaningful affairs, and travel the world before committing to anything as serious as a marriage or an MBA.

Here I was, living in a cornfield, with no meaningful work, being supported by my wife. In my mind, my story was over. Despite it all, I came up with a script idea for a movie called *Jacob's*

Ladder. It began as a dream that came partly out of my own fear and despair. I'm in a subway late at night, traveling through the bowels of New York. There are very few people on the train. A terrible loneliness grips me. The train pulls into the station and I get off onto a deserted platform. When I walk to the nearest exit and discover the gate is locked, a feeling of despair pulses through me. I hike to the other end of the platform, but that exit is also chained shut. I am trapped and overwhelmed by a sense of doom. I know with perfect certainty that I will never see daylight again. My one hope is to jump onto the tracks and enter the tunnel, the darkness. The only possible direction is down. I know that the next stop on my journey is Hell.

I could have given up my filmmaking goals and settled into a different kind of lifestyle. I was teaching at the university, and they probably would have allowed me to keep doing that. And that would have been my story. My obituary would have read: "Okay, you tried." Instead, I woke up from my subway dream and said, "That's a great opening for a movie." And then I tried to write my way out of Hell.

I nearly failed the only screenwriting course I ever took at New York University. The professor had a theory of screenwriting that involved a concept called "triangularity." I never understood what that meant. It had something to do with the three points of conflict required for a scene to work effectively and somehow came into play even when there were only two people on the screen. I hated the class and despaired that I would never be a writer if understanding triangularity was the measure of success. I have always been weak in the left brain, or whichever side controls logical thought. Structures and stratagems are a continual mystery to me. Plotting a script in logical fashion has almost always proved mind-boggling. I work mostly from intuition and my best work occurs when I trust it to lead me.

Jacob's Ladder was the first movie I wrote that was delivered, by which I mean I had nothing to do with it. I just sat at the typewriter and wrote. I typed as fast as I could because it was just coming through. I didn't understand where it was coming from or why, but it was pouring through me and scaring the hell out of me as I wrote. I remember one afternoon Blanche came into the room and stood behind me while I was writing. "What are you writing that for?" she asked after glancing at the typewriter. "I don't know," I said. But I couldn't stop.

About halfway through the script, I got stuck. I remember pacing the room with enormous frustration because I didn't know where the script was going. I was writing a movie about a man who had died and was stuck in Hell. Perhaps it was an intermediate state between death and rebirth. Tibetan Buddhist teachings call this the Bardo. I couldn't see a way out of the darkness. As a storyteller, I want to put stories out into the world that uplift or ennoble people. This film was definitely not heading in that direction.

Then one afternoon it hit me. I was writing a version of *An Occurrence at Owl Creek Bridge*, a brilliant short film by Robert Enrico based on a short story from 1890 by Ambrose Bierce that I had seen in college. A Civil War soldier stands on a bridge waiting to be hanged by Confederate soldiers. He is shoved unceremoniously off the bridge and begins falling to his death. We wait for the noose to catch and choke him, but he keeps falling. He plunges into the river below and, against all odds, soldiers shooting at him, he swims to shore and makes his way home, where he sees his wife. Arms outstretched, he runs toward her. She sees him and walks closer. Joy and awe flashes across their faces. Just as they are about to embrace and kiss, the man jerks backwards. He is on the bridge, being hanged. The noose tightens. He is dead. The journey home to his wife took place in a fraction of a second in his head.

The moment I realized that with *Jacob's Ladder* I was writing a feature-length version of that story, I was filled with so much energy that I couldn't even sit. I stormed around the house like a madman for over an hour saying, "Oh my god oh my god oh my god. This is it this is it this is it." I finally understood what I was doing. I had my movie. I just wrote. It poured out of me.

I finished the script in the fall of 1981. My New York lawyer from the *Brainstorm* days, Charlie Shays, had a friend, Cindy Degener, who had once been a Hollywood agent but left her career to get a doctorate in medieval ecclesiastical history. She had been married to Sterling Lord, a literary agent for Jack Kerouac, Art Buchwald and Lawrence Ferlinghetti. I knew immediately that she was the agent I needed. Cindy loved my script and began submitting it to studios. I felt optimistic for the first time in years.

Miraculously, around the same time, Doug Trumbull and Joel Freedman got *Brainstorm* away from Paramount and set it up at MGM. The studio had brought in another writer named Robert Stitzel. His new draft of the script was a real diminishment of what Phil Messina had written and I was embarrassed by it, but the studio seemed happy and gave the film a green light. They said no to Doug's Showscan process but okayed 70mm for the experiential shots whenever the helmet was worn. I was excited by the cast, which included Christopher Walken and Natalie Wood, whom I had loved ever since I was a kid. I had even once photographed her and her husband Robert Wagner for my high school newspaper. Also in the cast were Cliff Robertson, a true movie star, and Louise Fletcher, who had won an Oscar for her role in *One Flew Over the Cuckoo's Nest*.

I desperately wanted to watch the movie being filmed, but wasn't invited to be part of the production – a common reality for writers in Hollywood. Unlike in theater, where the writer is king, Hollywood considers them expensive annoyances once they have delivered the script. I used to refer to the metaphor of the totem pole, where writers would normally be at the very bottom of the pole. In Hollywood, however, they are the part below ground. Without them, there would be no totem pole and no movie, but the less visible they are, according to most directors and executives, the better. Regardless, they couldn't keep me away. The week before Thanksgiving 1981, I borrowed money from my mother-in-law and flew to Hollywood to watch my first film being made.

I was overwhelmed to be on the set, seeing this vision of the future that I had dreamed up years earlier, writing nightly in my New York loft. The sets were even similar to the Indiana University cyclotron where I had hoped to shoot the film when we were living in Bloomington. I was thrilled by every detail, especially the *Brainstorm* helmet that could read people's minds, emotions and memories. I stood breathlessly as Doug called action on the first shot of the day. A moment later, I was horrified – because Christopher Walken wasn't speaking any of the lines from the script. He was making everything up as he went along. I remember thinking, *He can't do that! He can't just change the lines. The dialogue is essential to the story. How is this going to work?* I wanted Doug to tell Chris he was saying the wrong words. Instead, he just said, "Cut! Good. Okay. Next scene." I was devastated. I never felt more powerless or useless. There was nothing I could do. I worried about how many other lines he might have changed during the course of shooting, and what the movie would turn into. I could only imagine what writers have forever been going through in the Hollywood universe.

While Natalie Wood was very sweet, Christopher was difficult to talk to and rather dismissive. He and Natalie would disappear into her trailer during filming breaks. I could hear them giggling when I walked by. I wasn't invited in. Cliff Robertson was easy to be with, but a polite hello was all I could get from Louise Fletcher, who was at the peak of her career. My one week on the set was emotionally complicated because I didn't know what my role was. Eventually I realized I didn't have a role. Still, it felt like a triumphant moment. I had a movie in production at a major Hollywood studio. Some of our soundstages had been used for *The Wizard of Oz*. My dreams were coming true. I returned home to DeKalb to a wondrous welcome from my family and one of the most satisfying Thanksgiving feasts I had ever had. I had every reason to be grateful.

Then, the day after Thanksgiving, my sister Marci called me to tell me that Natalie Wood had died in a boating accident. No one knew exactly what happened, only that Robert Wagner admitted to having a fight with Christopher Walken on the ship that night, arguing about Natalie's career, and it ended with Natalie getting into a rubber dinghy and rowing into the night. She was found dead the next morning. The movie, it seemed, died with her and the studio shut down production. Nearly all of her scenes had been shot and I was sure there was a way to finish the film. But no one was talking to me.

It felt like the universe was conspiring against me. I had just turned forty, my first movie had ended in tragedy, and then, adding insult to injury, nobody wanted to buy *Jacob's Ladder*. Sidney Lumet, Ulu Grosbard, Michael Apted and plenty of others I had never heard of had read and loved the script, or so I was told, but no one thought it could be made. Thom Mount, president of Universal, said he loved the script, loved the writing, but that it wasn't for him. Those words were a constant refrain. The most exciting possibility had long been my dream candidate, Ridley Scott, who had made *Alien* and was finishing *Blade Runner*, which contained Doug Trumbull's remarkable special effects work. Marv Minoff, my old agent, contacted Ridley for me. He loved the script and for about a month it looked like we might make it together. The idea was to shoot it right after he completed his next film, *Legend*. Then *Legend* ran into scheduling problems and he decided that he couldn't commit to *Jacob's Ladder*. It became a twilight zone period in my life, with fame, fortune and success just over the horizon. I gradually resigned myself to the fact that *Jacob* would join the pile of unproduced screenplays on my bookshelf.

I could have given in to the despair, but instead I went back to writing. I had an idea for a movie called *Secrets of the Astral Plane*, about a ragtag team of psychics – a psychic *Dirty Dozen* – who try to stop a Russian terrorist, also a psychic, from taking over the mind of the American president. I developed the story down to the last beat. My agent got it to a producer in Los Angeles named Bob Sherman, who was excited about the concept. He flew me out to pitch the story to the head of Warner Bros. I had never pitched anything in my life and was nervous. I had heard a story about a writer entering his first pitch meeting. After a few minutes of preordained small talk, the studio executive turned to the writer and said, "So what have you got?" The writer stared into the executive's eyes, sat motionless for a moment, and then fainted dead away. I didn't want to be that writer.

So I did the opposite. I talked and talked. I told the head of Warner Bros., Robert Shapiro, and his vice president, Lucy Fisher (who would later produce my film *Stuart Little 2*), every single beat of my movie. It took me two hours. A pitch is usually ten minutes, often less, but I hadn't learned that yet. When I had finished, Robert got up, went to the liquor cabinet, and offered me a drink. Then he said, "That was amazing, and we'd like to think about it and get back to you." That seemed very promising to me, but when we walked out the door Bob Sherman said, "When they say they'll think about it, it's not going to happen." And he was right. They passed the next day. Bob suggested that I go home and write the script because he said he could sell it more easily as a finished work. I went back to DeKalb and wrote like mad. The finished script floated around for a while, but nobody jumped at it. I remember one executive read it and said, "It's swell." That was like a knife in the gut. "Swell" does not sell movies.

MGM didn't want to finish *Brainstorm*. Their instinct was to take the insurance money and call it a day. There was even talk of destroying the negative. Then Doug Trumbull did a heroic thing. He locked himself into the vault with the negative and said, "Nobody is going to touch it unless I can finish the movie." He persuaded Lloyds of London, the insurers, that the film could be finished, that Natalie had completed enough scenes, and that finishing the film would cost them less money than abandoning it and paying off MGM. They eventually gave him the money to finish shooting and we all got T-shirts that read "BRAINSTORM: a Lloyds of London Production." MGM was no longer our parent in this process.

There was an arbitration for writing credits, and I was told that only two writers would receive credit. Someone convinced me that a "Story by" credit was the best way to go, since I would retain ownership of the original idea. I still don't know if that's true. I was also told when I joined the Writers Guild that I couldn't use my given name as a writer in Hollywood because there was already another Bruce Rubin with screen credits. He hadn't done much (he was best known for a movie called *Zapped*), but he was there before me, so I had to use my middle name, Joel, as my Hollywood signature. Like my mom, dad and sister, I was now a family member with a different name: Bruce Joel Rubin.

The movie came out in September 1983. My friend Joel Freedman, the producer, didn't have enough money to fly us all out or even to get us transportation to the opening, so Blanche and I flew to Hollywood for the premiere on money borrowed from Blanche's mom. We pooled our funds and paid for a limo, into which we packed fourteen people. When we arrived at the Cinerama Dome on Sunset Boulevard it looked like a circus car, where clown after clown keeps popping out. It so typified my experience with the movie that I could do nothing but laugh. Sometimes in life things just aren't meant to work out.

I actually liked *Brainstorm* as I watched it and was affected by the sight of my name, full size, in huge 70mm. I was even glad that I had added Joel to my name, as it completely filled the screen. Two things made the film successful for me. One was the scene where Natalie Wood puts on the helmet and sees how much her estranged husband loves her. Their marriage is falling apart because he is too focused on his work and isn't able to express his love properly. She has every reason to want to leave him. Then he says, "Here – I made this for you," and gives her a tape of all his memories of their time together so she can see into his heart. That saves their marriage. James Horner's score added tremendous emotion and elevated the entire movie. Louise Fletcher's performance was the other thing that stood out for me. I think she deserved an Oscar.

Early reviews were glowing. *US* magazine's reviewer was ecstatic, calling the film a breakthrough in the same league as *Star Wars*. But the euphoria didn't last long. I spoke with an old colleague, Howard Kissel, a film critic for *Women's Wear Daily*, at a screening in New York. His first words to me were, "So Bruce, I see you were involved with that unspeakable abomination, *Brainstorm*." I don't think I caught my breath for a week. Most other critics agreed with him. Unfortunately, so did the public. I quickly learned that a movie that makes no money, no matter how good, is a failure.

No one wants to talk about it. So finally a script of mine had been made and there was a huge billboard for it on the Sunset Strip, but it changed nothing. *Brainstorm* was supposed to start my career. Instead, it pretty much ended it before it had begun.

While we were in LA, Blanche and I had lunch with Brian De Palma, who had remained an important person in my life. In earlier years, Brian kept telling me that I was getting too old to be a part of the movie business, that you had to be youthful, in your twenties, to withstand the rigors of Hollywood. But this time was different. He had seen *Brainstorm* and loved it. "You're never going to have a career as a filmmaker," he said, "if you don't move to Hollywood." He was direct and clear. Clear enough that Blanche heard him. I was terrified about moving to LA, because the idea of not making it as a screenwriter in Hollywood was somehow worse than not making it as a screenwriter in DeKalb.

The first thing Blanche did when we got back to DeKalb was quit her job, put our house on the market, and announce to anyone who would listen that we were moving to Hollywood. I have never seen such selflessness, determination or courage. I was stunned by her willingness to risk everything in support of my career. I was beyond frightened. People at work told her she was crazy, that she was just a year away from getting tenure and living the rest of her life in DeKalb, but she was undeterred. We took photos of our house, printed FOR SALE signs with tear-off tags on the bottom with our phone number, and posted them in local supermarkets and anywhere that had a community billboard. In years past I had followed quiet inner voices directing me to follow my spiritual life. I had quit my job at NBC to find a teacher in India and I had quit my job as a curator at the Whitney Museum to move to an ashram in Indiana. Now my wife was pushing me to leave all security behind in support of my Hollywood dream. I couldn't believe her strength. It was an unforgettable offer. Within a month, our house sold.

Luckily, perhaps magically, a friend of Blanche's, Gil Clark, from Indiana University's Department of Art Education, heard about our plans and knew that neither of us had any promise of work in LA. He told Blanche about a short-term art evaluation study being done by the J. Paul Getty Trust. It used a qualitative approach to analyze what kids in public schools were learning about art, including history, criticism and aesthetics, in addition to making art. This was exactly what Blanche had studied. Blanche and I flew to LA so she could conduct the study in local schools. This also gave us a chance to look for possible homes. We couldn't believe the cost of housing, but Jerry Mandel, a friend from Bloomington, had a cousin who was a realtor in the San Fernando Valley. She found us a house in Northridge – a simple one-story bungalow on a full acre with a pool in the backyard and a train line that ran behind the house. It appealed to us and was affordable. With a sudden surge of good luck, the Getty loved Blanche's study and offered her a full-time job in their new program. We rented the Northridge house and Blanche officially quit her job at Northern Illinois University. What began as the biggest leap of faith in our lives started to look like a brilliant choice.

Sixteen

Arriving – Hollywood

During my DeKalb years, Brian De Palma recommended me to his agent, and the guy offered to represent me. "I'm interviewing a number of possible agents," I told him. "Do you mind if I do that and then decide?" His response was quick and brutal. "You just blew it, kid. Nobody gets an invitation from me and says he wants to consider other people. Goodbye."

After that, another agent showed up who seemed excited about my work. I flew out to Hollywood to meet him. We talked about my movie ideas, including a new one for a film called *Ghost*. Back in Illinois, I kept waiting for him to call. The day we sold our DeKalb house, he finally did. "I don't want to represent you," he told me. "Your stuff is too metaphysical. Nobody wants to make movies about ghosts."

Luckily, in 1983, *American Film* magazine had published an article by Steven Rubello in which *Jacob's Ladder* was described as one of the ten best unproduced screenplays in Hollywood. That seemed a dubious distinction, but I was pleased to have it acknowledged at all. I was surprised to discover that the ten scripts weren't chosen by Rubello. They had been picked by top Hollywood executives, culled from thousands of selections.

Admirers of Bruce Joel Rubin's Jacob's Ladder *flat out refuse to describe this screenplay. Their only entreaty? "Read it. It's extraordinary."*

And it is… Page for page, it is one of the very few screenplays I've read with the power to consistently raise hackles in broad daylight… Rubin proves a confident trickster-dreamer with a lighter hand than either William Peter Blatty or Paddy Chayevsky.

Steve Rubello

Soon after that I was approached by Kyle Counts, a writer for *Cinefantastique* magazine, who asked if he could do a story on *Jacob's Ladder*, "the thought-provoking script… that no one dares film." Suddenly there were two magazine articles about my script, so by the time I got to LA in 1984, people wanted to see me – not because of *Brainstorm* but because of *Jacob's Ladder*. I interviewed with several agents, but there was one who stood out. Geoff Sanford said that *Jacob's Ladder* was the kind of script that made him want to be in the business in the first place. He was also the only agent who didn't flinch when I told him I could last for only four months in LA without work. After that, my family and I would be living on the beach – and he knew I didn't mean Malibu. He was confident he could have me working shortly after I arrived and was willing to take me on knowing he had the weight of a family's survival on his shoulders. I signed with him right away. A few days later, he got me my first job.

I began writing a script for Embassy Pictures called *Little Brother*, a take on Orwell's dystopian *Nineteen Eighty-Four*, about a young boy who discovers that his all-seeing/all controlling Big Brother computer is programming him. I answered to three different executives over the course of that project. One of them was Embassy's vice president Lindsay Doran, who even before I met her played a formidable role in my life. It turns out she was one of the people who recommended *Jacob's Ladder* for the *American Film* article. She was the first genuinely creative executive I ever met and the best story editor I have ever known. She was also kind, generous and smart. After a marathon meeting with her at the studio one day, I realized I didn't have enough cash to get my car out of the parking lot. I sheepishly asked if I could borrow some money. She was astounded that I couldn't pay for my car and gave me some cash. Several hours after I got home, I got a phone call from Geoff Sanford saying something unheard-of had happened. Lindsay had called him, so ashamed that one of Embassy's writers didn't have enough money to pay for parking that she and the studio had decided to "give" me an additional $15,000 for my script. Needless to say, such largesse does not occur regularly in Hollywood.

We were getting close to my son Joshua's bar mitzvah, which was being held at a local temple we had just joined. We couldn't afford much of a party and I joked that it would be the first peanut-butter-and-jelly bar mitzvah in Jewish history. Lindsay's generosity made it possible for us to rent a room at a local golf club and have a real celebratory event.

Lindsay's role in my career would be what I can only describe as angelic. A few months later, she called me. "I have good news and bad news," she said. "The bad news is that I'm leaving Embassy and won't be able to help you finish *Little Brother*. The good news is that I'm going to become a vice president at Paramount Pictures and will hire you to write movies there. You'll make a lot more money than you're making here." I laughed – but it all came true. It was eventually through Lindsay that my films *Ghost* and then *Jacob's Ladder* came to be made. Happily, the executives at Embassy loved my finished script of *Little Brother*, but the studio went out of business before it could be produced. Around the same time, my friend Marvin Minoff got me a job writing a TV movie called *Student Affairs*, about a girl sleeping her way to a good grade, or something like that. I had trouble getting past the sleazy underpinnings of the story, but I tried to make it work. Luckily, it was never made.

Then Bob Sherman offered to hire me to write a horror film. Based on a book called *Friend*, it was the story of a girl murdered by her father and the brilliant boy next door who loves her and brings her back to life. He extracts his pet robot's brain and transplants it into hers. Things don't end well for anyone. "I can't write that," I said. "I have integrity. I didn't come to Hollywood to make shlocky movies like this." The next morning, while meditating and feeling very smug about turning down the job, I heard Rudi's voice in my head, as clear as could be. "You schmuck! There's more integrity in providing for your family than in turning down jobs. Get up right now, go to the phone, call the producer, and say you're going to do it." I've had a long enough spiritual practice to know that when your teacher speaks to you from beyond the grave, you listen. I got up instantly from my cross-legged meditative pose, wobbled to the phone, and called Bob Sherman. I told him I hoped the job was still available because I wanted it. He laughed and said it was mine. I suspect no one else was interested.

Once I began, I realized I wasn't just writing some kind of *Frankenstein* tale but a love story, about love lasting beyond death. A teenage boy wants to bring the girl he loves back from the dead. It was right up my alley. There was real emotion to be found, a human story beneath the horror. To my surprise, Wes Craven, whose *A Nightmare on Elm Street* had been a huge hit in the horror market, was hired to direct. He was anxious to try something different and was delighted that I was focusing on the human elements in the story. Now he would have an opportunity to inspire and explore emotions other than fear. Lucy Fisher, vice president at Warner Bros., called to say she loved the script and had found it surprisingly emotional. It had even made her cry. I hadn't expected that, to put it mildly.

Friend, as the script was originally called, was filmed on the Warner Bros. backlot, twenty minutes from our house. Every evening Blanche and I would pack the kids in the car and drive to the studio to watch them shoot. Wes always greeted us warmly and Joshua and Ari became set mascots.

We had our first test screening and I thought it went well, but Mark Canton, the new Warner Bros. vice president, was disappointed, and felt that audience feedback was lackluster. The truth is that it wasn't much of a horror film in the Wes Craven tradition. Canton announced that he was going to give us money to re-shoot additional scenes, with the understanding that each had to be gorier and more frightening than the last. Wes enjoyed the challenge and sat down to devise horrific elements, including having Samantha, the girl with the new brain and enormous strength, tossing a basketball at one of our villains and knocking her head off her shoulders. For half a minute she ran around headless, blood shooting everywhere. At the next test screening, young men were standing on their seats yelling and screaming hysterically, watching this headless body careening in all directions. I had never seen anything like it. Mark Canton and Wes seemed elated. I didn't know what to think. It surprised me that I had actually written this movie, the title of which was changed from *Friend* to *Deadly Friend.*

Canton figured we would make a fortune, but the ratings board had other ideas. We were given an X and told what we had to cut to get to an R or PG rating. Wes looked at me with surprising clarity and said, "Every frame we cut from this film is another million dollars lost at the box office." We clearly removed too many frames. It was no longer a love story or a horror film, and dwindled into a more modest and less appealing work that made very little money when it was released. It could easily have cost Wes and me our careers, but we were both lucky. He went on to make the *Scream* franchise, which reignited his status as one of the premiere horror film directors. The last time I saw him was at the premiere of his film *The Serpent and the Rainbow.* I was in a bathroom stall and he unknowingly sat next to mine. When we realized it was us, we both laughed and spoke for what turned out to be the last time. Other than glimpsing his feet, I didn't see him then or ever again. He died a few years later. It seemed a memorable ending to our brief but joyful time together.

Deadly Friend, the culmination of a childhood dream, wasn't just a joy to make – it became a continuing gift. During the writer's strike of 1988, when I hadn't seen any income for five months and our bank account was down to $400, I received a residual from *Deadly Friend*, a check for $3,400 which arrived in the mail. Blanche received it with even more gratitude than I did. "Look closer," she said. I did – and realized there was another zero. The check was actually for $34,000. It allowed us to make a down payment on the purchase of our rented Northridge house.

The *Deadly Friend* offices were across the hall from Joe Dante's. He and his producer Mike Finnell hired me to write a film called *Way Station*, an adaptation of a science fiction novel by Clifford D. Simak, a charming story about a depot for intergalactic travelers established on Earth during the Civil War. When the story begins, the way station is being run by Enoch, one of the last surviving veterans of the war. His interactions with aliens have exposed him to secrets of the universe, including his own immortality, and opened his eyes to humanity's possible destruction. It will be up to him to save us. *Way Station* was right in my wheelhouse, and I loved writing it. Unfortunately, Joe Dante's recent movie *Innerspace* didn't do well at the box office and the president of Warner Bros. announced that they wouldn't be making any more science fiction films. *Way Station* was shelved.

Writing movies that don't get made is a common experience in Hollywood. I probably have a three to one ratio – which is pretty good. The trick is staying employed. There are two ways to do that. One is to write a movie that makes a ton of money. The other is to write what studio executives consider good scripts, stories with tight plot lines, good characters and strong dialogue that catch the attention of actors, directors and producers. Anything less and careers tend to sink as fast as they rise. Supporting a family with those kinds of pressures was difficult. Fortunately, Blanche was working for the Getty Foundation and loving her job, but she was National Program Evaluator for their Institute for Education in the Arts, which meant traveling all over the country, so I became responsible for raising the kids at home, as well as writing. It was a struggle, but a joyful one. My boys delighted in my burgeoning

Hollywood career. I loved watching them fall in love with Los Angeles. It was a perfect fit. And not just for them. Within a few years of our living in LA, my brother Gary and his family moved there as well. Other cousins soon joined us there and the wonderful energy of my childhood family experience re-emerged in Los Angeles. Even Mark Greenberg moved to LA and found a job at the Getty Museum as head of publishing. It was a sublime reunion of friends and family. We hosted everyone in Northridge for holidays, just as my parents had done when we were kids.

A number of film projects kept me going, and money started coming in. Michael Shoemaker, when he visited one day in our early years there, saw the train go by behind the house and said, "It will keep you humble." I grabbed hold of those words. Staying humble in Hollywood is a life-saving mechanism – a saving grace. If anything, I learned that the ego-diminishing power of being a writer in Hollywood would be the biggest gift of my career, at least in a spiritual sense. Letting go of identity, of specialness and ego-inflation, is part of the path to awakening. Lightening the load of self-centeredness is a road to enlightenment. Hollywood helped with that.

I got a few interesting writing jobs in my early days in LA. One, a film for producers Harry and Mary Jane Ufland, was an opportunity to write for Robert De Niro, a project in which he would star with Whitney Houston and co-direct with Quincy Jones. This was heady stuff for me. The fact that Whitney hadn't yet committed to the project was of little significance – we always referred to the film as "the Whitney Houston project." I was hired to write the story of a man who finds a girl with an electrifying voice in a church choir, becomes her manager, and falls in love with her, even though she's in love with someone else. In some unspoken ways it felt more like a love letter from Bob to Whitney, but that was never said out loud.

It was fun to be back in the world of Bob De Niro. We hadn't seen one another since our time with Brian on *Hi, Mom!*, when I was assistant director. He still seemed shy and soft-spoken and often inarticulate, but this was now part of his public persona.

I had lost touch with both De Niro and Scorsese in the early Seventies as their careers soared, although at one point, when I was moving into the Bloomington ashram, Brian had encouraged me to come out West. They were having a fantastic time together on the beach at Malibu – Brian, Marty, Lucas and Spielberg, all those young hot shots, the Movie Brats, about to have their moment. It was an evolving group that hung out in Margot Kidder and Jennifer Salt's house. Brian said that he taught Marty, newly arrived from New York, how to drive. I wondered what would have happened if I had joined them. I imagine it would have been premature. I was mostly a writer at that point, and they were all directors. If I had gone and lived that Malibu life with them, I would probably have ended up as a footnote to their extraordinary careers. Not for a second do I regret the choices I made. My career flowed as it was supposed to. But finding myself suddenly writing a movie for De Niro all those years later felt affirming. Everything in its own time.

My boys were with me visiting Bob at his house in Malibu one day when Sean Penn and Madonna dropped by. I remember Joshua and Ari looking at me like I was God. For the first time, I felt I really was part of Hollywood. I remember Madonna being shy and introverted. I couldn't picture her performing in stadiums full of thousands of people. Much later, Joshua and I saw her perform in a huge stadium – and she most definitely filled the space. That day in De Niro's living room it was Sean who filled it for her, and for the rest of us. It was hard to breathe because he consumed so much air. He was a real movie star.

Quincy Jones, like Sean, also filled whatever room he was in. His dynamism was intimidating. We talked about the movie I was writing, and to help me develop the characters, Quincy introduced me to his music business friends. That was never my world and I was a bit out of my element, but I'll never forget the day I spent with Michael Jackson in a studio. His recording sessions seemed highly sexualized in ways his stage performances only hinted at. His hands were all over himself and his engagement with the material was full-bodied. Elvis would have looked away. I went to see Joan Baez in concert at Carnegie Hall, then spent a day with her. I wasn't so much starstruck as awed by her openness, authenticity and gentility. She helped me get a sense of the main character of the film I was writing.

Meeting Whitney Houston was crucial, since it was hoped that she would star in the movie and that her actual life story might somehow inform the script. We arranged to go as a group and see her perform at the Coliseum in LA. When we arrived, Blanche and I and the producers were shown to our seats way up in the gallery, while De Niro, Quincy and Joe Pesci (I don't know why he was there) were taken down to the third row next to the stage. We were a mile apart. It felt like everyone was meant to know their place. But it was a great concert, even from a distance.

After the performance we were allowed entry into Whitney's dressing room. The dominating force was clearly her father, who seemed in charge of everything, including Whitney, who cowered in front of him. De Niro seemed to have romantic designs on her, which I realized in that moment was the real reason I was writing this film. Years later she admitted to being pursued by him. Still, meeting Whitney was fascinating, and seeing her with her dad became a useful dramatic element in the story I was writing. The backstage experience was a defining moment for me, capturing much of what I found distasteful and disturbing in the music (and movie) business, especially the undercurrents of self-serving greed and egoism.

De Niro, who was involved in making several films at the time, became less and less available during the writing phase. He called me just as I was sitting down at the computer. "Just two words," he said. "Fate and Magic." I spent weeks trying to interpret Bob's cryptic message and finally found a way of weaving it into the script. I was pleased with the end result, and when I was finished I couldn't wait to get his response. "What did you think of fate and magic?" I asked. "What's that?" he replied. I knew then I was in trouble. I wrote several more drafts and submitted the script. MGM liked it but had suggestions that would have made it a different movie. I don't think Bob's relationship with Whitney was going anywhere, and the fate of the movie seemed tied to that. The whole thing was a bizarre experience, but it helped pay the bills and I was grateful for the insights about the effect Hollywood could have on people's psyches – mine included.

Some friends, Skip Shepard and Debra Franco, wanted to talk to me about writing a movie for them and flew me to New York. I pitched them a script I called *Armies of the Lord*, about a far-right American militia that takes over an army base in North Dakota and prepares to battle for white supremacist American freedom and again the ragtag common folk who stand up to resist them. Then *Red Dawn* came out, a Patrick Swayze film with somewhat similar themes, and Skip and Deb backed away from my script. Overnight, I was out of a job. They asked me if I had any other ideas. I read them a list a mile long. They listened to everything I had to offer and decided that what excited them most was something called *Ghost*. In the end, they didn't go forward with it. But their spark of interest awoke something in me. It put a pin in the idea. I couldn't stop thinking about it.

Seventeen

Sharing – *Ghost* and *Jacob's Ladder*

The original idea for *Ghost* was a question: *What would it be like to tell a ghost story from the side of the ghost?* I knew from my acid trip and decades-long spiritual journey that life doesn't start at birth or end at death. What I didn't know was how to dramatize that. Then one day, after watching a production of *Hamlet* and seeing the ghost of Hamlet's father standing on the parapet, telling his son to avenge his death, I came up with the idea of a story about a ghost trying to solve his own murder. Up to that point, my treatments were like outlines for novels, but the one I wrote for *Ghost* was very sparse, very simple. It had three acts, not twenty chapters. The characters were present tense, action-based, in the moment. I abandoned novelistic narrative tropes to describe them. Their back stories, their personalities, evolved as the story unfolded. You could read it and see the entirety of the story at a glance.

I spent two years pitching *Ghost*. Everyone said no. I honed my pitching skills over time. Studio executives are like jaded kindergarteners who listen to story ideas all day long. The hard part is getting their attention, so I decided something different was required. At the moment in the story when Sam gets shot, I clapped my hands loudly. It startled them every time, and I had their full attention for about two minutes – long enough to deliver the rest of the story. The pitch also evolved. When Bruce Evans and Ray Gideon, writers of *Stand By Me*, heard me talking about the psychic who can hear Sam the ghost, they laughed. The psychic was originally a con man and a straight character. They thought it would be funny if he was a fake who discovered a hidden talent for communion with the dead. I thought that was brilliant. I made the psychic black, female, and named her Oda Mae.

A word of advice for anyone making a pitch at a studio. When you enter the room of a studio president or vice president, which is often filled with a small group of lesser executives, and they ask if you would like a cup of tea, always say yes. Just before you start talking, take a long sip. Sit quietly for a while and let the room settle. That's very important. Get everyone centered and focused on you. Have your opening pitch lines in place and ready to go so you feel assured. And then tap into the core of the story, and let it tell itself. I never memorized a whole pitch – I just let it flow and find its own way. Not that I wasn't prepared, but I opened up to the moment. Every group has its own collective energy. You need to *meet* that energy. Feel the room. Every person has to be included. Look into their eyes. There is a spiritual version of this related to chakras, the energy centers in every human being, but if you haven't studied that, just sense that you're opening your mind and heart to the people around you. That sip of tea you take before you start will open the throat chakra, so the words flow through you with simple and articulate ease. And fully embrace your story. It's the way I was taught to sell cameras: *caress* your pitch. Make it special. Deliver it with tenderness. Be willing to withhold. Pause for a moment and let listeners find their way in. Make them hunger for what comes next. It works, I promise you.

As I pitched *Ghost*, the story became richer, and I became more and more connected to it. I really had it down to an art. At one point my agent, Geoff Sanford, set up five meetings at five different studios, all in one week. Everyone wanted it. At Paramount, we pitched it to Lisa Weinstein. While I was telling her the story, she started crying. And I immediately knew, *I want to make my movie with this woman.* Lindsay Doran loved my pitch and took the project to Dawn Steel, president of Paramount, who instantly said yes. And that was it. I started writing the script immediately. It was the beginning of the best experience I've ever had in Hollywood.

I had an office in the writer's building on the Paramount lot, down the hall from three writers – Scott Frank, J.J. Abrams and Phil Alden Robinson – all of whom built major careers for themselves. We cheered each other on. Working as a professional studio writer for the first time – driving through those gates every day, having a designated parking space, getting paid to write – was an amazing experience. I even bought a new car. My Ford Taurus didn't feel right in that parking lot, and with Blanche's encouragement I bought a used Mercedes 560 SL convertible. Lindsay Doran's husband, Rod Kemerer, told me I needed it if I wanted to be a player in town, and now I felt like one. But underlying that was the worry that my fancy car would endanger whatever humility I still had from my spiritual life. Rod assured me that expensive visits to the Mercedes auto shop would keep me humble.

One time I was sitting with Dennis Feldman, a writer friend, having lunch at Paramount, and a high-level producer came over to him. "Eddie Murphy decided to do your movie," he announced. Dennis lit up. *The Golden Child* would be Eddie's first film following *Beverly Hills Cop,* his biggest hit up to that point. Everyone in Hollywood was waiting for him to announce his next project, and it was in every newspaper across the country that week. Part of me was jealous, part of me was amazed that I was present at that moment. I could feel the universe at work. I had a strange feeling it was preparing me. Maybe I would be next.

I wrote a full script for *Ghost* in ten weeks. That's three or four pages a day. The plot unfolded with ease, following the blueprint I had created with the treatment. It was a simple story. We meet Sam and Molly moving into a New York loft with the help of their friend Carl. Molly is a potter, Sam is a banker, Carl works for him. Sam and Molly are deeply in love, but Sam finds it hard to express his love in words. Whenever Molly tells him that she loves him, Sam always responds, "Ditto." His inability to say "I love you" seems a minor failing, but it's what drives the movie. We can tell from the first scene that Carl is attracted to Molly and loves Sam. They all feel deeply connected. One night, coming home from a play, Sam and Molly are confronted by a gunman who wants Sam's wallet. There is a fight and BOOM – the gun goes off. Sam runs after his attacker but can't catch him, and when he returns to Molly he is horrified to discover his own dead body being cradled in her arms. He is a ghost. He wants desperately to communicate with Molly, to let her know he loves her, but doesn't know how. He is helpless. Then he meets a fake psychic in Harlem named Oda Mae, who is shocked that she can hear him. Sam persuades her to visit Molly, but Molly doesn't believe her for a second. Then Sam asks Oda Mae to tell Molly that he loves her. "He would never say that," Molly insists. "Tell her 'ditto'!" yells Sam. Molly's eyes light up and the movie clicks in. (Spoiler alert). Eventually we discover that Carl is the villain. He has financial troubles and needs secret codes that Sam keeps in his wallet to help steal money from the bank. He hires someone to rob Sam, but the robbery goes wrong and Sam is killed. From that set-up, everything follows.

When I handed in the script, everybody liked it, except our producer Lisa Weinstein, who said, "It's not a movie yet." Lower-level executives seemed excited. I remember walking out of the Paramount commissary after having lunch with one of them. He said that my early draft of *Ghost* was the best script he had ever read. It was hard to bring my head back to earth after that. Several days later, I was walking out of the commissary with a friend and the same executive was in front of me talking to another writer. I was close enough to hear him say, "Your script is the best script I've ever read." The sky opened up. I never took praise in Hollywood the same way again.

It took a long time to get the third act of *Ghost* right, and I was frustrated that I couldn't figure it out myself. Lisa kept repeating, "It's not a movie yet," but I didn't know what she meant. Eventually I understood that nobody in Hollywood knows what works, only what *doesn't* work. I kept writing and writing and writing. In earlier drafts, Oda Mae, the psychic, dies at the end, shot by Carl, and her ghost re-inhabits her own dead body and kills Carl, saving Molly. At some point, I decided to have Sam use his evolving physical powers to kill Carl. That way Sam has his "I love you, Molly. I've always loved you," ending and Oda Mae remains alive to comfort her. Lisa read the draft and said, "Okay – now it's a movie!"

None of us were prepared for the avalanche of excitement that greeted the script. Dawn Steel called me personally to say she would drive me to the premiere. During this time the "success" of *Ghost* made its way around Hollywood. It's amazing how word travels. I'm told that Jeff Katzenberg, head of production at Disney, was at a party at Dawn's house and heard her talking about the script. Excusing himself, he stepped into the hallway and called my agent. Without even seeing the script or having met me, he offered me a three-picture deal at his studio. In the end it wasn't a deal I took, on my agent's advice (he insisted far more lucrative deals would be coming down the road), but it's a good example of how such things work in the business. We immediately began a search for a director. I figured we would be in production in a few months. I had once again forgotten that it can take years to get a film up and running, even when a studio wants to make it.

While *Ghost* was becoming a major project for Paramount, I got a call from Tracy Jacobs, an agent at ICM, asking if it would be all right to send a copy of *Jacob's Ladder* to Adrian Lyne. "Are you kidding?" I said. I loved Adrian's work. I thought *Fatal Attraction* was brilliantly directed. I loved its visual power and his sense of cinematic language. A week later I got another call from Tracy. She was panting. Adrian had just called her from France to say that *Jacob's Ladder* was the best script he had ever read and that he wanted to make it. I had learned not to get too invested, but was over the moon excited. I didn't hear anything for a month, until I got a call from Bruce Evans and Ray Gideon inviting me to a party at their house. Adrian would be there. At the party, a place opened up on the couch next to him and we sat together. He seemed happy to meet me. The TV was on and people were watching the Mike Tyson/Michael Spinks fight. Adrian was totally into it. I kept hoping he would turn to me, but we barely spoke. It felt like a wasted evening. But then, at one point, his wife Samantha leaned over to me and whispered, "He's going to make your movie." That's how I learned I was getting another film made.

Days later I found myself having breakfast with another Hollywood producer, Scott Rudin, who congratulated me on my deal with Adrian. This was news to me. I asked him where he had heard about this. From Adrian, he told me, at dinner the previous night. "He loves your script." Adrian called me the next day and we arranged a breakfast at Art's Deli on Ventura Boulevard. It was like meeting an old friend. We spoke for two hours, shared our love for *An Occurrence at Owl Creek Bridge*, and agreed that he wouldn't make the movie with a studio unless they understood and embraced our shared vision for the film. We both agreed that the script, at 135 pages, was too long and that I should try to cut it down, but when I showed him the cut draft, he wanted to put everything back in. He grew increasingly impassioned about the script. He was in the throes of deciding whether to make *Bonfire of the Vanities* before *Jacob*, but after replacing the excised scenes, said, "Fuck 'em. I have to do this movie. I'm calling my agent right now."

Adrian went straight for the phone and called ICM. He said he didn't want to read the new draft of *Bonfire* so no one would think he turned it down because he didn't like it. I told him about the *Cinefantastique* article, which described *Jacob's Ladder* as the screenplay no one dared film. "I dare," Adrian said, smiling.

I wanted to make *Jacob's Ladder* at Paramount. Lindsay Doran was very close to Ned Tannen, the new president of production and a personable, down-to-earth guy, and she was sure she could get the film set up there. Besides, Adrian had made *Flashdance* and *Fatal Attraction* at Paramount, films that had earned over $600 million for the studio. I also thought it would be great to have two films going at the same time at the same place. Lindsay showed Ned the script. He read it overnight and called her in the morning. "Buy it!" he said.

A massive negotiation began and ended in 24 hours. Lindsay's promise to me to get more money at Paramount than I had ever made before came true. Geoff negotiated for even more money than I had fantasized about with Cindy nearly ten years before: a million dollars. It was a major financial coup.

Adrian and I began an intense examination of the script. While we both agreed that it was long, Adrian did not seem anxious to cut it, at least not at this point. He knew that a script is like a complex fabric. If you pull one thread, it might unravel, with unexpected consequences. Before we took out the scissors, we had to be intimately aware of the overall design. As we began to work together, it became clear that we had different visions for the look of the film. For nearly a year before we began shooting, we had long philosophical discussions on the subject. I envisioned a biblical, William Blake mood, but Adrian did not. We kept struggling for the right imagery. When I initially wrote *Jacob's Ladder*, Joe Dante had just completed *The Howling* and Ken Russell had made *Altered States*. Both films explored a new make-up technique in which one could watch the human body go through amazing, fully-realized, biological transformations. I was thrilled by the technique and wanted to apply it to *Jacob*. Adrian hated prosthetic make-up. Anything that reeked of rubber or latex, anything with slime running down it, appalled him. He was determined not to use anything that looked unreal.

One word that emerged in our conversations was "thalidomide," a drug used to treat morning sickness in pregnant women that unexpectedly caused deformities in their children. It perfectly defined the demonic imagery Adrian had trouble describing. Instead of Hieronymus Bosch-like images, we gravitated toward the painter Francis Bacon and photographer Joel-Peter Witkin. Although I struggled to let go of my biblical imagery, which Adrian said would be too familiar to audiences, a new look for the film emerged. He felt that when a nurse's cap fell off and Jacob saw horns protruding from her skull, they should look more like abnormal cancerous growths. He argued that demonic horns were too easy for an audience to dismiss. Growths were more horrifying and harder to look away from. The same was true for the tail emerging from the man's pants on the subway. For Adrian, it would be less like a lizard and more like a massive phallus. He wanted to put the audience into a state of primal terror. I had to shift my sensibility from the written page to the screen and view the movie through his eyes. It was an instructive experience. I was holding on to old patterns. He was demolishing them.

I began writing new drafts to capture this vision. Adrian and I loved these fresh ideas, but the studio was worried that the film was becoming too dark. They wanted more emotion, so Adrian had the idea of giving Jacob a son who had died. I fought for a while, then found as I began writing that it worked beautifully. But the new emotional scenes somehow seemed to make the film sadder. The studio was having difficulty with the direction we were headed. Then Ned Tannen left his job as president of production and after much hand-wringing, the new studio brass pulled the plug on the film. Two hours before we were due to leave for London and Zurich on a pre-production trip, Adrian and I were told that *Jacob's Ladder* had been put into turnaround.

For about two weeks it looked like no other studio would step in to take over the film, that once again it would be the script no one dared to make. Then Adrian and I had a fateful luncheon with the heads of an independent company, one that was rapidly becoming a new power in Hollywood: Carolco.

Mario Kassar and Andy Vajna had turned a small company into a giant corporation by making a string of films with Sylvester Stallone and Arnold Schwarzenegger. The *Rambo* films had reportedly filled the company coffers with more than $400 million. Even so, our luncheon was unsettling. The players were intimidating and the stakes were high. Jeff Berg, president of ICM, and Jim Wiatt, his executive vice president, joined us at the table along with Mario and Andy. No one ate.

The conversation, while polite, seemed unguided and for a while no headway was being made. Then Jeff Berg took charge. I sat with my mouth open as he explained why Carolco had to make *Jacob's Ladder*. He emphasized Adrian's brilliance, the gripping nature of the script, the hunger of audiences for a film so mesmerizing. If I'd had $25 million in my pocket, I would have given it to him then and there. Before I fully understood what was happening, we were shaking hands and the deal was made.

Except for one thing. I was told that there was one impediment to the deal. Andy and Mario felt I was getting too much money for the script. I was told that if I didn't cut my fee by one quarter before 5pm, there would be no deal. I froze.

I was desperate for advice. I called my agent. He was with his wife visiting wine country in Napa Valley. I called Lindsay Doran at Paramount. She was out Christmas shopping. I called my lawyer, Charlie Shays, in New York. The office was closed. He wasn't at home. I tried calling every confidante I could think of. No one was available. Finally, I realized that this was the entire point. I would have to decide for myself. In the end I realized that I was my own teacher. I had to access the deepest and most profound voice I could find inside myself. It felt like a culmination of years of meditative practice.

After an agonizing and troubled hour, I came to a clear and absolute decision. Screw 'em! If they wouldn't pay me my money, they couldn't have the script. I called Adrian to say I was sorry if I had killed the deal, but what they were asking was wrong. He said I didn't need to apologize to him. He thought I was doing the right thing. I called Jim Wiatt and told him what I had decided. He said I was a fool, that I was destroying a major opportunity, and that I would regret it. "So be it," I responded. An hour later we closed the deal and not another word was ever spoken on the matter. Soon afterward, each of my advisers returned my call and each one said I had made the right decision. I was now playing hardball in the big leagues. And I had hit a home run.

Ghost needed a director. Frank Oz, who had voiced and developed many of the Muppets characters along with Jim Henson (and was also the voice of Yoda), was interested. He had made two movies – *Little Shop of Horrors* and *Dirty Rotten Scoundrels* – that I especially liked, and I wrote a new draft of the script for him, incorporating his ideas. We were both happy. But Frank insisted that Sam's ghost not cast a shadow, and wanted every one of his shadows in the movie digitally removed. This raised the budget to astronomical levels. I took him to see *Heaven Can Wait*, in which Warren Beatty's ghost casts a shadow everywhere, but that didn't change Frank's mind. I took him to see *Blithe Spirit* on Broadway. Same thing. Lots of shadows and nobody cared. But Frank cared, and eventually the studio said they couldn't afford to go with his vision.

Then Miloš Forman, a superstar whose films *One Flew Over the Cuckoo's Nest* and *Amadeus* had both won him Oscars, said he wanted to direct. I was both terrified and hopeful, because I knew that with him behind the camera, I wouldn't have much leverage in terms of what might happen to my script. But I also knew that if Miloš wanted to make *Ghost*, it would get made. The studio flew me to Connecticut to meet with him at his home. It was winter, and there was no heat in his house. And no food. "I don't eat lunch," he told me. I did, or wanted to, but that didn't seem to register. I sat there for seven hours with no food, freezing (he did offer me a blanket), listening to his ideas. The first thing he said was that he wanted Molly to commit suicide at the end – to jump out the window so she and Sam could be together for eternity. *Well, it's over*, I thought. Miloš was one of the biggest directors around and I was certain the studio would throw me off the picture if I didn't agree with his vision. His ideas only got worse. On the way back to my hotel in New York, I drafted a letter to Lindsay Doran, detailing every idea that Miloš had come up with. "Thank you," Lindsay and the other Paramount executives said after reading it. "We're moving on to another director."

Not long after that, I got a call from Lindsay. "I have your director," she said. I was breathless, waiting for her to say Spielberg or Scorsese. "Jerry Zucker," she announced. I was confused. Did she really mean Jerry Zucker, director of *Airplane*? The movie *Beetlejuice* had just come out and done well at the box office, and I assumed the studio wanted to do a similar all-out comedy version of my script. I told the studio executives I couldn't accept that decision. I was convinced they were going to kill my baby. "Just meet with him," they said. "Hear what he has to say." I went to dinner with Jerry and set one ground rule: I told him we could talk about anything except *Ghost*. Over the course of dinner, we discovered that we had a lot in common. I had even spoken to him on the phone once before, when a mutual friend connected us during my trip to Los Angeles to watch the filming of *Brainstorm*. He remembered that conversation and so did I. It was a rather innocuous memory, but it was enough. Right away, we became old friends.

But things deteriorated quickly after that. Jerry started telling me his thoughts for the movie – and I hated them. *This is worse than Miloš*, I thought. I wrote nineteen drafts for him, one after another, and for a while the story got further and further away from where I thought it should be. Jerry was trying all these different things, and none of them fit the movie I wanted to make. About nine drafts in, I thought, *I should walk away from this. I can't kill my own child.* Luckily, Jerry kept saying, "No, you're right. This isn't working." Slowly, we started working our way back to the original idea. Only now, it kept getting better and better.

Somewhere around the eighteenth draft, something still wasn't working with the Oda Mae character. It's hard to explain what it was. I think Jerry was hoping for a really funny scene. It had to do with the moment when Oda Mae is at the bank. I had this idea that she would talk to the banker as the ghost of Sam is standing beside her giving her all his personal information. When I was a kid, my mother was in a one-act Noël Coward play called *Hands Across the Sea*. I spent time coaching her on it. There is a scene at a party where a couple arrives that neither of the hosts know, although the couple seem to know both of them very well. They have to figure out who these people are, but the couple never leaves their side, so the hosts sit at a piano and begin to make up a song with lines like, "If these are not them, who are they?" and "I haven't the faintest idea." It's a hilarious moment that sort of led me to the bank scene. I wrote it in a few hours and drove over to Jerry's and Janet's house. Jerry took the pages upstairs to his bedroom as Janet and I sat and talked. We could hear him laughing, almost roaring out loud. Then he came downstairs and kissed me on the head. It felt like a blessing. I recalled my arduous, weeks-long effort to get Muktananda's forgiveness by kissing his foot. As Rudi said, it gave me my career. If I hadn't persisted with Jerry and written nineteen drafts, you wouldn't be reading this book.

Ghost had become what Hollywood refers to as a "four-quadrant film" – one that could appeal to everybody. By that point Jerry understood every scene the way I did. We had been writing and rewriting together for nearly a year and were on the same page. He ended up shooting the script we had created beat for beat.

The only thing we couldn't figure out was the final scene. "We need a line of dialogue at the end of the movie," said Jerry, "Something people will remember." We called it the *Casablanca* line, like Humphrey Bogart saying, "Louis, I think this is the beginning of a beautiful friendship," or his line to Ingrid Bergman, "We'll always have Paris." Something like that. I kept thinking and thinking, but couldn't come up with anything. One day Jerry and I were working at my house in Northridge, then drove to the pharmacy to get some medicine for Ari. We were talking about Molly and Sam's loss at the end of the movie – the loss of their relationship – and I said, "You can't take it with you." Then right away, I said, "Wait a minute, wait a minute – you *can* take it with you. The love inside – *you take it with you*." Jerry yelled out, "That's it! That's it! That's the line!" If I leave any kind of legacy when I die, it might be that line. "The love inside – you take it with you." I would settle for that.

Ending the movie with that line pointed to one of the most important things Jerry taught me. "All movies," he said, "have two halves. Everything up to the end... and the end. If the end doesn't work, half your movie doesn't work."

Making *Ghost* was the best creative experience of my life. But it didn't start out so easily. Casting was a problem. Finding Molly was simple. Both Jerry and I wanted Demi Moore for the lead, and she wanted to do it. Piece of cake. We were so happy. But finding someone to play Sam turned out to be a nightmare. Every major actor in Hollywood turned us down. Harrison Ford said he read the script twice and still didn't get it. Why would anyone want to play a dead guy? Paul Hogan, a huge star after *Crocodile Dundee*, turned it down. So did Michael J. Fox. The list goes on and on. The only actor who Jerry didn't go to was Patrick Swayze. "Over my dead body," were Jerry's exact words. But we were running out of possibilities, and it looked like the movie might be shelved. Then I saw Patrick being interviewed by Barbara Walters and at one point he started talking about his dad. Suddenly he was crying. But he was crying like no one I had ever seen before. Here was a real man crying real tears, and it moved me so deeply that the next day I called his agent, Nicole David, and asked if he might read for the role of Sam. I didn't ask Jerry's permission and sensed it was the wrong thing to do, to go behind his back in this fashion. But I wanted our film to be made and felt this might be our last chance.

When I got to the production office the next morning, Jerry said I wouldn't believe what had happened. Patrick wanted to read for us. I feigned surprise and innocence. Jerry was still insisting he would never go with Patrick, but I said, "Jerry, when a major movie star offers to read for you, don't say no." Jerry agreed, and Patrick arranged to come in. I secretly told Nicole that I needed to talk to Patrick first, and we arranged a phone call, which took place as Blanche and I were driving

downtown to the opera. I told Patrick to wear a suit and tie to the audition and carry a briefcase, to look like a banker. I also suggested he read the final scene of the film, his good-bye to Molly. He agreed.

The next day he came into the producer's office wearing a suit and tie and carrying a briefcase, and read his goodbye speech to Molly. Lisa Weinstein started crying. We all had tears in our eyes. We thanked him for auditioning. As he left the office, Jerry came up to me and whispered, "Whenever I say, 'Over my dead body' – that's who we hire."

The Oda Mae part was more complicated. "Anybody but Whoopi," I told the casting agents. I was afraid of an over-the-top comic performance and didn't trust that Whoopi could deliver the part. And so we saw every major black female actress in Hollywood. None of them could deliver. We even had singers like Tina Turner try out. It just didn't work. I began to think I had written a terrible part. Finally, Jerry said he wanted to audition Whoopi, and I relented.

Patrick was also on board with Whoopi. The two of them went to audition her and came back saying she was perfect.

I watched her audition tape. I've never been so wrong about anyone. Whoopi was funny, humane, deep, caring and loving – more perfect for Oda Mae than anyone I could have imagined. Jane Jenkins, one of the casting agents, came over to me and reiterated Jerry's line: "Whenever Bruce says, 'Anybody but Whoopi,' that's where we go first."

Casting the role of Carl was also hard. He was clearly an evil guy with designs on Molly, but the audience has to be blindsided. They have to love him at first. We were despairing after meeting with a lot of people in town, none of whom quite measured up. Then one night Joshua, a senior in high school, came in while I was watching audition tapes and sat down to join me. We looked at all the Carl casting tapes again and were both struck by one actor, Tony Goldwyn. He was in a courtroom drama and really jumped off the screen. Joshua and I looked at each other and said, "Him." I took the tape to Jerry, who had the same reaction. The fact that Tony was married to our set designer, Jane Musky, added to the rightness of the choice.

The only remaining casting issues were that Jerry wanted his mom, dad and sister to have roles in the film. I asked if my family could be in it, too. "Director's get their families," he said definitively, "writers get their mothers." So my mom was given the role of the nun who gets the $4 million from Oda Mae, then passes out in the street. She had been in many local theater productions, but had always dreamed of being an actress on the silver screen. There was one problem: she had never in her adult life appeared in public without make-up, not one single day. And nuns don't wear make-up. Finally, her screen debut – and everyone would see her face naked as the day she was born. It was probably the bravest thing I ever saw her do. We made sure she got star treatment. She dressed in Demi's trailer and had a police escort to the set on Wall Street, which was crowded with Swayze fans. Her performance was stellar, and she always gets one of the biggest laughs when she realizes the size of the check she's been given. The theater marquee near her home in Detroit listed the stars of the film followed by her name in the same-sized letters: PATRICK SWAYZE, DEMI MOORE, WHOOPI GOLDBERG, SONDRA RUBIN.

Jerry not only allowed me on set when he was filming, he *wanted* me there. I was beside him for every shot, and every time we got the reading we wanted, we both did a thumbs-up to show our agreement to each other. Actors started looking for those two thumbs-up, so Jerry and I learned to keep such things to ourselves. We both knew the story so well after so many drafts that it was always immediately and thrillingly clear when we had it right.

It was fun to be with the cast. Patrick was like a buddy. We talked about everything. I wondered how much he had to work out to get that body. "I never work out," he told me. Maybe it was the dancing, maybe he was just born that way. He confessed that he wasn't as intellectually developed as he would like to be, which bothered him. When he was younger, he would wear a pair of reading glasses he had bought at a drugstore to make people think he was more "intellectual." He paid a price for that: blurry vision, just to convince people he was smart. He was aware of how it came across, and that endeared me to him. Patrick was a wonderful presence during the making of the film.

Whoopi, too, was a joy, a constant source of laughter. She was very free in sharing her life story and opened her heart and home to all of us. I hadn't conceived how brilliant she would be as Oda Mae. Every line delivery was better than I had imagined. When she said to Molly, "You in danger, girl," the entire set nearly fell on the floor laughing. I could feel the script come alive every time she spoke.

Demi was more complicated for me – more of a star and less approachable. I often felt her annoyance or anger. The moment where Carl says, "Molly, you're not the one who died," and she slaps him across the face, wasn't in the script. I wasn't happy, and we shot it again without the slap, but her instinct was right and mine was wrong. In the movie the slap turned out to be a real deepening of the character and worked in ways I hadn't imagined. I learned to trust Demi's sense of Molly. It turned out she was always right.

Tony Goldwyn was the nicest guy in the world, a perfect trait for the character he played. No one would believe that he could be so conniving, which is why it's so shocking when it's revealed to the audience who he really is. It so contradicts the essential good nature of his persona.

The most famous scene in the film involves pottery. You know the one. I originally wanted Molly to be a female artist who made big and imposing work, and had written her as a sculptor. My thinking was that if she would be left alone at the end of the movie, we needed to feel she would be strong enough, self-motivated enough, to survive on her own. The sculptor Marisol became a model for me. But then Jerry decided he wanted Molly to be a potter. Blanche was a potter, so I knew something about pottery, and I couldn't picture Molly making bowls and pots. I wanted something more dynamic. But Jerry insisted, and Demi went off to pottery school. In the end she became so good at throwing pots that she was making large ceramic pieces.

The scene of Sam coming into Molly's studio late at night and sitting behind her was supposed to be a prelude to their making love. Patrick was supposed to sit there and admire her, and when he touched the spinning and somewhat phallic pot she is making, we all watched in astonishment. When the pot folded in half, Demi's instant smile and sense of forgiveness lit up the scene. As they started to build the next pot, the merging of their hands covered in moist clay was clearly going in an erotic direction. That wasn't planned or anticipated, but Jerry let it roll. Walter Murch, our editor, decided to move straight from the pottery to the dancing and lovemaking. The scenes were shot maybe a day apart, and because of that when we cut to the dancing, their hands are clean. But the energy was so hot between them that Walter knew nobody would care.

The enduring legacy of that sequence for Blanche and me is that everyone thinks the scene is autobiographical, that Blanche makes pottery and I sit behind her at the wheel, and we end up nightly on the floor making love. Actually, I'm not a clay person, and making love on the floor covered in wet mud is no turn-on for either of us. But then again, we've never tried it.

One of the key elements of the scene is the song "Unchained Melody." We all knew we needed a strong piece of music, but were at a loss as to what it should be. One day producer Lisa Weinstein walked into our production offices carrying a cassette player. "I have our song," she announced. We all gathered around, and the Righteous Brothers began to sing. It was surprising to see such instant agreement among a creative group. Sam plays it on the jukebox before the pottery scene. In a sense it has become the theme song for all of our lives. I imagine that when we die, it will be playing at our funerals.

The only difficult moment during the shoot was when Carl seduces Molly. As written, it was a simple scene with him reaching over and putting his arm around her. But even with Demi and Tony, it just didn't work. It was like a brother and sister about to make out, or a family friend being seduced. There was nothing seductive or romantic about it. At that moment the production stopped cold. Jerry glanced at me with a *what-should-we-do?* look in his eyes. I had no idea. The producers, somewhat panicked, told me to figure it out. The stoppage was costing $30,000 an hour. I went to the production trailer to come up with a rewrite. Luckily, I had seen

Tony shirtless and knew he was very sexy, so I started the seduction scene with him accidentally spilling coffee on his shirt so he could take it off. Then it hit me: Have him do it on purpose. I was told later that audiences hated him more for that coffee spill than for arranging for Sam's murder. It was insidious. And then having him pull off his coffee-stained shirt so fast and asking for one of Sam's to wear – that was especially manipulative and evil. I typed up the scene as fast as I could. I think the whole thing took me a couple of hours, but at $60,000, it was worth it. Jerry grinned happily as he read it. The producers were thrilled.

Music arrives late in the film process, as if from another dimension, after nearly everything has been locked. You already know the look and feel of the film. You know the performances. And then the music is added – and everything is transformed. The movie is enhanced, experienced anew. Nothing quite prepares a writer for it, and so to hire someone like legendary French composer Maurice Jarre (*Lawrence of Arabia*, *Doctor Zhivago*, *Fatal Attraction*), which we did for both *Ghost* and *Jacob's Ladder*, is money in the bank. It gives you great comfort. Jerry's first words to Maurice were, "Look Maurice, we need something brilliant here, so don't give us any of that *Lawrence of Arabia* crap." Maurice burst out laughing. His work *was* brilliant. Watching the film with his score for the first time was otherworldly. It far exceeded the vision I had lived with for years.

Jacob's Ladder was scheduled to shoot after six months of pre-production. Tim Robbins' agent had wanted him to play Sam in *Ghost*, but Jerry and I didn't think he was right for the part. But the moment Adrian and I met him, it was clear he was born to play Jacob. The same for Elizabeth Peña as Jezzie, Jacob's girlfriend. It was another instantaneous "yes" for us both. Another wondrous piece of casting was Danny Aiello as Louis. Louis Savas, my chiropractor in New York, introduced to me by Rudi, was a true healer. I once had a lower back injury so severe that I needed a wheelchair to visit him. He worked on me for twenty minutes and I walked out a new man. He loved to talk, and when I wrote the character of Louis, I was simply emulating his penetrating wisdom. Danny Aiello, who met him, copied his every verbal intonation and physical gesture. It was probably the first time in American cinema that a chiropractor was a hero in a movie.

Philosophical discussions raged anew, and I found myself increasingly isolated, with Adrian and producer Alan Marshall allied against me. While conversations were always very British and polite, there was a growing sense of entrenchment on both sides. Adrian would begin every sentence with, "All due respect..." and he was, in fact, always respectful. We just saw things differently. He was worried that the audiences would think Jezzie was the Devil, and disliked the idea of that character being played by a woman.

I insisted she was an angel of death, but he considered that too intellectual and said audiences wouldn't buy it. He was also worried about the ending of the film, the biblical images of Jacob's Ladder going up to Heaven that had been so central to my writing of the script. He found the whole concept too impersonal and wanted to humanize it. The imagery, he said, was too rooted in classical descriptions of Heaven. I had been fascinated by the opportunity to introduce archetypal imagery into twentieth-century experience, but Adrian wanted none of that. This was a struggle that went on for more than a year. His inability to communicate exactly what he *did* want was especially frustrating. He only knew what he *didn't* want. He felt the end battle between Jacob and Jezzie couldn't be shot as written. He referenced my line "The room crumbles beneath them and disappears into the void" and asked how many carpenters it would take to build the void. Adrian had no interest in making a special effects film and didn't want any process shots. Everything would be actually filmed by the camera. I didn't know what to say.

I also had to contend with a chorus of critics made up of secretaries, assistants and anyone else who might have a passing opinion on the film. Adrian was open to all comers, which in many ways was to his credit. He didn't want to get stuck in one viewpoint or perspective. As director, he needed to be a sponge, absorbing ideas and points of view. But while I respected this approach to the process, it was diminishing for me, the film's actual writer. Various scenes were cut before production began, including one between Jacob and his former college professor talking about mythological and theological demonology. Neither Adrian nor I wanted to alter or eliminate it, although we both knew it was almost totally expositional. The scene established the brilliance of Jacob's mind, his background in philosophy, specifically Existentialism, the fact that he has a PhD, and the reasons for his becoming a postman. As much as I loved it and felt it added tremendously to the film, I lowered the axe on it myself. Adrian was sensitive to my discomfort and bought me a present, a copy of *Heroes of the Kalevala*, by Babette Deutch. Somehow he had remembered me mentioning it as the first book I had ever adapted into a script, in Mr. McCarty's seventh grade class. Inside was a loving note. He asked me to trust him and not to worry. "It'll all come out in the wash," he wrote.

It's a writer's dream to have two films shooting at the same time, and I was loving it. I was on the set of *Ghost* every day in Los Angeles, while *Jacob* was filming in New York. Then, for a period of about a month, both films were filming in New York at the same time. I was being pulled in two directions, just miles apart. It was a complex gift. Adrian, who knew I was being torn between being on both sets, took me aside and said, directly and lovingly, "Go be on *Ghost*. Jerry needs you and I don't." I laughed. The truth was, I knew that I really wasn't needed anywhere at all. My real work had already been done. Still, I tried be on both sets as often as possible just to bathe in the pleasure of this unique opportunity. The two movies were even being processed together at Technicolor Labs in midtown Manhattan, so at night I would take a cab over and watch dailies for both of them – thirty minutes for *Ghost*, two hours for *Jacob's Ladder*, because Adrian always shot so much footage. On the set I watched him film the same line over and over and pushing the camera in two inches for each new take. He would ask for endless reading of the same line, all with subtle differences, then do it again from a different angle. It was excessive, but it gave him an enormous palette when he was cutting the film.

I hadn't appreciated the full iteration of Adrian's visual brilliance until I watched the dailies. They were full of terrifying visions that I was sure audiences would respond to. These were images inspired by my ideas, but raised to a whole new level. Jerry was a different kind of director. Being a comic writer, he knew when and where the laughs came, when the delivery was right. When he had the reading he wanted, he knew it. He was done. He didn't need to craft his film in the editing room. I loved watching both men at work, each artists in their own way.

One of the most exciting experiences filming *Jacob's Ladder* was the two weeks we spent in Puerto Rico recreating Vietnam. I had never worked on a war film before, or been in a jungle, or witnessed explosions, gunfire and helicopters filled with soldiers. I had written those scenes with a vivid imagination, but the actual realization of those images was impactful. I was startled by Adrian's ability to capture the inner terror and disassociation of combat. It was a lesson for me to see a director take people into such spaces and make their emotions so real on camera. He artfully molded performances for every character, and I doubted that anyone working with Adrian would ever regret the high level of demand that was placed on them. Great directors are few and far between, but Adrian is one of them. He wasn't always able to articulate his vision or speak on behalf of his own gift, but it appeared in every frame, unspoken, yet totally realized.

Whenever there was a break in shooting *Ghost*, I would jump into a cab and race to Brooklyn to watch Adrian filming *Jacob's Ladder*. In the morning we shot Sam and Molly's loft in SoHo, and in the afternoon it was Jacob being chased by a speeding car full of demons near the Brooklyn Bridge. The juxtaposition was astounding.

Adrian and I struggled over the ending of *Jacob's Ladder*. In the final scenes of the original script, Jacob is set on fire by Jezzie, and his charred remains lie on the ground. His eyes open and we see that he is still alive. Then his flesh falls away, piece by piece, and he becomes a being of pure light. He steps out of his body as peeling flesh falls to the ground and sees a stairway, surrounded by angelic beings, that reaches down from unknown heights, radiating an infinite power and grace. Jacob is beckoned over, and he ascends the ladder up to the starry heavens. The screen fills with light, and he becomes one of the angelic forms, amidst billowing, glowing clouds. The light condenses, and we see the glowing electric light hanging above an operating table in a jungle triage tent. A doctor pronounces Jacob dead. At that moment the entire film reveals itself as the inner journey of a man killed on the battlefield in Vietnam. The doctor says, "He put up a good fight," and closes his eyelids.

Adrian didn't want to do it that way. He didn't want the charred body, the light emerging from the flesh, or the ladder going up into Heaven. He said it was too Spielbergian. In the end, he decided to do something much simpler – to have Gabe, Jacob's dead son, reach out and guide him up the stairs, transforming the simple staircase into Jacob's ladder.

I knew it would be doomed to failure – I could never show enough sunbeams. So I shot a scene showing a father and his child together, almost as a family reunion. Maybe the idea came from my own feelings about being reunited with my father, who died 15 years ago. He didn't like me much, and I didn't like him much. But I've always hoped that if we ever had a second time around, maybe we'd make our peace with each other.

Adrian Lyne, *Los Angeles Times*, October 30, 1990

Most viewers thought that Adrian's ending – Jacob ascending the stairs with Gabe – was beautiful. That image of heaven-as-home really worked on an emotional level, counterbalancing all the suffering that had come before it and delivering a more familiar concept of life after death. But it took me years to understand it that way. I always saw what wasn't there, what might have been. We shot pieces of the scene with Jezzie showing up in the apartment at the end of the story, but I could tell Adrian was doing it in such a way that meant it would never make it into the final cut. His heart wasn't in it. I saw the film a few years ago, the first time in decades, in a movie theater with a devoted crowd. It had been so long that I had forgotten what had been cut out of the film. I just saw the movie that Adrian made. In its own way, it worked for me. I cried at the end.

Now when the bardo of dying dawns upon me,
I will abandon all grasping, yearning and attachment,
Enter undistracted into clear awareness of the teaching,
And eject my consciousness into the space of unborn Rigpa;
As I leave this compound body of flesh and blood
I will know it to be a transitory illusion.

The Tibetan Book of the Dead

Many people are unsettled by the end of *Jacob's Ladder* and wonder what it means. Let me be as specific as I can. The film is about a man's realization that he has been liberated by death. We're in the mind of someone who has just been mortally wounded in Vietnam. We witness his death as he observes it himself. Most people who think about dying at all have what I refer to as a Sunday School idea of what awaits them: Heaven, Hell or perhaps just nothingness or blackout. Very little in Western culture prepares us for the bardo experience described in Tibetan culture, where dying involves the process of untangling oneself from all the illusions and delusions of the life just lived. The bardo journey is a shedding of the story, the narrative we have just passed through. My LSD trip and decades of meditation have shown me how difficult our story is to let go of, how hard it is to get back to the Source,

God, Nirvana, or whatever you want to call it. But I had the visceral experience of doing just that on acid, and it continues every time I meditate to this day. That's why I wanted to tell the story, to share it in a movie. I wanted to create something that would reveal the complex and often frightening experience of unraveling, or letting go of one's life. Most of us are caught up in the intense experience of day-to-day living, and the mind engages this experience with enormous attachment. The mind weaves it all together. It creates the sense of our reality, but obscures a Greater Reality that lies beyond – or so it seems in my experience and that of many teachers of centuries past.

Rudi used to say that the mind was the slayer of the soul. We identify ourselves so closely with our minds and emotions that we can't recognize the oceanic depth of the moment we are in right now. The only way we experience this vast immeasurable awareness is to go beyond the mind, to let it go. I believe that is what happens as we die – often in a violent and merciless way. Better to engage with the work of doing it *now*. In the best of worlds, *Jacob's Ladder* is a glimpse, perhaps a doorway, into spiritual awakening, or maybe just an inducement to begin the process of searching.

In my experience, most people are afraid of letting go of their distractions, and use them to deny the reality and inevitability of death. They seem to believe that death will never happen. Or they create a belief system that explains it all for them, so they don't have to do any of the preparatory work. Which is fine, until death happens, at which point, I suspect, many are totally unprepared for the magnitude of what is taking place.

When I took LSD, in an instant all my Sunday School beliefs flew out the window. They couldn't hold up against the vastness of what was revealed. I was totally and irrevocably lost. But in the dismantling that took place over what seemed like eons of time, I began to see the Mystery, God, Truth, unfolding all around me.

It had been there all the time. This is the journey, the teaching, of *Jacob's Ladder*. The ego must be dismantled before you can return to the place of pure Being. If you don't prepare for that dismantling, it's going to be a painful transition and it will be excruciating for you to let go. The universe will be tearing you apart, molecule by molecule, and you'll be saying, "No, no, no." But you can't leave this world in a body. You can't leave the world enmeshed in mind, in your history, in your personal story. It all must go. We must learn to let go.

"If you're frightened of dying and holding on," says Louis in *Jacob's Ladder*, borrowing from Meister Eckhart, "you'll see devils tearing your life away. But if you've made your peace, then the devils are really angels, freeing you from the Earth." Many people have known this truth since the beginning of time. When the narrative of our lives is burned away, what survives is pure and indestructible Being. This seems like an odd subject for a Hollywood movie, but it tells the world what I saw when LSD yanked open my eyes. It was something I needed to share.

When *Ghost* and *Jacob's Ladder* were released, I did a lot of interviews. Everyone kept asking me the same thing: "Why do you keep writing movies about death?" I responded, "Because it's only through embracing death that you get to know life." When you understand that death can come at any moment, you see life for what it really is: totally, unendingly precious.

Several months before *Ghost* opened, my grandpa Dave died. He was 103. Dora had preceded him by many years after a long period of dementia. David stayed healthy to the end. He even found a new girlfriend, whom the family loved. It was almost as if he became a new person. He loved cooking lentil soup for everyone and watching Johnny Carson. He attributed his longevity to prunes and regularity, as he called it. That was as close as I came to wisdom from him. I loved that he was generally happy and content in old age, at least as far as I could tell. I sensed that he had faced certain existential truths and made peace with them. But that turned out not to be the case. On the last day of his life, when he was sent to the emergency room with a failing heart, the doctors said they could attempt an operation to try and save him. Heroically, I thought, he said no. He had lived enough and was ready to go. But then, hours later, as death approached, he started begging the doctors. "Save me!" he cried out over and over. But it was too late – there was nothing they could do. Full existential terror arrived at the last minute. Perhaps putting it off that long is a blessing. To me, however, better to face it when there is still time to embrace eternity, impermanence and all the other issues that surround the one inevitable truth of our lives – that we die. My obsession with death may seem overplayed to many people, but for me it has been a clearheaded way to approach, and hopefully accept, the inevitable.

While *Ghost* and *Jacob's Ladder* were still in pre-production, I was hired to do rewrites on two films, *Deceived* and *Sleeping with the Enemy*. It was lucrative, but no fun. For *Sleeping* I flew to Wilmington, North Carolina, and never even left my hotel room. The second lead actor had quit because he thought the script, or his character at least, was poorly written, so I had one week to write a new second act with a more engaging character – and it had to be seductive enough that they could quickly recast the role. I did some work and showed it to Joe Ruben, the director. He didn't like what I was doing, so I sat back down and quickly wrote another draft. Joe loved it. And Julia Roberts, who was starring in the film, did too. The next thing I knew they had a new actor and a green light for the movie. Joe Roth, the studio head, called me from LA saying, "You saved the movie." Then they asked me to doctor the first and third acts of the script. What I remember most is the scene where I introduce Julia's new love interest. I had her staring out the window at a neighbor mowing the lawn, as he sings "I Feel Pretty" from *West Side Story*. It was so unexpected and innocuous that her character starts laughing. I laughed, too, as I wrote it. A whole character came alive through a song choice.

I received no credit on *Sleeping with the Enemy*. Maybe I was naïve, but I tried to write the film in the voice of the original author, Ron Bass, who got full credit and hopefully some major residuals. For me, the best thing about the film was that I formed a lifelong friendship with Joe Ruben. Even though our names are spelled differently, we suspected our families were from the same Russian shtetl. Apparently, I look exactly like his grandfather.

I barely remember working on *Deceived*, except for an odd encounter with Goldie Hawn at a table read in Toronto. For some reason she didn't like parts of the script I had written, parts the director had wanted and approved. Her annoyance with me turned into unbridled rage, which was surprising and out of character for the actor and person I had imagined her to be. I felt shamed and was reduced to tears by her outpouring of anger, when I had only written what I was told to write. The intensity and duration of her rage felt misplaced and overwrought. I gather she sensed that, because she finally got up and walked over to me, offered an insincere apology, then planted a huge and inappropriate kiss on my lips, as if that would erase the mistreatment from the hour before. It did not. I told the director that I could write just as easily from home and left the room, grabbed my suitcase from my hotel, and flew back to Los Angeles the same day. It was the only time I ever acted like a spoiled star, but the truth is, it felt great. For my credit, I used a name I had made up for myself as a kid, Derek Saunders. I remember telling the name to my dad, who mockingly told me that I looked like a "derrick," some heavy-duty construction machinery.

I was overweight at the time, and though he thought it was funny, I felt judged and diminished. I never used the name again, until *Deceived*. For that film, it felt right.

Eighteen

Transformation – Openings

While I was working on *Deceived*, I got a phone call from Frank Mancuso, the head of Paramount. "We're so excited about *Ghost*. Thank you for everything you've done." This was the first feedback I'd had about the film. It was the beginning of a golden period in my life and career. I'd had so much rejection for so many years that I hardly knew how to embrace his words. I was nearly fifty years old.

The week before *Ghost* opened, my family and I were in Detroit. Interviewers at a local TV station asked me what film I was promoting. I told them *Ghost*. "You mean *Ghost Dad*?" they asked, a film opening around the same time, with Bill Cosby in the starring role. No, I said, *Ghost*, with Patrick Swayze and Demi Moore. "Oh, that one," they said disparagingly.

There appeared to be no word of mouth or general excitement for the film outside of the studio. On that Saturday there were going to be preview screenings in Detroit and thousands of theaters across the country. I wondered if anyone would show up. The Detroit preview followed a screening of the Tom Cruise/Nicole Kidman film *Days of Thunder*. That showing was so crowded that Blanche, the boys and I had to sit in the third row from the front. When the film ended, nearly the entire audience left and the theater was empty. My heart sank. I sat huddled with my family and a growing sense of despair, unable to turn around to face the empty seats. All those years of effort, and nobody cared. But then a couple took two seats in front of us, in the second row. I wondered why they would choose to sit so close to the screen. Slowly I turned around and discovered that those were among the only seats left. The auditorium was full to capacity. I couldn't believe it. Then a voice came over the loudspeaker: "The fire marshals prohibit any sitting in the aisles!" And then, once the film started, I could tell from the opening moments that people were loving it. They laughed and cried and even cheered when Carl was killed. When I called Jerry in LA that night, he told me that every single preview was sold out.

The night of the actual opening of the film, Paramount hired a van for all of us, including the actors and the president of the studio. As we were driving to Westwood and the Bruin Theater, we saw long lines of people nearly three blocks away. We all figured there must be a rock concert nearby. But no – the Bruin had added a midnight screening for the overflow for *Ghost* and people were lining up three hours early to get in. The next morning Jerry called to say that the numbers for the opening were huge. The question was whether they would hold up the following week. They did. *Ghost* opened on Friday, July 13, and months later was still the number one film in theaters. It was still playing at Christmas. Most of the reviews for *Ghost* were so-so. The critics didn't love it, but we were the number one film in the country and probably the world for 1990, and became one of the most commercially successful films of all time. Adjusted for inflation, a film made for $27 million grossed something approaching a billion dollars.

Jerry called me every Sunday morning with the projected box office receipts from around the country. "Are you serious?" were my first words each time. Blanche would roll over in bed and listen to my calls. Her eyes beamed. Nothing in the world prepared us for a hit like this. We weren't meant to be a summer blockbuster, a *Jaws* or a *Star Wars*, but we were amassing the same money as those films – and more. It made no sense to me.

Soon the receipts were coming in from all over the world. *Ghost* was a huge success everywhere. I couldn't contemplate what all this meant or would mean for the rest of my life, my family's life. Financial security didn't exist in the Rubin lineage, but for the first time I was experiencing a new kind of foundational comfort. My percentage of the grosses didn't equal that of the director or the stars, but it was more money than I could ever have imagined. My sense of awe and gratitude were hard to contain. I smiled day and night for a year.

Decades after it premiered, the History Channel listed the opening *of Ghost* in 1990 as the most important historical event to have happened on that date in history. I didn't know what to make of that. Lindsay Doran argued that perhaps the death of Jean-Paul Marat was a more momentous occurrence, but who were we to argue? *Ghost* has certainly become a piece of world culture. When Captain Sully's plane crashed into the Hudson River, one of the survivors told *The New York Times* that as he got off the plane and was standing on its wing, all he could think about was Patrick Swayze in *Ghost*. He said he kept looking back at the plane to see if his body was still on board. I thought, *If someone is confronting death and the first thing they think of is the movie* Ghost, *then perhaps it really has had some impact on the world.*

Ultimately, *Ghost* gave me the opportunity to live up to the pronouncement I heard so dramatically after my LSD trip: to tell people what I saw. I had wanted to talk about how life doesn't end at death, and possibly doesn't begin at birth. I wanted to share that larger context for our world, so I wrote this simple – almost mythic – story about a man who comes back from the other side to save the woman he loves. In order to do that, he has to go through a journey of empowerment. He must learn how to conjure up this primordial energy in his naval chakra. That came directly from Rudi's teachings. "You've got to push everything down into the pit of your stomach," says the subway ghost, "then let it explode like a nuclear reactor!" That's a real spiritual teaching in the middle of a Hollywood film. Focusing on the navel center produces a fire in the belly, the power to get things done. In the material world it helps people take charge of their lives, take action. In *Ghost*, it helps Sam learn to move solid objects and save Molly. Movies are entertainments, not teaching tools, but hidden below the surface are thoughts, feelings and emotions that can impact lives. It's a gift to be part of that world.

One would think that having written such a popular film I would meet hundreds of people who saw it, especially in the months after it opened. The opposite was true. I met very few. I remember being in a taxi in New York when *Ghost* was at its height. The driver asked what I did, and I told him I wrote movies. "What movies?" he asked, and I told him I had written *Ghost*. "Oh, I think I've heard of that," he replied. Another night, around the same time, I was standing in line in a restaurant and a woman behind us was talking to friends. "Have you seen that horrid film, *Ghost*?" she asked? And that was it. That's all I heard. That lack of feedback was a phenomenon I experienced for most of my film career, as if the universe didn't want to inflate my ego. If anything, my Hollywood journey was about dismantling my ego, not feeding it. In the end I had no trouble with that. My career and spiritual life were so intimately entwined that I didn't look for approval. If anything, I was just grateful for the opportunity to become a full-time writer and be supported in that effort.

Jacob's Ladder's opening was more complicated than *Ghost*'s. Test screenings weren't great, but when the studio tried cutting the movie down by a fifth, removing much of the final twenty minutes, the audience's reaction didn't change. That prompted a discussion about whether or not to excise those twenty minutes, since it didn't seem to affect anyone's response – except mine.

In those final minutes of the film as it was released, Jacob talks with Michael, a character who seems to have been following him throughout much of the film and who, it turns out, is the inventor of a drug given to soldiers in Vietnam. He has been observing Jacob, one of the few survivors of the opening episode, when many of his comrades were killed on the battlefield. Jacob then goes to his family home, where his wife Sarah lives, and where he sees his deceased son Gabe, who takes his father's hand and leads him up the staircase. With tender emotion, they ascend together, hand in hand, up Jacob's Ladder, on a stairway to Heaven. Light fills the screen. Cut to the battlefield hospital and doctors announcing Jacob's death.

What never made it into the film was Michael explaining that he has an antidote to the drug, and he and Jacob going to a hotel room, where Michael administers the antidote to Jacob through an eyedropper. Jacob experiences a hellish episode that transforms into a heavenly vision. Michael becomes an angelic being, rescuing him from the horrors of his own mind. But the remedy wears off, voices return, and Jacob eventually finds Michael killed.

> The ceiling begins to rumble. Cracks split wide open. Huge crevasses tear through the plaster. JACOB's world is crumbling. He stares in horror as DEMONIC FORMS attempt to surge through the rupture above him. Piercing eyes and sharp teeth glimmer in the darkness. Hooved feet and pointed claws clamor to break through.

JACOB
HELP ME!

Instantly MICHAEL appears standing over him. He is holding the vial with the antidote. He draws an eye-dropper full of the fluid and holds it over JACOB's mouth.

MICHAEL
Take it!

JACOB fights him but MICHAEL forces the entire contents of the eyedropper down his throat. JACOB tries to spit it out, but can't.

Suddenly the ceiling erupts in violent clashes as whole chunks break off and collide with one another like continental plates. The collisions wreak havoc on the DEMONS, chopping and dismembering them. Body parts fall from the ceiling like a Devil's rain. Horrible screams echo from the other side.

Flashes of light and dark storm over JACOB's head, thundering like a war in the heavens. It is a scene of raw power and growing catastrophe. It builds in fury and rage until suddenly the ceiling explodes.

Matter atomizes instantly. Trillions of particles hurl chaotically in all directions. The walls shatter into a dazzling brightness. For a moment there is a sense of intense forward movement, a rush toward oblivion. And then, suddenly, it stops. There is absolute quiet and stillness.

JACOB's eyes stare into the formlessness sparkling around him. All space has become a shining void. Gradually faint pastel colors appear like colored molecules, dancing and spinning, redirecting space into new formations. They weave patterns of intricate complexity and stunning beauty.

As the colors grow brighter and more vivid their abstraction gives way to solid form. A GARDEN SCENE emerges. It is a GARDEN OF LIGHT, a vast, almost mythic, Rousseau paradise. It radiates an intense shimmering light.

JACOB's eyes are captivated by the vision before him. A sudden movement catches his attention. He looks up and notices MICHAEL still standing beside him. MICHAEL, however, is rapidly changing form. It is a full, plastic, three-dimensional metamorphosis. His very flesh seems to expand and glow with its own inner light. His face shines and radiates an almost transcendental beauty.

JACOB is nearly blinded by MICHAEL's presence and must shield his eyes to look at him. MICHAEL smiles an extraordinary and joyous smile that radiates such intense luminosity that JACOB has to squint to see it.

Suddenly MICHAEL steps off the ground. He rises into the air and floats above JACOB. JACOB can barely breathe as he watches him. MICHAEL rises into a sky filled with orbs and blazing lights. The lights shine on JACOB'S head. He effervesces and shimmers in their glow.

One of the orbs sends a burst of light exploding over JACOB. So intense is the light that JACOB grabs his eyes. As he opens them again he sees that the GARDEN is fading back into pure light. MICHAEL, too, is fading.

Another burst of light and the GARDEN is reabsorbed by the void. Only the brightness remains. It is many seconds before we realize that the HOTEL ROOM is coming together, reconstructed by the light. In moments it is fully formed. Sunlight is pouring through the window. MICHAEL is sleeping lightly in a chair. He hears JACOB stir and sits up.

JACOB is sitting on the bed. He does not seem to know where he is. His eyes are filled with awe. They move slowly around the room, taking everything in. He doesn't speak. MICHAEL gets up and sits beside him. He respects his silence.

Some of Adrian's best filmmaking was in these final scenes, but even he acknowledged that they could be removed. They added glorious cinematic moments, yet barely moved the story forward. It was a lesson for me, since I understood that those antidote scenes, while elaborating and deepening the story, didn't advance it. In fact, they held up the ending. The audience didn't want another spin around the track – they wanted resolution. They wanted to go home. Besides, I could tell that cutting the film down was a done deal, and I went with the flow. There was also a push by the producer to have a card before the end titles explaining that there really had been drug experiments in the military during the Vietnam War. I thought that was completely unnecessary, even if it was true. I didn't want the film to become some kind of military exposé. For me, it was a spiritual journey into the death of a single soldier. I lost that battle as well.

I don't think anybody ever really understood *Jacob's Ladder*. The people at Carolco thought it was a horror film and didn't know what to do with it. Once *Ghost* came out, *Jacob's Ladder* became a prestige project for them. They called me into the office to meet with their entire executive department, and asked, "How should we market your movie?" I suggested they try to sell it as an art film rather than a horror film, which is what they did. It still didn't get much of an audience.

The day *Jacob's Ladder* opened, it was showing at a theater in Westwood. I decided to go by myself and wait outside to see how the audience responded as they left the screening. I stood in the lobby and heard the last lines, the end of Maurice Jarre's score, then backed out the door onto the street to await the verdict. Before Maurice's end title music had even started, a young man burst out of the theater and stood under the marquis. He was fuming. I had never seen anyone so upset by a film. He looked at me and then at no one in particular. There weren't many people around. And suddenly he yelled in total anger and frustration, "If I ever meet the guy who wrote that film, I'LL KILL HIM!" And he stormed off. I didn't wait for anyone else to exit. I turned and walked to my car, and drove home in silence.

The reviews were damning, except for Roger Ebert in the *Chicago Tribune*. He had seen the film at a press screening where Joan Laser, Blanche's oldest and best friend, also saw it. They went down in the elevator together. Ebert turned to her and asked, "What the hell was that about?" Joan, who had long been a fan of the script, told him. He was wide-eyed with fascination. "Really? Really?" he said. Whatever she said, it struck a chord. "The movie left me reeling with turmoil and confusion, with feelings of sadness and despair," he wrote. "Those are the notes it strives for... It evokes a paranoid-schizophrenic state as effectively as any film I have ever seen... Powerfully written, directed and acted."

I suppose that some movies need to be explained. Perhaps I shouldn't have run away from the man who wanted to kill me for writing the movie. I could have introduced myself and offered to talk about it. Maybe a conversation over coffee would have helped him understand what he had just seen. *Ghost* is a sugar-pill movie that goes down easy. *Jacob's Ladder* is a film that makes you work.

Over the years I have heard from people that *Jacob's Ladder* has become a rite of passage for college students, who get stoned and watch it. I've also heard that it has been taught in film classes around the country. I have no idea if these things are true. But it pleases me that decades later, *Jacob's Ladder* is still somehow part of the conversation.

A few months after *Jacob's Ladder* opened and closed, *Ghost* was nominated for a slew of awards, including Golden Globes, BAFTAs and Oscars for Best Picture, Best Supporting Actress (Whoopi) and Best Original Screenplay. At the Golden Globes ceremony, because we were seated at a table a long way from the stage, I hoped we wouldn't win. (We didn't.) At the BAFTA awards dinner, Blanche and I sat next to Francis Ford Coppola. That was quite a night. We spoke for hours. Blanche's sister Rhoda had gone to college with him, so he felt like instant family. He told us stories, including how, in a fit of anger, he had thrown away all his Oscars, and how his mother had retrieved them from the garbage. To this day, he said, he is grateful to her (and the Academy) for teaching him to find humility in the recognition he has been given. He was, in fact, touchingly humble.

A few weeks before the Oscars, Jerry Zucker had a dinner at his home with screenwriters Ron Bass (*Rain Man*) and Tom Schulman (*Dead Poets Society*). Both predicted I would win because mine was the only original script that was also nominated for Best Film. I wanted desperately to believe them.

Nothing focuses more attention on the fragility of the ego than knowing that a billion people might be listening to you and hearing the thirty seconds of brilliant hyperbole you've been storing up for decades. It doesn't matter how much spiritual work you've done

– the ego mind is unbelievably dominant in a situation like that. When we rode to the Oscars in a long stretch limo, Blanche said I was shaking. I was scared that I would lose. I was scared that I would win. I feared how I would be perceived. All that high school stuff – the fear of being rejected, of not being acknowledged, of not being loved – came back in a very vivid way. Blanche and I got out of the limo and stepped into our red-carpet moment, only to discover that not a single camera was pointing in our direction, and I was once again reminded that no one cares about writers. Once past the red carpet we entered the theater and took our seats in the fourth row on the aisle. After a few moments, I stood up at the front of the auditorium as people were still entering, and quietly and unassumingly delivered my acceptance speech to mostly empty seats. I figured, if nothing else, I would give myself the moment I had dreamed of since I was a kid in the shower accepting my Oscar. It didn't matter that no one but Blanche was listening.

When Anthony Hopkins and Jodie Foster announced my name as the winner, I went up on stage and nervously delivered that same speech. I said I was grateful for writing a film that not only acknowledged the spiritual nature of man, but also affirmed it. I sensed a groan from the audience. I thanked Jerry Zucker and said how his beautiful heart was on every frame of the film. I thanked everyone at Paramount, "past and present" – which got a laugh because there had recently been a regime change at the studio. I singled out Lindsay Doran, who happily was still there. I thanked Whoopi, who also won that night, and said she deserved every award she received. I thanked my parents, my children, and especially Blanche, who, six years before had quit her job, put our house on the market, and brought us all to Hollywood. I'm looking at this big clock counting down, telling me how many seconds I have left, and then telling me to get off the stage. I have a recollection that it actually said "GET OFF THE FUCKING STAGE," but I can't be

sure of that. At the very last second, I held the Oscar up in the air and said, "Thank you, Rudi." In the lobby during an intermission, I ran into Marty Scorsese. His film *Goodfellas* was nominated that night, and he was, too, for directing. It turned out to be *Dances With Wolves*' night, with Kevin Costner taking home the gold. But it was touching to see Marty. He congratulated me on being there, on the journey we had begun so long before. That full circle experience was very moving to me. There is no script I could have written in our early days at NYU that would have put us in that celebrated space together. I certainly didn't imagine winning an Oscar before he did, or that I would have won an Oscar at all. It was a magical feeling of overriding gratitude.

The next day I had lunch with Martin Bregman, the producer of *Platoon*, who told me, "Now your tombstone is going to say 'Oscar-winning writer Bruce Joel Rubin.' Nobody can take that away." That's when I realized it was already a past-tense thing. It was done, finished. I had completed that journey. Everything in this lifetime had been building to that moment, and now I could put it all behind me. It was a totemic event for me, like sitting on Victoria Peak. I sensed I had created what the voice in the desert of Afghanistan had instructed me to do. Even if *Ghost* wasn't a masterpiece, it had been acknowledged as something worth creating.

I sensed that going forward, my life would be about eliminating rather than accumulating. "You can't let go of what you haven't had," Rudi said. Now I'd had it – and the rest of the ride was going to be about letting go. From that moment forward, I was on a journey toward becoming nothing, or at least less and less. This idea, the recognition of the strange emptiness of reality, underlines much of what I have learned about the spiritual journey. In experiential terms it would become even more central to my life as I moved further down the path. When I got home that night, I put the Oscar on the nightstand by my bed. It stayed there for decades, quietly, deeply personal, uncelebrated, and out of sight. But I smiled when I saw it. Now it's in my basement mixed in with Blanche's pottery. It looks good down there.

The real and enduring surprise of *Ghost* was its ongoing success at the box office. Because I was an associate producer as well as its only writer, because the studio could only hide so much of its income, and because the producers came together to audit the Paramount returns, Blanche and I were financially comfortable for the first time in our lives. We considered moving to Beverly Hills, but still couldn't afford more than a small bungalow there. In Northridge, by the train tracks, we had a sizable ranch house on an acre of land, although in need of a lot of work. We decided to rebuild what we already had. We tore down everything except the fireplace (so it would be considered a remodel instead of a new house at a higher tax rate) and expanded the space dramatically. Construction took a year, while we lived nearby in rented quarters.

The new house quickly became the gathering space for a huge swath of our Midwest family that had ended up following us to Los Angeles. It also became the full-time home of Fann, my mother-in-law, who arrived for a vacation and told us as she entered the house that she was never going back to New York. Our family instantly expanded from four to five, and she lived with us until she died, nine years later. Fann's presence was an enormous amount of work for Blanche, but I think she loved having her mom so close.

In addition to family, I had a new and expanding group of students for my meditation class. I had stopped teaching for the first year or so of our move to California because I felt I had to devote myself to writing and establishing a life for my family. But one day, two friends from Bloomington now living in LA asked if I would start teaching again. More and more people started coming to class and the house became a regular meditation center. Soon the living room was too small a space to accommodate everyone. In that regard, *Ghost* was a real gift. In the rebuilt house, we created a dedicated classroom that fit fifty people, a large open space with the floor covered in Oriental carpets, the walls filled with antique Oriental art, and piles of meditation pillows. It also became the "pillow room" for groups of little cousins who would race up there to play when family gathered for the holidays. Phil Alden Robinson famously said, "If you build it, they will come." And they did. The classes filled up and our social life was now a mix of family, friends and students. That balance, that intertwining, has been a defining factor of my life ever since I met Rudi.

The new house expanded to a second floor and the former detached garage became my office. We landscaped the whole property and built a wall to enclose it, with a gate to the railroad tracks where we could go out and take long walks. Those tracks became a metaphor for my journey in Los Angeles. I was embarrassed by them at first, but came to understand that they would indeed keep me humble. Every time my head expanded with career success, a train came roaring past the house and brought me back to earth. Once I decided to stay in Northridge, to accept my home, my simple but comfortable life, the tracks became something special, magical even. When my grandchildren were born, the trains were a real attraction. My granddaughter Thalia and I would sit and wait for them to pass by, making puppets out of twigs and drawing faces on them to greet the trains as they sped toward us. The engineers would blow their horns as we waved them on. It was all a pure delight.

Nineteen

Certainty – *My Life*

After the Oscar win, I could have done anything, and I wanted to direct. I had an idea called *Multiples*, about a person with multiple personalities, one of which was God. I didn't quite know where to go with that one. Then one night I had a dream about a man who was dying. His wife is about to have their first child and he knows he won't live long enough to see that child born, so he decides to make a videotape about his life to leave behind for his unborn baby. In the process, he discovers himself. I woke up and said, "That's a movie." And I immediately started writing *My Life*.

For a long while it was a script that I couldn't get right. I wrote and wrote and wrote, but something was missing. I couldn't figure it out, and almost abandoned it. I had my main character, an advertising executive named Bob Jones who isn't ready to die and is unable to cope with the reality of so much loss. Because I was obsessed with death and everything one can learn from facing it, I felt I had the perfect story to tell – the waking up to ultimate existential truth. Why I thought that might be the subject for a Hollywood movie I'll never know, but it spoke to me. I had explored death through the fantasy and horror genres, and now wanted to explore it from a more humanistic point of view. Long inspired by Truffaut and the French New Wave, I wanted to create a realistic and more grounded human story. I knew it would never be as big a hit as *Ghost*, but was grateful that *Ghost* had given me the chance to make something personal and meaningful, something I was unlikely to be able to do again. The only problem was that I didn't know how to tell the story in a way that wasn't predictable and morose. I struggled with draft after draft and was beginning to think I should just let it go. I suspect I was also afraid of directing. I had long imagined that writing successful movies would open that door, but now I was terrified about walking through it. It was a challenging moment.

Around that time, I took my family to Africa, a great place for figuring things out. The visual effects supervisor on *Ghost*, John Van Vliet, told me he and his wife had taken a trip to Africa that had changed their lives. "It's so pure," he said. "It's like going back to the Garden of Eden." I imagined Africa would look like a Disney documentary. I discovered that in the African bush it's carnage all day long, in every direction. Lions eat zebras and antelopes and ostriches for dinner and don't even clean up after themselves. Wherever you look on safari, there are half-eaten bloody carcasses. It takes a strong stomach to be a tourist in the African veldt. I wasn't prepared for that. For the first time, I saw myself as part of the food chain.

I had a dream while we were in Tanzania in which Rudi appeared. He was sitting and teaching, then beckoned me to come forward. As I approached, he exploded into a wild dog with razor-sharp, gnashing teeth. I jumped back, my heart racing, cowering with fear. Then he was Rudi again, and said, "You aren't ready for this. If you're afraid of me in that form, then you won't be able to accept me in my true form." From that moment on, I was unable to find him, even though I always felt Rudi's presence every time I meditated. We were in Africa for ten more days after that, and I felt no energy, no connection, no nothing. I felt cut off. It was as if Rudi, declaring me unworthy, had abandoned me because I was afraid. I was afraid of the brutality of nature. I was afraid of the wildness and destructive Shiva side of life. I wasn't ready for Africa, for the dark reality of this world.

We took a safari through Kenya and Tanzania with our friend Mike Broten, who was living in Nairobi. We were often off-road and far from the beaten path, and the days were filled with the unexpected. We took a balloon ride over the Serengeti. We danced with tribal Maasai warriors. Blanche and I outwitted a group of hyenas blocking our way back to our cabin, and one night I heard strange noises outside. I cautiously opened the door and all I saw was blackness, until a massive eye appeared. A giant hippopotamus stood staring at me. My heart was racing. I felt alive.

On one journey we saw an abandoned factory on the side of the road. As we approached, we saw a strange mass of something crumpled up on the factory floor. It took us a moment to realize that it was six dead men, freshly executed, blood still pouring from their heads onto the concrete floor. I thought we should go closer to see if there was anything we could do, but Mike said it was possible the killers were still nearby and we should move on, quickly. We were many miles from civilization, and urgently set off for our lodge to report what we had seen.

We were about half an hour away from the factory when the road, which was more of a dirt path, came to a dead stop at a flood plain about a hundred yards long. We didn't know if Mike's Land Rover would get through it. One option was to turn back toward the factory and risk running into the killers. The other was to take our chances and drive into the water. If we got stuck, no one in the world would know where we were. We realized that this situation was potentially life-threatening, so we decided to take a vote. If anyone wanted to risk turning back, we would. Joshua and Ari were empowered by the choice, and we debated it seriously. I could see a new maturity dawning in both of them. It was a defining moment, a real experience of what it meant to be a family.

We decided to risk going forward. It was a ten-minute crossing, with water lapping at the edges of the vehicle. We all held our breath and each other, and cheered and hugged Mike when we got to the other side. After a few hours we reached the lodge and reported what we had seen. Later, the police told us that we had probably stumbled onto the results of a war among poachers. By the time they got to the factory, the bodies had disappeared.

The last day of the trip was Rudi's birthday, the 24th of January. I knew I had changed a lot over the past couple of weeks, that I had confronted the wildness of nature. But I still hadn't reconnected to Rudi's presence or even reconnected with myself, and was still very conscious of my Rudi dream and the wild dog. I remember waking up and feeling sad. "Rudi, I need a sign from you that you haven't abandoned me," I said. "Please, give me a sign." I didn't want to leave Africa without it.

A few hours later, we were in a jewelry store in Nairobi. Blanche and the kids were watching the shop owner make bead necklaces, and I was watching this dog – a kind of wild-looking German shepherd. He seemed to be staring at me. All of a sudden – with no provocation – the dog shot up at me, teeth bared, growling in my face. To my surprise, I remained completely still. I didn't flinch. "Rudi!" the owner yelled. "Get down!" I gasped when she said his name. It felt like a message from the other side. The dog stared at me with a strange intensity. I stared back, straight into his eyes. "Thank you, Rudi," I said. "That's all I needed." I felt like I had passed a major spiritual test. Africa had opened me up. It taught me to face the darkness in life straight on, without giving in to my fears. And it was Rudi's birthday. What better sign could I have? The teaching embedded itself into my psyche. Rudi never left me again after that.

Back home, I went to work on *My Life*. "You have one week," I said to myself. "If you don't figure out how to make the movie work, you have to abandon it." Over the next three nights I had a series of recurring dreams about a character named Dr. Ho. Each night, he appeared in a different scene from the script.

At first, it looked like Dr. Ho was going to heal Bob Jones and save his life. That gave the script a new rooting interest – the possibility that Bob might live. I immediately wrote those scenes, and it felt like the script had turned a corner. Then, in the third dream, it became clear that Dr. Ho couldn't save Bob. I knew he had to die. What dawned on me, however, was that the man who died wasn't the same man from the earlier part of the story. He had evolved. Dr. Ho achieved something miraculous. He helped turn Bob into a loving and aware human being. He had, in fact, healed him in the only sense that really mattered. The bittersweet nature of the ending was sad and uplifting at the same time. When I added those new scenes and showed them to the producers, Jerry Zucker, Gil Netter and Hunt Lowry, and to Columbia studio executive Amy Pascal, there was a sudden consensus. Everybody said, "This is the movie we want to make."

My Life is about the gift of pain. When suffering, most people search for a release. They look for doctors or healers. But in the face of death, the only release from suffering is to accept suffering as it is. In many ways this was the lesson of Africa. I have always sought comfort, and my entire life have feared suffering. But my dream of Rudi and the wild dog, learning to accept wildness and death without flinching, opening to the reality of life and death, was at the core of the movie I was making. Bob Jones' experience of dying teaches that the acceptance of suffering and loss is a key to liberation. Accepting the thing that seemed so unacceptable takes you into a place of great depth and wisdom. Rudi had said that pain is God's love. We see that in Bob's journey.

Bob has shunned his Ukranian-born family for their customs and traditions. He holds a heart full of grudges and anger, leading him to move away from Detroit and abandoning himself in the process. His wife Gail encourages him to go back, to visit his family. The trip home is where all his toxicity reveals itself. He has to return to his childhood self to see the inner being he has repressed and ignored his whole life. He needs to make peace with who he is. I loved that he had to go back to Detroit, my hometown, and experience so many physical spaces and dramas drawn from my own life. His experience with the circus in the backyard, his fear of roller coasters, are my stories too. Although the film isn't autobiographical, it is deeply personal, and Bob, in many ways, is me.

My mother was a true bhakti, a lover. She had a massive heart. So did her mother. When my grandma Minnie held me, a tiny boy, in her arms, as she was dying of breast cancer, she changed my life. I wasn't even four years old, and my mom had taken me for one final visit. She was lying in bed, propped up by pillows, looking frail but emanating an enormous amount of light. We shared a birthday, exactly fifty years apart. My mother put me in the bed with her, and my grandmother took me in her arms and held me for the longest time. She kept saying to me, "Bubela, bubela, bubela," which means "honey" or "sweetie" in Yiddish. She knew that she was holding me for the last time.

I felt the enormity of the moment without really understanding it. I think that was my very first direct transmission of love. She downloaded her entire human heart into a little child. Days later

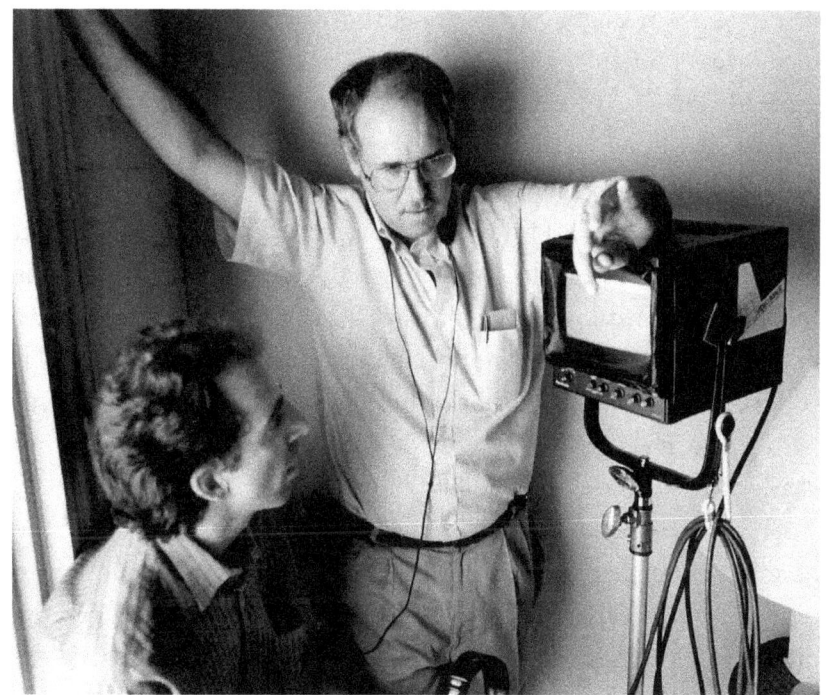

she died – and has never been absent from my life. I don't have to look deep to find her. Luckily, the same depth of love found a foothold in my mom, who kept it flowing her entire life. There hasn't been a single day when I haven't been embraced and comforted by it. Years later, Rudi told me that true love is what you feel for your mother when you're four years old. That made good sense to me. Like my grandma, my mom is my conduit to an ocean of love. When I teach, the core shaktipat energy is that oceanic space. It connects with anyone who is open to receive it – and often people who are not. Blanche and I like to sit near windows in restaurants. I can feel the shakti pouring out of my heart to passersby on the street, even when they can't. I feel well used.

But uncovering love isn't easy to do. Connecting with my father was difficult for me. There was a point in my life when I realized that I didn't love him. It was as if a valve in my heart was shut. It just wasn't working. I started using Rudi's practice and digging into memories of my father. It took a while, but I recovered a memory of the two of us on a train ride to Cleveland to visit his brother Harold when I was about five years old. I remembered being on that train and looking at him as this godlike being that I really loved. Once I remembered that train ride, the love reignited in me. I had tapped back into a source I hadn't known was there, and for the rest of his life, that renewed love flowed through all of my dealings with my dad. It didn't happen by itself. I had to dig, open and let myself receive what had long been forgotten, buried deep inside. It was hard work. That has been a valuable lesson for me ever since. A tiny spark of connection opens many doors.

I wrote the movie *My Life* to explore these issues, to show families reconnecting, discovering bonds of unspoken or even hidden love. I wanted to show the work involved, how Bob must dig deep and work hard to manifest the kindness that ultimately fills his life. The story is like a road map for someone who doesn't even know he's on a journey. I know from Grandma Minnie and my parents what unending love lies at the heart of the family experience, if one is willing to unearth it. I deeply wanted to put these lessons on film as a way of honoring and sharing what had been given to me.

Casting the film was a challenge. I had somehow imagined Tom Hanks as Bob Jones and went to meet with him, but in the end Tom felt that *My Life* was too wake-up-and-smell-the-flowers for him, and did *Philadelphia* instead. Not a bad choice, I suppose, since he won an Oscar for his performance. My second choice was Michael Keaton. He and Bob Jones were a good match. Michael wanted a meeting with me, and I went to his office in Santa Monica. Walking down the street, heading out to lunch, he was stopped repeatedly by everyone who loved *Batman*. I didn't quite sense how big a star he was until that moment. It was his smaller films, like *Clean and Sober*, that most interested me. We had a couple of visits where I think he kept sizing me up. The more time I spent with him, the more perfect he seemed for the film. The warmth he exuded was often overshadowed by a kind of stand-off guardedness. There was nothing simple about him. He was oddly open and shut at the same time. He made me want to get inside his mind, to find his heart.

When it came to the part of Gail, Bob's wife, I began to see the limited range in so many actors. Warm and loving was easy for most of them, but not many could do sad and despondent. It wasn't until Nicole Kidman walked through the door that I saw what real range was. She had every note down, every nuance. She was more than I had written, and she made the script sing. I couldn't believe my luck.

As for Dr. Ho, I really didn't know how to cast him. I remember Ian McKellen reading for the part, which laid bare all the problems in the character. Everyone who came in to read made me more and more nervous about my own writing. And then I met Haing S. Ngor. I knew him from *The Killing Fields*, and I knew his story as a victim of the Khmer Rouge in Cambodia, a country I had visited two decades before. They had cut off the tip of one of his fingers, something you can see on screen when he begins to work at healing Bob. His presence was the essence of the character I had written. His authenticity touched me instantly. Although his English wasn't great, he took direction well and really animated each line. In a sense, the movie found its spiritual center in his performance, and even more in the essence of the man he was.

The other difficult casting moment was finding the hospice worker who takes care of Bob. I don't know why so few people emanated a sense of true kindness that I felt the movie needed at that moment. One actor after another left me sad and depleted. But when Queen Latifah walked in, my worries evaporated. There was a powerful goodness in her. All she had to do was show up. No acting required. Bradley Whitford's inner kindness and expansiveness walked into the audition with him. You just wanted him around. Richard Schiff brilliantly played Bob's father as a young man. Little did I know that by choosing these guys, I was also casting *The West Wing*.

Directing *My Life* was a brutal experience. I had always fancied myself a director, but when the time came, I realized how little I actually knew. Although I had been on many movie sets over the years, I had never really learned the core elements of directing. I had no problem speaking with actors or guiding the crew, but I lacked the basic sense of how to stage a scene. Peter James, my cinematographer, took me aside the first day of shooting and said, "Bruce, this is a master shot, this is how you cover it, these are the sight lines you don't cross, this is a two shot…" etc. I was humbled and grateful.

I became aware on day one of how very disciplined I needed to be. I would dream up compelling shots, then realize I wasn't Orson Welles or David Lean. My friend and now producer, Jerry Zucker, told me I wasn't shooting enough coverage and that I was limiting my choices in the editing room. I tried to add a series of shots to the first day's shot list, then suddenly the sun was going down and we had to rig lights outside the windows to match the lost light. Hunt Lowry, the co-producer, called me aside and said that he had spoken to the studio about going into overtime. They said that if I didn't get those shots in the next hour, I was fired, and they were going to shut down the film. I've never experienced as much panic and tension. With only minutes to go I dropped the new shots and managed to get everything in the can. Learning under fire is an indelible experience. Day by day I became more confident, and by the end of the production I was expressing a new level of visual creativity. Some of my more complex shots even made it into the film.

One fun thing about making *My Life* was that Tom Cruise visited the set. I was still awed by movie stars. Bruce Willis would join Demi on *Ghost* and hang out in the background, just a guy supporting his wife. For Tom, supporting his Nicole meant hiring a helicopter to fly over her trailer on her birthday and toss a ton of rose petals over half of the Columbia lot. I would have married him just for that. We shared a few meals, including at their home, and I was always aware of the person more than the star. That was unusual in Hollywood. He was uniquely charming, in ways that so few stars manage to be, although the petals were a bit excessive. We talked about other films that I might write for him and Nicole, but those ideas went the same way as their marriage.

I ran into a small problem during editing. When we were casting *Ghost* and Jerry Zucker said a writer could cast his mother, but the director could cast his entire family, little did I know that one day I would have the opportunity to immortalize mine. When Bob goes back to Detroit, I cast my own family to play his. My mom got to appear on screen for a second time, this time in full make-up, greeting Bob and Gail at a family gathering. She welcomes them into her home, standing at the front door the same way my mom would greet our family when I was a kid. She is surrounded by her children, my brother and his family, nieces and nephews and all my cousins. When Richard Chew, the editor, told me he needed to cut the scene down, I was resistant because it meant cutting my cousin Wendy out of the movie. There was a long tracking shot in the film in which my dad delivered the final words. It was a complicated setup, and his line was important, at least to me. Unfortunately, he forgot it every time. We must have filmed it eight times. Long tracking shots aren't easy to pull off. So much can go wrong – and did – every time. When we made it to the end of each take, my dad often looked stymied, searching for the words. When my mom tried coaching him from the sidelines, I had to remind her that this wasn't a play and we could hear her yelling out his lines. He finally got it right, but the shot was too long and after a lot of discussion Richard convinced me to cut it from the film.

A few of us gathered in the Sony screening room to watch the first cut of *My Life*. I was beyond anxious. When it was over, I felt sick, humiliated, sad, betrayed by my own script, ready to run away from my career. The film was horrible. It had no pacing, no emotional energy, no rhythmic power, even though it followed every word I had written. I couldn't believe how bad a writer I was – to say nothing of my directing. I could tell that Peter James, my director of photography on the film, was aware of my suffering. He explained to me later that this kind of despair hits everyone. But in the moment, he turned to me and said, "This is only a rough cut, a first assembly. There is a reason they call them rough. Now go and make your movie." It was lifesaving. I remember looking at Richard, my editor. He smiled. "Let's go do it," he said. And we did. We went right up to the editing room and essentially started over. Everything was there – it just needed to be pruned, rearranged, expanded, contracted, eliminated. For two months I sat in the editing room with Richard and Christy, his assistant, reviewing every outtake, every frame of the film that might be better than the shots we had selected. Richard had a way of finding great material, including expressions on actors' faces before I had even called "Action!" He made the movie. He found its rhythm, its emotional life. His ability to dig emotional moments out of the literal wastebasket of discarded film was astounding. That so much of the movie works is because Richard retrieved shots I didn't even remember were there.

My mom died of a brain aneurysm while we were cutting the film, and I flew to Detroit for the funeral. We were mixing in the sound studio when she passed, and her loving greeting of Michael and Nicole as they arrive at her home was the very scene we were working on when I returned to work. It was the sound of her voice that I heard whenever I arrived in Detroit and she answered the door. For a week after her passing she was greeting me over and over again. It was heart-wrenching to watch. I'm grateful I was able to immortalize her loving greeting, her full-hearted welcome, in *My Life*.

We had a small budget and limited shooting time. A few elaborate shots made it into the movie and I began to see my own possibilities as a director, but I would clearly need many more years of practice. It was clear to me that I was a better writer than I was a director, and I saw that a more talented and experienced director would have made a better film. Still, I was proud of the work. I think Nicole Kidman, Michael Keaton and Haing Ngor give impressive performances, and the film has a deep and satisfying emotional core. I was excited to share it with the world.

My Life opened the same weekend as *Home Alone 2* and Brian De Palma's *Carlito's Way*. Brian called me to express how excited he was that we both had movies opening the same day. I hadn't heard from him in years, so it was fun to connect. We both felt doomed to second or third place by *Home Alone 2* but happy to be sharing the weekend together. We didn't even think about *Mrs. Doubtfire*, which was previewing that weekend. It was only when I saw the full-page newspaper ads for all four films, including mine, that it dawned on me. After a hard week at the office, people going out on a Friday night would be more interested in seeing Robin Williams in drag or Al Pacino as an honest ex-con than Michael Keaton dying of cancer.

Home Alone 2 won the weekend, Brian's film did respectably, and *My Life* flopped. Hollywood agents used to collect reviews in big thick books. I thought I was strong enough to handle it. I went through them one by one, and they just kept getting worse and worse. After an hour, I felt like such a failure I could barely breathe. I doubted all my choices. That feeling lasted a very long

time. I never saw Michael again, although many years later he was quoted in *The New York Times*: "People have come up to me about *My Life* and certain things that I've done and commented on what it meant to them. So you can say: 'There's *that*. At least I did *that*.'"

I didn't see Nicole again either, although she lovingly remembered holidays and birthdays for years. When the DVD came out, the studio had somehow failed to put my name on the packaging. Here was a film without a writer or director. I didn't think I would ever work again.

One weekend, months after the film came out, I went to a party. A woman there said she wanted to talk to me. "I understand that you wrote the movie *My Life*," she said. I nodded yes. "Well, I want to tell you something. Do you have a moment?" I nodded. "My husband died of cancer three years ago. I had an eleven-year-old son, and he couldn't talk to me about the death of his father. About a month ago I learned that I have terminal breast cancer and only six months to live. I knew I didn't want to leave this world without having a meaningful dialogue with my son, but I didn't know how to do it. Then we saw *My Life*. During the movie, my son was sobbing. When we got home, he crawled into my lap and we had the conversation that has made it possible for me to leave this world." She took a long, emotional breath. "I want to thank you for that."

I choked up. In that moment I realized why I had made *My Life*. I made it for her and her son. That was enough. There is a Talmudic injunction: "Whoever saves one life saves the world entire." We think we make our movies for the masses, but perhaps it's not as grand as that. Touching one other person may be all we are here to do.

Weaving in and out of all these productive years are endless stories of my boys Joshua and Ari, essential threads in the true fabric and tapestry of my life. Eight years apart, they are amazing human beings and very different people. Both of them wanted movie careers and both are excellent writers. Joshua has written novels and screenplays, Ari mostly movies and TV shows. Joshua left film after writing the script for the video game *Assassin's Creed 2*, which was nominated for a Writers Guild of America Award. He built on that success to launch a career in video games as a writer and narrative director, and won an Interactive Emmy for writing and producing a branching Netflix show. Ari spent years writing for big-name talent, but like many Hollywood projects the films didn't get made, and writers with unproduced films don't last in the business. After much soul-searching he decided to go to Georgetown Law School and graduated having already published several law review papers. I always imagined he could become President of the United States someday, but don't know if I wish that on him. He is presently a federal prosecutor in Washington D.C., and recently married an extraordinary woman from Antalya, Turkey, named Burcu. In many ways she has completed his life.

It's slightly painful for me to think that my career both inspired and frustrated my boys, and I feel guilty about having made the path look easy, even though nothing happened for me until I was in my early forties and it was *never* easy for me, even after the success of *Ghost*. The odds are against screenwriters from the start, and a life of material achievement is rare. I have tried to teach Joshua and Ari the more important lessons that Rudi taught me over the years: how to engage reality as it arises and how to find support and refuge within our deeper selves. The great lesson of Hollywood is not what movies we produce, but who we become along the way.

Twenty

Struggling – *Deep Impact*

After *My Life* I spent several years writing screenplays, some of which got made and some of which didn't. One of the more interesting was *Deep Impact*, which I wrote for Steven Spielberg. It was produced by Richard Zanuck and David Brown, the team that twenty years earlier hadn't understood the end of my script *Quasar*. One of my favorite childhood movies, and Steven's too, was *When Worlds Collide*, about a rogue planet on a collision course with Earth. I stood for two hours on a Detroit street corner with a friend after we watched it, having the first philosophical talk of my life. At the age of ten, I was beginning to sense the impermanence of the world.

A planet on a collision course with Earth felt somewhat unlikely in our current scientific sense of space, so I suggested we turn the planet into a comet or asteroid, and Steven agreed. Somehow a threat to earthly life offered an opportunity to write about what the world might look like if humanity could actually come together, which for me was a much more forceful and emotional idea than just killing everyone off. I hoped I could use this threat of human destruction to show what was meaningful about being human. Steven and I were on the same page. We had a series of meetings at his Amblin office on the Universal lot.

I had been to Amblin once before because a friend from Bloomington, Pauli, was a chef there. She called me one day to say that Scorsese was working at the studio on a television series that Spielberg was producing. She knew we had been friends, so asked if I would like to have lunch with him. I hadn't seen Marty in decades. We ate in a private dining room, just the two of us. He was now a household name, but was having a hard time. For all their recognizable artistry, the films – *Mean Streets*, *Taxi Driver*, *Raging Bull* – weren't Hollywood blockbusters, and he was wondering how best to move forward. He had been offered a movie called *The Color of Money* with Paul Newman, but implied that it represented a kind of selling out, or, at least, a step away from generating his own artful work. I didn't know how to advise him. I like to think I encouraged him to do it. That's what Rudi would have done. Clearly my days of helping Scorsese were long over. Still, it was a pleasure to be with him. I filled him in on my life. I had yet to have a major film produced other than *Brainstorm* and he was deeply empathetic and encouraging. The last time we had spoken was after a friend showed him my script for *Jacob's Ladder* and he called me in DeKalb with complimentary and encouraging words. Our lunch at Amblin was a defining moment for me – two guys from film school, chatting. I admired Marty tremendously, although I thought it was a bit odd that he ended up making *Kundun*, about His Holiness the Dalai Lama. It was my LSD trip and burgeoning spiritual journey that had separated me from Marty and most of my film friends. I seemed to be on a different path from theirs, one they didn't fully understand at the time. It's curious that in the end my spiritual journey brought me to Hollywood and that Marty's brought him to the Dalai Lama.

It was wonderful working with Spielberg. For one thing, he and my brother look almost exactly alike. Their personalities are different, but they have many similar mannerisms and the facial similarities are striking. Gary is often mistaken for Steven. In France once, on a family vacation, a woman in a restaurant came up to us and bowed to Gary. "*Enchanté*, Monsieur Spielberg. *Enchanté*."

We all smiled. While I was writing *Deep Impact*, Gary took over my office on the Universal lot since I always wrote at home and had no use for it. He was an aspiring screenwriter, and having an office at Universal added heft to that dream. One day Spielberg walked by his open door and stopped in his tracks. "My God, you do look like me," he said. They both laughed.

But working with Spielberg isn't like working with your brother. Every now and then I was reminded by a gesture, a comment, that this was *his* domain. I was told by insiders that office personnel weren't allowed to look up when he walked by. That may have been a myth, but Steven *was* mythic. Amblin was, in its own way, a palatial space. The statuary in the entryway was awesome, packed with Oscars, Golden Globes – you name it. There was no question that you had entered the heights of Hollywood, almost sacred ground. Steven was always warm to me, but you couldn't escape the feeling that he was "Spielberg." One time, eating lunch at his home in the Hamptons, a plate of oysters and a plate of shrimp were set on the table before us. Steven finished all the oysters. I wasn't exactly told they were all for him, but it was clear and unspoken that the shrimp were mine. The oysters were all his. Our conversations had a sense of the hierarchical about them, even while always friendly and congenial. Occasionally I would slip up and feel that I was with my brother, but that wouldn't last long. A roll of the eye, a hand gesture, and you remembered where you were and who was running the show. He was the manifestation of Hollywood power.

Working for Steven opened every door I wanted to walk through. Researching *Deep Impact* was my favorite part of the project. It quickly became clear that I needed science to back up our storyline of a comet colliding with Earth. We needed to research how a foreign body from outer space could conceivably impact our planet. Amateur astronomers claimed to be able to spot asteroids and comets that might do terrible damage, but professionals didn't generally devote time to the issue, even though there was consensus that an asteroid collision with Earth had wiped out the dinosaurs 66 million years ago. It was Gene and Carolyn Shoemaker who documented the impact origin of Meteor Crater in Arizona. They also became famous, along with David Levy, for discovering Comet Shoemaker-Levy 9, a potential planet-crossing comet. Using Spielberg's imprimatur, I spent a week with them at Palomar Observatory, working out the science and, in some ways, the potential reality of a true *Deep Impact* occurring.

I spent time in newsrooms and on assignment with Andrea Mitchell at NBC and Tom Brokaw. I spent time in the White House with George Stephanopoulos, White House Communications Director under Clinton (who wondered if I could help get a relative of his into a meeting with Spielberg), and in Al Gore's office, with its wall-size image of Earth, as seen from the Moon, dominating the room. In the White House, I sat at the President's Oval Office desk and visited his private quarters. I understood how someone occupying that space could believe ultimate power resided in them. But it was the room itself that exuded power. I experienced something similar in Hollywood with executives who had no sense of how empty they were as human beings or how egoistically full of themselves they became when sitting at their desks. I remember watching the pompous vice president of a major studio leaving the room and seeing his power instantly dissipate as he stepped out the door. It was as if his suit was suddenly six sizes too big. He had no idea how much he had shrunk. He stepped out of his office and his power remained behind.

I went to NASA and rode up in an open elevator alongside a huge rocket. I watched a lift-off from the NASA control room. All you had to do was mention Spielberg and the world opened up. I began to see how important comet/asteroid research was and even had a series of meetings with members of Congress about the real import of this Hollywood movie. Not long afterwards, as the subject of cometary collisions became more seriously discussed and not simply sensationalistic, more federal funds were channeled into scientific research. In 2022, a much-publicized space mission (DART – Double Asteroid Redirection Test) successfully sent a rocket to collide with a comet, hoping to divert it from its course. It proved that a comet could be deflected from a collision course with Earth. I felt like *Deep Impact* and a similar film released weeks later, *Armageddon*, may have had a real hand in alerting mankind to the threats that errant comets and asteroids pose. Speaking of *Armageddon*, before I knew that Disney was contemplating producing that film at the same time as us, I was invited by the president of the studio to have lunch. He pressed me about *Deep Impact*, and I proudly volunteered stories about the amazing research I had been doing. Before I knew it, one of my primary consultants left our film and went over to consult for *Armageddon*. I had been played by a studio head. Clearly, I was still an innocent kid from Detroit. On the other hand, perhaps the double whammy of *Deep Impact* and *Armageddon* did some good when it comes to the future of the planet.

Steven and I began to develop different ideas about the structure of the story. He wanted it told exclusively from the point of view of the newscasters covering the unfolding event. I wanted to be more expansive. My original script was long (Steven wanted a three-hour epic) and involved kids (amateur astronomers) who discover the comet on a collision course. All the political and news coverage was interwoven around those characters. My version also involved the effort to save a portion of the human race in underground facilities and the formation of a group of scientists and astronauts who would attempt to stop or deflect the comet with nuclear weapons before it could hit Earth. The science behind that was up for grabs, but enough people supported my research to make it a through-line of the story. The interweaving of these stories fascinated me and I loved writing the script, but in the end it wasn't what Steven wanted. When I was asked to refocus the story on the news media alone, I declined. Shortly after that, I was removed from the project. I thought after the success of *Ghost,* after winning an Oscar, I had graduated from this kind of career pain. But now I was being fired from a Steven Spielberg film and no longer invited to hobnob with royalty. I felt I had put my soul into the film, and it had been discarded.

Shortly after I left *Deep Impact,* Blanche's mother, Fann, passed away. She had lived with us for nine years. Fann had been a troubled woman much of her life. She had lost two sons, one in early childhood and one at birth, experiences that shaped her life. She later lived to see the death of her first grandchild. It wasn't an easy ride. As she aged, she expressed a deepening anger and seemed to hold grudges against anyone who had done her wrong. I had never known anyone so caught up in her own negativity. Her years living with us were complex. But after she began having small strokes that affected her mood and memory, a transformation took place. Much of her anger and repetitive negativity began to subside. It was as if her altered brain, her body, was releasing her from all the accumulated tension in her life. Her grudges, her sadness, her frustrations all disappeared. She forgot who she hated, who had done her wrong, and why she was so angry. Her time with us became sweeter and softer.

In January 1997, she was in a hospital not far from our house. I went to see her one morning with no sense that it would be the last time I would ever visit her. As I entered her room, she was sitting up in bed, weak but present. She smiled as she saw me, then shrugged a "what can you do?" shrug. Her smile cut right through me. It was an acceptance of her whole life. It was an act of total surrender. It was so loving, so absolute. There were no words, just that shrug. She died later that afternoon. I took her shrug as a great lesson, up there with anything Rudi had ever given me.

Fann had every right to enter the hereafter with her antagonisms in place, but the woman who had outlived her anger was, I suspect, much like the sweet child who had been born 92 years before. In later years, after her strokes, she didn't know exactly who we were, but she would sing and laugh and bless everyone: "I love you all around!" She spent her final years filled with a joy and profound simplicity that rivaled what I had aspired to with my life of meditation. The lightness and acceptance I witnessed in her death reminded me of what I had sensed when her husband Arnold died. They hadn't meditated for half their lives or pursued much else other than a Jewish tradition of geniality and kindness. "Trying" to become that liberated person had been the core of my decades-long meditative life. Fanny and Arnold arrived at that space simply by being good people.

Fann's death didn't empty out our home. My dad Jimmy moved in a few years later and stayed for six years. In the end Blanche and I had fourteen years of providing parental care. Jimmy had an odd journey. Shortly after my mom's passing, while I was still editing *My Life*, he began to date. That seemed inappropriate enough, but the women he chose were equally unsuitable. It was an early sign that his mind was going and a signal that life with him was about to get weird. Wanting to meet women and to graft onto my Hollywood celebrity and career, he had cards printed declaring himself a talent agent. His company was called Talent Galore, an absurd name for someone who represented no one. He would hand them out to any woman he met. A few believed him. The most he could do was introduce them to me, at which point I would have to disabuse them of his promise to start their careers.

One woman he met was a large blonde, perhaps in her early forties. I suspect she saw me as a doorway to fame and fortune for her son, a singer, whom she immediately introduced me to. She attached herself to my dad and they became a strange kind of couple. It made no sense, but seemed innocent enough and he appeared very happy. For a few years she lived off the money we were giving him, but as his mind deteriorated, I could feel the relationship unraveling. In a moment reminiscent of Blanche's mom's arrival at our Northridge home, one day my dad arrived at our front door with his "girlfriend," who proceeded to drop him off and quite gingerly say goodbye. She wanted nothing more to do with him.

Thus began his residence in our Northridge home, with a new round of caretakers. Unlike Fanny, Jimmy didn't get sweeter and more joyful as he aged, just more confused. Blanche was an amazing helper and took care of all his doctor's appointments and managing the minutia of his life. He aged quickly. But he loved being surrounded by all the Detroit transplants, all his nieces and nephews and their offspring who lived near us and visited regularly. He felt like he was back in Detroit. He spent his waning years creating collages with photos of family and images cut out of *Life* magazine articles, combining them all into surprisingly interesting compositions. But gradually he was unable to do anything. He mostly sat in the backyard staring at the pool. When he died of gastro-intestinal reflux at the age of 87, we transported his body back to Detroit and buried him next to my mom. The burial plot was now full – my mom's parents and sisters all lying cozily side by side, the vast expanse of my childhood pushed underground into a tiny plot of land. It was too big and too small to contemplate. It was a relief to have them resting together, side by side, and to feel they were home. For the first time since our kids moved out and our parents were gone, Blanche and I were alone with each other. It was surprisingly liberating.

My next film didn't become a movie, but it should have. *In Your Dreams* was a script by a friend, David Saltzman, whom I had met years earlier. David and my cousin Mark Levin stopped at our home in DeKalb for a couple of days on their way to California. We talked about nothing but movies. David later became my assistant on *My Life* and a student of Rudi's work.

I loved the premise of *In Your Dreams*, but felt it had some problems I thought I could fix, and I wondered if I might try my hand at punching it up a bit. It's about a man who almost dies in a car accident but is miraculously saved by a beautiful angel. When he finds out that this savior isn't really an angel, but an actual woman who pulled him from the burning car, he wants to thank her for saving his life. But he can't find her anywhere – the mystery woman has vanished – except in his dreams, where he falls in love with her. When he does finally meet her in the reality of New York, she's actually a meter maid and nothing like the angel of his imagination. I felt it was a story about the power of dreams and the truth that lies beneath the surface of our daily experiences, and that encourages us to listen to the inner voices beyond our conscious mind.

David was happy with the changes to the script and especially happy when Jerry Zucker and Sony Pictures expressed interest in making it. We ended up with an office on the Sony lot and reached out to top female stars, including Sandra Bullock, who felt she had already done a movie with similar themes, Julia Roberts, who passed, and Cameron Diaz, who was thrilled to do it, then pulled out just days before we were about to start production. Those were the only stars whom Sony felt could get the film made, and almost immediately the film was dead and our offices shut down. The blinding speed of Hollywood disappointment is hard to fathom.

I had been through enough loss over the years that such pain simply became part of the process. But for David it was hard. I felt for him and everyone else who was suddenly back on the sidewalk looking for the next break, the next paycheck. Rudi taught me that it's harder to let go of what you haven't had than what you have. David stepped away from the loss of *In Your Dreams* and never let his experience with the project define him. In that sense, he became my teacher. In all my years of witnessing people getting close to the brass ring and failing to grab it, I often found that those who held on to regret really were damaged. I hated the way Hollywood treated all the people who crashed and burned there. But those who managed to move on often discovered a wholeness in themselves, an authenticity that defined them and made them more complete. I was, and remain, deeply inspired by David. He turned back to his family and found joy in another career – marketing film – that made use of his creative talent. If I had to vote for Hollywood stardom or becoming a true human being, my vote is on the human side of the equation. The struggle to have both is rarely achieved.

While I was working on *In Your Dreams*, Michael (*The Player*) Tolkin was hired to write Steven's version of *Deep Impact*. His version didn't work for me, and probably Steven too, because the script was rewritten yet again by John Wells (showrunner for *ER* and *The West Wing*), who is uncredited, although I begged him to take credit since he did such a beautiful job on the script and, in many ways, resurrected much of what I wanted and hoped the movie would be. He declined. Steven also backed out of the project and Mimi Leder stepped in as director.

I'm told that Steven thought *Deep Impact* would be a loser. Early screenings supposedly tested badly, so they went back and re-edited the film, focusing on the emotion I had always felt was at the core of my story. Watching the astronauts offering to give up their lives to save the planet, watching them say goodbye to loved ones, all the heartfelt scenes – that was the movie I had written and hoped would get made. And it was. I was happy and proud to have my name on it. In the end *Deep Impact* brought in $350,000,000, became the biggest box office success for a female director up to that time (a title it held for over a decade), and helped make DreamWorks, the company that Steven had just formed with Jeff Katzenberg and David Geffen, the powerhouse it is today.

Years later I was watching another Spielberg blockbuster – I don't remember which. As I left the theater, all I could think was that one day I would love to write a huge movie like that. Ari looked at me like I was crazy. "You did, Dad. You wrote *Deep Impact*." To tell the truth, I had completely forgotten. It's hard to express how little imprint a film can leave on a writer. It's fun while it lasts, but they do have a tendency to bunch up in your mind, then fade away. The joy, mostly, is in the writing.

Twenty-One

Grace – *The Last Mimzy*

I decided to write a novel. It was a way of recapturing a sense of authorship that had been diminished while working in the collaborative and sometimes contentious world of Hollywood. The book, about a famous Las Vegas magician who discovers real magic, was called *Magician*. I had met David Copperfield and David Blaine, and was captivated by their lives and personalities. They sparked something in me. My opening line was: "Sebastian was not aware of ..." I loved writing images that weren't present tense or filmable, things the main character wasn't seeing or mindful of. I reveled in the third person voice, in describing what wasn't perceived rather than what was cinematically visible. The novel form was liberating.

I was about ninety pages in when a futurist I had worked with on *Deep Impact* called me out of the blue and told me that something called Y2K could be one of the true great human calamities, far more immediate and terrifying than a comet hitting the planet. And it was just a year away. He predicted that everything controlled by computers would stop working because they weren't programmed to move into the twenty-first century. It was impossible not to take him seriously. Having been warned about Y2K before people were talking about it, I became very apocalyptic. All I could think of was finding a house where we could manage our lives, grow food, store supplies, and make room for family, students and friends. We looked for houses all over Southern California. By now Blanche had horses, which she boarded at a local ranch. We wanted a property that had space for them as well as us. But we couldn't find anything.

Around that time, we took a trip to a hotel in New York's Hudson Valley called the Mohonk Mountain House. Blanche and I had visited Mohonk early in our relationship and fallen in love with its antique beauty. It has been around since the 1860s, and we have a photograph of Blanche's family vacationing there in the 1920s. We decided that if we ever married and had children, we would take them there, and by now we have visited with our parents, siblings, children and grandchildren. What I love about the place is that it doesn't change. It's a snapshot of a moment in time, a storehouse of feelings and memories, with the same carpets, pictures on the walls and dining room fixtures as when we first visited. I can walk through the dining room and remember sitting at a particular table with my parents, another with Blanche's mom, her sister Rhoda and her husband Joe, my brother Gary and his wife Suzy, and my boys. Since we loved the area so much, on this particular trip we decided to search for a possible Y2K house nearby.

We discovered a 100-acre estate with a house built in the 1700s, added onto in the 1800s and then again in the 1900s and 2000s, with 22 rooms, horse facilities, a swimming pool, three ponds, a caretaker's house and miles of walking trails, all along a stream which bordered the property. This would be enough room to keep fifty or more safe if the world ended, and maybe, somewhere down the road, house a commune like the Big Indian ashram. It was called Bear Hollow. Joshua and I, walking along the path past the expansive horse fields to a huge open glen, both said simultaneously, "This is magic," or something to that effect. Unfortunately, we couldn't afford it.

Shortly after seeing the house, when I got a call from Bob Shaye asking me to look at a script he thought might interest me, I saw a path to buying the Bear Hollow estate. I put down the novel I was writing and read the script. Little did I know that I would probably never pick up the novel or write anything original again. Instead, I would spend the rest of my career supporting a lovely but far too expensive bi-coastal life.

Bob's script was based on a short story called "Mimsy Were the Borogoves." I recognized the name right away, both as a line from *Alice in Wonderland* and as a TV show I had seen as a kid. The show, based on a short story by Henry Kuttner and C.L. Moore, was about two kids who find toys from the future. My brother and I watched it in complete awe, transfixed by the ideas of toys from beyond. But the half hour ended abruptly, and even back then, long before I became a writer, I felt something was missing from the story. I tuned in to the show again the next day, thinking that maybe I had only seen half of the story, but there was no second half. Forty years later, I picked up the short story thinking, *Oh boy, I'm finally going to find out how this ends!* But it ended in the same place as the TV show. These two kids disappear into the future and we never find out what really happens to them. "There's no ending," I said to Bob Shaye. He looked at me and said, "So make one up." Such strange karma that forty years later it would fall to me to create an ending for the story. Unfortunately, at the time, I couldn't figure out what it should be.

Several people had written drafts of the screenplay, including Toby Emmerich, who later ran New Line Cinema and became president of Warner Bros. Toby's version worked well for the first third, then misfired completely. I had to figure something out, so I started with a vague idea about bringing Tibetans into the story. I had always been fascinated by the idea that Tibetans identify the reincarnation of a lama, most especially the Dalai Lama, based on

on whether or not they recognize toys from a previous lifetime. As I understood it, toys from the previous lama's past are mixed in with lots of other toys. If the child picks out the toys from his past lifetime and avoids the others, it's proof that he is the true reincarnation and, in the case of the Dalai Lama, is destined to lead Tibetans in their continuing journey in this world. I knew there was something there, but I struggled to put it all together into a coherent story.

The pitch meeting was scheduled for the following Monday, and I still had no ending. All I knew was that I needed to buy Bear Hollow and protect the people I loved from Y2K. Even as I was driving to the meeting, the ending hadn't arrived. But I had learned to trust the process, to believe that if I opened my heart and head chakras, the answers would be delivered. I opened deeply as I drove along the 101 Freeway to the New Line offices on the Warner Bros. lot. I still had no idea what I was going to say. But then, in the parking lot, it began to gel. I went into the conference room, took my customary sip of tea, and the story of *The Last Mimzy* delivered itself.

The central concept was that the toys were from many eons in the future, when the human race was dying. The toys were looking for a pure child whose DNA could resuscitate humanity and save the world. It was about finding a child, in this case a little girl, whose genes would renew and repopulate mankind. As a teacher in the future tells us at the end of the film, this is a story about a little girl from the distant past who became the mother of us all.

As I spoke, I could tell that the story was flowing. Bob Shaye, who was attending the meeting via video transmission from New York, seemed to like it, too, but he stayed silent. When I was done telling the story, Bob wished everyone well and signed off. The next thing I knew, one of the executives was called out of the room to speak to Bob privately. A few minutes later, he came back and said,

"You've got a deal." I started writing the movie and we bought the house in upstate New York just weeks before Y2K – all based on an idea that arrived on the way to the pitch meeting. I spent the next eight years writing and rewriting the story to satisfy the powers that be – mostly Bob.

Shortly after I began work on the script, I learned that Bob, in addition to being the president and founder of New Line Cinema, had decided to direct *The Last Mimzy*. This meant that in addition to dealing with him as a studio president, I had to handle his creative micro-managing as a first-time director. Maybe that's why the film took eight years to get made. He was obsessed with it being perfect. As studio president he would have gotten it out the door as quickly as possible, but as the director, every element had to be just right. Bob was always in charge. There was a familial warmth between us, but he was like a forceful older brother. He was definitely the boss.

Bob finally felt the script was done. The film was budgeted and casting began. We were shooting in Vancouver, filling in for Whidbey Island in Seattle, where the story takes place. But Bob couldn't stop fiddling with the script. At one point, just before shooting, he had a meeting with Steve Jobs, where they talked about the success of the Pixar movies. Jobs said the secret to good storytelling was cutting out everything that isn't absolutely essential. That makes sense, of course. It's what I try to do whenever I write. My final drafts are streamlined and tight, as far as I'm concerned. Jobs told Bob that a good script shouldn't be more than ninety or a hundred pages, so Bob told me my screenplay was too long and I needed to cut twenty pages. I tried arguing that such cuts would destroy the story, but to no effect. After eight years of writing and finally arriving at an actual shooting date, I was told to upend everything I had done. What I had written for Bob was, at its core, a Buddhist movie thematically, but he wanted to remove every Buddhist element from the story, including several major Tibetan monks who were central to identifying the young girl. They were all erased. The script was collapsing in on itself. Eventually, after a series of drafts, we were down to less than a hundred pages and only a couple of weeks away from shooting. It was a completely different script. After eight years of on-again, off-again writing, I was devastated by the movie we were about to shoot. I struggled to cut elements from the story that seemed foundational to me. It was agonizing.

But in the end, the amazing thing is that the essential spiritual dynamic of the movie couldn't be eliminated. Characters could be lost and scenes tightened or cut, but the core reality of the story was impossible to extinguish. To my amazement, the deepest and most important narrative structures in the movie were intact. I missed the excised scenes, but saw the story's message rising on its own without attachment to the Tibetan monks whom I had believed were central to delivering it. The underlying story was bigger than the words on the page. I handed the new script to Bob and within days we were shooting.

One of the great pleasures of working on the film for all eight years was the presence of its producer, Michael Phillips. Michael had produced some of the biggest films in Hollywood, including *The Sting*, *Taxi Driver* and *Close Encounters of the Third Kind*. You would think there would be an enormous arrogance accompanying such achievement, but in fact Michael was humble and profoundly human. It turns out he's a major collector of Buddhist art, so he was sympathetic to the underlying spiritual content of what I was proposing with the script. When I first walked into his home, I was surrounded by a collection of Asian art that immediately reflected his persona to me. It was Michael who fought to keep *Mimzy* alive all those years and infuse the film with its spiritual aura. It would never have made it to the big screen without him fighting for the purity of its vision.

The biggest surprise for me was how good a job Bob did as director. I remember watching *Mimzy* for the first time and being knocked out by the assurance of his choices. The deeper underpinnings of the movie managed to shine through. It's a real mythic fairy tale that makes me feel like a child every time I watch it. I'm endlessly grateful for its simple, loving, almost magical beauty. I don't know how Bob did it, but he pulled it out of the hat. Perhaps the Buddhist insights of the story impacted him and he learned to get out of the story's way.

A year after the film came out, I was a participant at a Writers Guild of America event called, "Writing Movies that Matter." The room was filled to the brim. Winnie Holtzman, writer of the musical *Wicked*, moderated. In the front row were two girls, maybe fourteen or fifteen. I couldn't imagine what they were doing there. Everyone else in the room was decades older. At the end of the presentation, I asked for questions and one of the young girls raised her hand. "Mr. Rubin," she asked, "what is the meaning of *The Last Mimzy*?" I, who am rarely at a loss for words, had no idea what to say. I stammered for a moment and then cleverly asked her, "Well sweetheart, why don't you tell me what *you* think the meaning is?" She looked at me with a profound seriousness and innocence, and answered instantly. "Well, Mr. Rubin, I think that the meaning of *The Last Mimzy* is that even young girls can save the world." I smiled a huge grin. "Right," I answered. "Absolutely right."

Twenty-Two

Questioning – Gun for Hire

New Year's Eve, at the turn of the century, entering the year 2000, we assembled as much family as we could shove into Bear Hollow. There was no space unpopulated. People slept everywhere, about 35 of us, everyone prepared for the world to end. We built a huge fire pit in the big field near the house, filled it with logs, and prepared to dance around it, like Rudi's puja ceremony years before where it rained three times. Unfortunately, no one had any idea how to start a fire. At midnight, we crowded back into the house and waited for the electricity to go off (even though we had a generator) and all our computers to crash. Nothing happened. The next morning, we woke up and the world was just as it had been the day before. The only difference was that I now owned two huge homes a continent apart, in the Hudson Valley and Los Angeles.

For fifteen years I wrote like mad to sustain our bi-coastal lifestyle. We loved the seasons in New York and flying back to the warmth and sunshine of LA when the East Coast started to ice over. It was the best of all worlds. Part of me had always longed for a baronial lifestyle. I had wanted to live in a Scottish castle when I was a kid. This house wasn't exactly a castle, but it served the purpose.

Because it wasn't that far from Rudi's ashram in Big Indian (now owned by his student and my friend John Mann), there were a lot of Rudi students in the vicinity, some of whom were teaching.

I joined the fray. Classes started immediately. Bear Hollow became like a small ashram, with meditation every Sunday and a flow of friends and students filling our lives. But that sense of abundance had to be sustained through enormous effort. My friend Larry said he never saw me so unhappy, although I don't remember it that way. I just had to work while everyone else played. We even rented an apartment in Manhattan, and I would teach there as well. It was nice to bring the class to the city. But the strain grew immense.

During one of our periodic family visits to Mohonk, Blanche and I sat with Joshua, chatting in one of the gazebos. At one point he asked Blanche for her mother's wedding ring and told us that he wanted to propose to his girlfriend of two years, Evanne. We were speechless. I don't know why we never expected this moment to come, but we didn't. Blanche's mouth was wide open with amazement. I grabbed my camera to capture it. I've never seen Blanche happier. We all loved Evanne. She was fun, vibrant and very witty. She had worked as a copywriter for ads and commercials selling Hollywood movies. Her work was often much better than the films she promoted. Most importantly, she made Joshua happy. He had gone to a party with a lot of women with piercings and tattoos – something he had always loved. Evanne was the only untatooed woman there.

Having my first son get married gave me an innate sense of completion. It was profoundly fulfilling. Being with them as a couple enriched our lives and a new level of joy filled our family. One year later, Joshua and Evanne married at Bear Hollow. It was a magical event. Family came from everywhere. It rained on and off the entire day but never even drizzled when anyone stepped outside. The ceremony was held around an expansive stone maze that Joshua and Evanne had constructed in the woods. It seemed to symbolize the mystery of what brings people together. Later, as we finished dining under a huge tent that Joshua and his friends had decorated, we witnessed a double rainbow that filled the sky and ended on our back lawn. It was a transcendent, magical sight, the kind of magic Joshua and I had spoken of on our first visit to Bear Hollow. I had never seen the end of a rainbow, let alone a double one. And I've never had one end in my own yard. Even minus the pot of gold, it seemed like a blessing.

Our New York home was some kind of symbol that I had "made it," a demonstration of my success. But to support this lavish lifestyle I was writing a movie a year – sometimes more – just so I could pay for everything. I never wrote anything that didn't align with my deeper feelings and beliefs, but I didn't create new material, either. I was writing whatever was profitable, nothing original. This is not unusual for successful writers in Hollywood. The price of writing an original screenplay, especially one that doesn't get made, is often too high in terms of mortgages, college tuition, supporting aging parents, etc. You need to keep making money. And having people wanting to hire you to write their movies can be a very attractive option.

Shortly after I finished *Ghost*, I was approached by Disney to work on a story for an animated film about a lion cub becoming king of his realm. The subject didn't speak to me, and I turned it down. I regret the failure of my imagination. It became *The Lion King*. I developed a story for a film that Marvel Studios and Kevin Feige wanted to make, a movie of the comic book *Dr. Strange*. I ended up writing the treatment while we were shooting *The Last Mimzy*. I thought it was a great concept, but it wasn't to their liking. I wrote a script for Will Smith about monsters and spent hours with him kicking the story around, but we could never quite agree on what it was about. Our creative differences couldn't be bridged, and I moved on. I wrote a ghost story with Country and Western star Garth Brooks. Like Will, he had many ideas that didn't gel with mine. Most specifically, we didn't see eye to eye on the rules of being a ghost. Luckily, I did write a fair number of screenplays that were successful and satisfying for me. Some got made. Others didn't. Such is the life of a Hollywood gun for hire.

Into the Light was a script I wrote based on a true story about a man named Mike May who, at the age of three, had an accident that blinded him, but still lived a life of unbelievable achievement, including winning a medal for downhill skiing. He had a beautiful family and the courage to travel on his own. Then, one day, he was offered the possibility of a new medical procedure, transplanting stem cells into his eyes. It was a radical idea and there was no certainty it would work, but, being an adventurer, he went for it. The power of the story was that the operation was successful, that he found vision again after nearly fifty years of blindness, but didn't like what he saw. The effort to interpret the visual world became exhausting and overwhelming. Seeing his wife and two boys for the first time was an emotional upheaval, beautiful and terrifying. And so, he decided to choose blindness, to witness the world the way he had for most of his life – in darkness. He understood more without sight than with it. In darkness, he knew life more clearly than most of us who see.

I rewrote a science fiction script for 20th Century Fox called *Slowman*, about a nurse at a psychiatric hospital who discovers a nearly comatose patient in a wing of the facility whose records suggest that he's been there for 150 years, although he appears to be only thirty years old. She discovers that since being shot in the head in the Civil War, he has been moving in a kind of slow motion. As she tries to wake him back up into the present, she discovers a hidden sense of time and reality that upends everything she has ever known or believed in. I loved it, and so did a few of the executives. Others thought it was too spiritual. End of journey.

I wrote a movie about an autistic child, based on a book called *Strange Son* by Portia Iversen, the true story of the Iversen family, whose son Dov was born autistic and unable to speak. Portia, a bold and determined mother, discovers an Indian family, a woman named Soma and her autistic son Tito, who is also mute but has learned, through his mother's aggressive teaching, to read and type on a computer. After a lifetime of being unable to communicate and silently observing the world, his mother's unique computer interface gives him a voice. He proves to be an excellent writer, wildly articulate about who he is. He explains that his body and mind lived different lives, and that even though he wants to discuss Shakespeare, his body wants to open and close paper bags and sniff the walls. Tito's skills offered Portia enormous hope for communicating with her own son. Their shared journey is breathtakingly moving. At a breakthrough moment late in the story, Dov learns to use the computer and dialogue with his family. When asked by his amazed dad what he has been doing inside his mind all these years, he types, "LISTENING." That brought me to tears and was enough for me to want to write the movie, which in the end no one wanted to make.

El Sistema, about a real-life wunderkind from Venezuela named Gustavo Dudamel, a member of a youth orchestra created by his mentor, José Antonio Abreu, was a real passion project for me. The orchestra trained a generation of underprivileged children from around Venezuela and became the world-famous Simón Bolívar Symphony Orchestra, with Gustavo as its teenage conductor. Getting to know Abreu and Dudamel was a gift, and spending time in Caracas researching the film was impactful. The intersection of poverty and joy – watching people of the impoverished favelas dancing and singing on their rooftops, which I could only visit with armed guards – was something I had never seen before. I only wish the movie had gotten made. It was a worthy story.

Stuart Little 2, based on the book by E.B. White, was produced by Doug Wick (producer of *Gladiator* and *Working Girl*) and his wife Lucy Fisher. I loved the idea of planting spiritual seeds into young minds and had long wanted to write a children's film. I was intrigued by the metaphor of flying vs. soaring, where flying is the initial effort to get a plane off the ground and soaring is when you let go and something far greater takes over. I see much of spiritual effort in life to be like that: an effort to get off the ground, then letting higher forces move you through the world. Unfortunately, that metaphor didn't make it into the film. Still, the critics loved it, and it's the best reviewed movie I ever wrote.

There were also a few forays into TV. One, a show called *Shelter*, gave me an opportunity to work with my son Ari. It was his concept, inspired by the moment in *Deep Impact* when people are selected to enter a series of underground shelters in the hopes of surviving a comet colliding with Earth. We took the show to the Sci-Fi Channel (as it used to be called), where Ari presided over one of the best pitches I have ever witnessed – smooth, focused, engaged – and sold it in the room. Unfortunately, the Sci-Fi president was fired from the network days after we handed in the script and the project evaporated with him.

Twenty-Three

Knowing – The Power of Now

At a certain point, the main challenge became how to balance my spiritual life with my screenwriting career. The career was paying the bills, supporting a household, putting my kids through school. I sat at a computer for years, allowing all these stories to come through and fill the empty pages. It was exhilarating to start every day with nothing, then slowly bring something into existence. Writing certainly enriched my life, but I knew that my spiritual life was more important than Hollywood. I continued to meditate, but began to feel that something was missing. I realized I needed more than the meditation practice I'd had for all those years.

During the time I studied with Rudi, I had developed a strong desire to grow. And in my mind, growing always meant getting closer to some kind of attainment or goal, something I thought Rudi had achieved. For years, I practiced deep, energetic meditation, and experienced moments of exquisite peace and beauty. Sometimes those moments would last days or weeks or months, but they never became permanent. I couldn't hold on to them. I knew I had to do something different. I thought that if I worked harder and meditated longer, I would get there.

One of the things I did to help deepen my meditative practice was a ten-day Vipassana yoga silent retreat. In all the years I had been meditating, I had never tried a retreat. I sensed it would be productive to sit for ten days, twelve hours a day, and not talk to anybody. Six silent hours into the first day of the retreat, my back started hurting. I have sciatic nerve pain, so my meditation for the next four days was excruciating. I saw people sitting there for hours on end, not even getting up for lunch. They seemed to have smiles that never went away. I felt like a spiritual failure. I finally said, "I can't do this." I packed my bag – silently – and went to tell the head teachers that I was leaving. "You're making a big mistake," they told me. "You're like a patient in the middle of an operation. The sutures are hanging out all over the place, and if you leave now, the operation will be incomplete." I wanted to say, "That's alright with me. Bye." But I didn't. They told me I could use a chair if I wanted. I figured that might help, so I took my suitcase back to my cabin, unpacked, and sat through six more days of a little bit less pain. The sciatic pain diminished, but my inner struggle did not. I had moments of stillness and comfort, but couldn't see this as a lifestyle, a life of endless contemplation, and wondered why it seemed so attractive to everyone assembled there. Part of me felt that some in the meditation group were looking for a kind of escape, while others seemed to have found that escape through deep communion with something I was able only to touch or glimpse. For me, it wasn't a permanent state. Rudi's practice was centered on ongoing spiritual growth. I never sensed that there was an arrival point other than death itself. Still, I was drawn to the idea of permanent bliss. Perhaps by sitting another few days, I would know what that was.

On the final day, when I was no closer to Nirvana than the day I arrived, we were finally allowed to talk. I met a guy who had been doing retreats for years. He told me this was his thirtieth one, and that some he attended had lasted months. I looked at him like he was crazy. Then he said that he didn't really care about the Vipassana practice. He said he just liked having a place where he could sit in silence, where someone else would provide food and shelter. I might have dismissed him as a drifter in the world, but he seemed too content for that. He said that his own personal practice was based on a book called *Consciousness Speaks*, by Ramesh Belsekar. He claimed that the book had changed his life and that I should read it. Something in me thought, well... maybe there was a reason for this retreat – and maybe that book was it.

The next day, back home in Northridge, I went to a bookstore and bought *Consciousness Speaks*. I didn't fully understand it, but I found it interesting. It was full of things like "No one can attain enlightenment" and "You are already the thing you're looking for." I had heard those teachings before, but I could never accept them, because I didn't want to be the thing I was looking for. How could this neurotic Jewish gay kid from Detroit be what I was looking for? I wanted to be enlightened, whatever that meant.

Enlightenment was something I had always perceived as an attainment, something a person would acquire – like superpowers. I thought that when I was enlightened, I would be able to see into other people's minds and master my own. I would cause miracles, heal the sick, turn hatred into love, and fear into courage. Most of all, I would be free. I would be happy. "You are already the thing you are looking for" didn't seem useful. But that message kept coming at me in different ways.

My son Joshua gave me a book by Ramesh Belsekar's teacher, a Bombay tobacco store owner named Nisargadatta Maharaj. I thought, *Why am I reading a book by the disciple when I can read a book by his guru?* As soon as I started reading Nisargadatta, I knew that this book was going to transform my life. I felt like I had discovered the graduate program for my spiritual practice. The book, called *I Am That,* was the start of a transformation.

The true knowledge of the self is not knowledge. It is not something that you find by searching, by looking everywhere. It is not to be found in space or time. Knowledge is but a memory, a pattern of thought, a mental habit. All of these are motivated by pleasure, and pain. It is because you are goaded by pleasure and pain that you are in search of knowledge. Being oneself is completely beyond all motivation. You cannot be yourself for some reason. You are *yourself, and no reason is needed.*

Nisargadatta Maharaj, **I Am That**

Nisargadatta was a non-dualist. He basically said, "You don't need to seek to find what you already are." That message was so alien to what Rudi taught us. Rudi's message was "work, grow, expand, evolve." He encouraged enormous effort, and spoke to us about the spiritual potential awaiting those of us who worked our asses off. In contrast, Nisargadatta said, "What are you working for? What are you trying to get to? You are already in that place. You already are the very thing you're looking for."

Nisargadatta instructed his students to keep repeating the phrase "I Am." When he used the word "I," he wasn't referring to a personal self, but his infinite being. He worked every day in his tiny tobacco shop, and knew that a personal ego-self existed, but when he spoke – when he used the word "I" – he knew that "I" was something vast, that it was the Infinite Eternal Absolute Totality of Being. His enlightenment had come when his teacher told him, "You are infinite truth. Just be that."

I started to become a non-dualist. I tried to absorb the message that "You are already the thing you are looking for" – not limited by your body, your mind, your history, your personality. I desperately wanted to awaken to that idea. I walked around for months, repeating, "I Am I Am I Am." Maybe it works for some people, but it didn't for me. I got the idea, but not the experience.

Sometime later I read a book called *The Power of Now* by Eckhart Tolle. My first thought was, *This is Nisargadatta lite.* When I learned that Eckhart was giving a five-day seminar at the Omega Institute, just down the road from Bear Hollow, I signed up.

The minute Eckhart Tolle ambled into the room, I felt different. He was a small, unprepossessing guy with a very quiet voice. He sat still for a long while before telling us a story about him trying to commit suicide and realizing that there was no one to kill. That's how he awakened. Then he said something that really got my attention. "Nothing that you're looking for is in the future." That sort of stopped me in my tracks. My whole spiritual life was about attaining something in the future. He talked about the presence of Now. That's when I realized that he wasn't Nisargadatta lite. This was something other than what Rudi had taught, because Now isn't attained through effort and growth. It's already here. You can't fail to attain it. I didn't know quite what to do with that idea at first, because I didn't want to dismiss Rudi's teachings, which are central to my life. So I spent the next several years trying to incorporate Rudi's work into the practice of embracing the Now.

The philosopher Descartes believed that he had found the most fundamental truth when he made his famous statement: "I think, therefore I am." He had, in fact, given expression to the most basic error, to equate thinking with Being and identity with thinking. The compulsive thinker, which means almost everyone, lives in a state of apparent separateness, in an insanely complex world of continuous problems and conflict, a world that reflects the ever-increasing

fragmentation of the mind. Enlightenment is a state of wholeness, of being "at one" and therefore at peace. At one with life in its manifested aspect, the world, as well as with your deepest self and life unmanifested – at one with Being. Enlightenment is not only the end of suffering and of continuous conflict within and without, but also the end of the dreadful enslavement to incessant thinking. What an incredible liberation this is!

Eckhart Tolle, **The Power of Now**

Tolle talks about what he calls "pain-body," a sense of self that is largely defined by affliction – anger, tension, depression, sadness – and around which we build our identity. Eckhart says the pain-body is nourished by suffering, which is why suffering always returns. The way to deal with this is not to run away, but allowing it to be. Resisting just feeds the process. You can perpetuate the misery or you can just say, "Okay, this is what is."

You come to a point in spiritual work where this is what you're working with. It's *all* you have to work with. It's not about what was or what will be, it's about what *is*, right now. Real spiritual work is learning to say "okay" to what is. The more you say "okay," the more present you are. Rudi's teaching of "surrender" is essentially the same thing. The need to make your life something "other" robs you of the opportunity to live the life that is. Living the life that is in front of you may not be easy, but it's a heroic act. Saying "yes" to your life is the end of the battle with yourself. It took me years to internalize that teaching. A film I showed at the Whitney Museum, *This is It* by James Broughton, contains a remarkable line: "This is it. This is really it. This is all there is. And it's perfect as it is. There is nowhere to go but here. There is nothing here but now. There is nothing now but this. And this

Knowing – The Power of Now

is it. This is really it." I always knew that was true, but didn't know what to do with it. Eckhart helped me with that.

Years later, I spent some personal time with Eckhart. We spoke about doing a movie together, which never materialized. But being with him, sitting in a space with a human being and not a "teacher," was an essential gift on the path. His humanity filled in many of the pieces that I had difficulty assembling as a student in a room full of hundreds of followers. Seeing him eye to eye was very different than seeing him separated, raised up, on a stage. Our equality, just sitting opposite each other, completed something for me.

Around the time *The Last Mimzy* came out, I was hired to adapt Audrey Niffenegger's *The Time Traveler's Wife* for New Line Cinema. I had read the novel in 2003 and loved it. When I heard that New Line had acquired the rights, I called Bob Shaye immediately and said I wanted to write it. It was the only writing job I ever pursued. He got me together with the producers at Plan B, who loved my take on the script, and I was certain that I had my next assignment. Then Bob hired someone else, a man who had recently written a successful film for his company. Some years later, Blanche, Joshua, Ari and I were on vacation in Costa Rica when I got a call from a young Hollywood director named Robert Schwentke. He asked if I would be interested in rewriting *The Time Traveler's Wife*. The project had come back to me. It felt like fate. I wasn't surprised when Robert said that the script hadn't come together the way he wanted it to. It was a hard one to write because the element of time travel created a nonlinear narrative that was potentially difficult for an audience to follow and get invested in. I had a simple solution to that problem: *follow the love story, follow the heart*. Nothing else mattered. The script wrote itself in three weeks. Robert and everyone at New Line loved it and we were positioned to go into production immediately – a rare event in Hollywood.

At the same time *The Last Mimzy* was opening, Bob Shaye arranged for me to be honored as Screenwriter of the Year at the ShoWest Writer's Conference in Las Vegas. We flew there in his private jet. Christopher Walken was on the flight. I hadn't seen him since *Brainstorm*, and had never really forgiven him for changing my dialogue. But there we were, sitting together on this plane, which I took as a sign. I don't like holding grudges, nursing old wounds, or feeling that my heart is closed, and I have learned over the course of my life that it's important to try to turn those feelings around, so I went over to Chris and initiated a conversation. I just sat and told him how I had felt all those years ago. He was very conciliatory, apologizing for what he said had been a kind of arrogance and naïveté on his part. I was grateful that the universe had engineered this moment. I could feel layers of heavy-heartedness floating away.

While I was talking to Chris, Bob Shaye was reading my draft of *The Time Traveler's Wife* for the first time. Everyone else at New Line had already read it. They were already casting the film, so clearly everyone was happy. But Bob was having trouble getting through it. He kept falling asleep. When we landed in Las Vegas, he said, "I think it needs a lot of work," and asked me to rewrite it. Then we all went off to a screening of New Line's new movie *Hairspray*.

The next day was the awards presentation. I asked the people at New Line if I should prepare a speech. "No," they said, "Just go up and say thank you." The ceremony took place in a huge ballroom and was attended by hundreds of film exhibitors from across the country. I remember looking around at the other tables and seeing all the people who were being celebrated that night. It seemed like everyone was accompanied by an entourage from their studios. They were all being supported. I, meanwhile, was sitting at a table with some distributors from Houston. Bob was nowhere to be seen, and neither was the rest of the crew from New Line. It was just me and my son Ari, who had flown in for the conference.

Quentin Tarantino and Robert Rodriguez got up onstage and did a big number about whatever movie they were promoting. Everybody kept going making huge speeches, and I started to worry because I hadn't prepared anything. I had no idea it was going to be such a big event. I decided to just tell the audience what I believe: "Without the writer, none of us would be here."

Finally, it was my turn to go up onstage. They played a five-minute reel of clips from all my films. It was surprisingly well done, and I was very moved. Then it was over, and I had to make my speech. Still no Bob. Just me and Ari and a bunch of guys from Texas. *What the fuck?* Finally, the host introduces me: "Without the writer, none of us would be here." I thought, *Oh no – that's my line... She stole my line!*

As I was walking up the steps, I had an idea. It was a very Zen idea: *Don't tell – show.* I walked up to the microphone, took the statue they had given me, and just stood there. I looked around the room for more than a minute, not saying a word. People started laughing nervously, but I still didn't say anything. I thought I was ingeniously communicating the message that without the writer, none of us in that room would be there. The nervous laughs got louder and louder as people realized that I really wasn't going to say anything. Then I said, "Thank you." And I walked offstage.

The minute I turned away, a little voice in my head said, "Bruce, that was the right speech – but the wrong audience." Then I thought, *Maybe I should turn around, go back up onstage, and say I was joking.* But the moment had passed. There was some polite applause as I went to sit down. It was done. Ari looked at me. He could tell I was nervous, so he said, "Own it, Dad." The wisdom of his words helped, but it took me over a year to internalize them.

When the ceremony was finished, Bob Shaye came over to me. "Was that all there was?" he asked. "Did I miss something?!" It was strange to me how I crumbled when facing him. I felt like I was back in Mumford. He was the senior and I was the freshman. He and New Line had gone to all this trouble to celebrate my screenwriting career, and in his world view I had crapped all over it. "I just kind of lost it up there," I said. He was angry, and just stared at me. So much for *The Power of Now* and *I Am That.* I realized that trying to teach a spiritual lesson to hundreds of mostly inebriated film distributors was hubris. In the end, the real lesson wasn't for them, it was for me.

Bob and I spent the next week in our hometown of Detroit. At first he wouldn't even ride in the same car with me. I tried to apologize, but he wasn't interested. After a couple of days, he warmed up a bit. We were both awarded plaques by the mayor naming us distinguished citizens of the city of Detroit, something I suppose New Line had arranged. Being together on our old stomping grounds allowed for a sense of rapprochement. After a while, I thought everything was good between us.

About a month later, I got a call from Toby Emmerich, president of New Line. "You have been removed from *The Time Traveler's Wife*," he said. "We're bringing in a new writer." I had delivered a shooting script that everyone at New Line was happy with. The film wouldn't have gone forward without my script. The director loved me. They were already casting the film. But I was unceremoniously removed from the project. That was my punishment for not saying "Thank you" to Bob Shaye.

I started to experience a level of regret that I had never experienced before in my life. I knew that I had blown it in a big, big way. All I had to do was say "Thank you, Bob" or "Thank you, New Line," and my whole life would have been different. I wanted to go back and make it right, but I couldn't, and the regret was eating me alive. I kept replaying the moment over and over, and every time it brought up the same pain and anger. It was horrible. I couldn't sleep at night. I felt so stupid. I tried to meditate my way out of it. I would sit and get to a place of stillness and peace. The minute I was done, the regret came flooding back. Every little thing would set it off again.

Eventually, I realized that I had *consciously* initiated my own suffering. When I arrived in Vegas for the writer's conference, I listened to a recording of a talk by a spiritual teacher named Adyashanti. Everybody else on the New Line team went off to the gaming tables, but I sat in my hotel room with this recording. Adayashanti talked about the value of suffering during the course of a spiritual life. As I listened, I sensed that I had lived a charmed life and that I was a stranger to real suffering. Some part of me felt that I could speed my spiritual journey along by entering into the realm of suffering, although I wasn't sure what that involved. On some level, I started preparing myself to find out.

My actions on that stage in Las Vegas produced a full year of prolonged regret and the emotional suffering that regret produces. In terms of my spirituality, it was the most important year of my life. Once I realized that the regret and pain and suffering weren't going away, I began to figure out how to use them. I had to work harder than ever before to transform my situation. Eventually, I came to understand how absolutely pointless regret is, because you can't do anything about it. You can't change what happened. When you finally understand that, you open yourself up to one of the greatest gifts that any human being can ever receive: acceptance.

Every time those emotions rose up in my mind – at four in the morning, in the shower, sitting on the toilet – I would acknowledge them. I would say, "I know you're here." Then I would watch them. I would watch the whole emotional routine, the attack on my ego and my mind. As I moved deeper into acceptance, I became more and more aware of the part of me that was doing the watching. I was discovering the observer within, the witness to my life – the real Self. That's when I realized that my suffering was the thing that could free me. Instead of beating myself up and using the regret as a cudgel, I simply said "Thank you" – and it became a tool for spiritual transformation.

The Time Traveler's Wife lost some of its magic in rewrites. I had tried to give the story a spiritual underpinning by using the idea of time travel to explore timelessness. If we're not rooted in time, where do we exist? I liked the idea that the hero's daughter was starting to time travel, showing us where the human race might go spiritually, so that one day we might be freed from the constraints of time and space. Those kinds of metaphysical ideas have been excised from nearly every movie I've written, and this one was no different. As a result, I don't think the finished film is as vibrant as the version I wrote. Still, it had the emotional resonance I had hoped for.

I had to fight for credit on *The Time Traveler's Wife*. The initial writer thought he deserved credit and so did the follow-up writers. I couldn't accept that. The original script was structurally unsound. I described the first draft to the WGA arbitration committee as being similar to the architectural plans for a building that never got built. The plans may have been nicely conceived, but they had nothing to do with the building that was actually constructed. Subsequent writers may have added nice carpeting and wallpaper, but they hadn't designed and built the walls, the plumbing and electricals that made the final structure inhabitable. I won the battle. Sole credit was financially meaningful to me and my family, and getting that check was a fitting end to an excruciating ordeal.

Reviews for *The Time Traveler's Wife* were bad. But the suffering didn't last. A day later, the pain was gone. I had worked through it, or risen above it, as Rudi would say. I realized then that I was experiencing something he had talked about years before. "In the beginning," said Rudi, "you will have patterns in your spiritual life that will take six years to process. Then it will take six months. Then six weeks. Then six days. Six hours. Six minutes. Six seconds." That's exactly what happened to me. I've gone through so many personal trials and public humiliations and had so many deep disappointments with some of my films. A movie opening is a wildly egocentric experience, and in the beginning I used to get very caught up in it. Over time, I learned to process it. I went from nine months of depression over *My Life* to eighteen hours over *The Time Traveler's Wife*. I took that as a measure of progress.

"To make a great film," said Alfred Hitchcock, "you need three things: the script, the script, and the script." Writers need to know that. They give birth to the entire industry. It relies on them, on their voice, their stories. But if you write for ego gratification and fame, be careful what you wish for. Life is a spiritual ride. It allows you to go through all the drama and suffering, and then, if you're lucky, you come out of it whole. You emerge awake.

Twenty-Four

Enlightenment – Awakening

Around 2010, I delivered two scripts to two producers and never heard a word. No "Thank you," no "Good job," no notes. Paychecks arrived, but nothing beyond that. "Would you like me to find you another job?" my agent asked me. "No," I said. It was the first time I had ever said no. When I hung up the phone, I turned to Blanche and said, "I think I just retired."

For a while after that, I woke up in the mornings and didn't know what to do. My days had always been centered around my career. My work had largely defined who I was, what I was about, and how I perceived the world. It gave me a level of comfort and safety. *Who am I without that?* I thought. *What's left?*

I always claimed that I needed to write to fulfill my LSD directive, to tell people what I saw. I also needed to write to support my family and, later, our lifestyle. But in many hidden ways, I think I needed to write to stave off nothingness. The arrival of true nothingness, in a certain sense, is the ultimate realization of a spiritual practice, and, to be honest, the thing I feared most. I had always hungered for purpose and meaning, and writing, to a large extent, fulfilled that. Taking it away or letting it go was a challenge I was preparing for my whole life. When I stopped writing, I realized that the end of my career was offering me an opportunity to embrace nothingness and enter the core, perhaps the fulfillment, of my spiritual existence.

"Enlightenment" and "awakening" are concepts used by Hindus and Buddhists to describe a person's arrival at a state of higher or even supreme consciousness. Most meditation is an effort to attain this exalted state, although it's a rarefied achievement. I imagined enlightenment to be akin to my LSD experience and that fifty years of meditating would help me arrive at a state of permanent awareness. I also believed that awakening happened to only a small number of people – and mostly in Asia. There were exceptions, like Adyashanti (born Stephen Gray) and Eckhart Tolle. But very few.

One day, out of the blue, I was sent a documentary about a group of ordinary Americans who had supposedly awakened. The producers wanted my endorsement of the film, and I was curious to see it. After listening to their stories, I couldn't deny that something significant had happened to them. I realized that maybe enlightenment was a more common experience than I had previously thought. It occurred to me that there might be many awakened people out there whose experiences go unrecognized and uncelebrated.

The story that really fascinated me was about a guy named Bart, who had been a soldier in Vietnam. One day, on the battlefield, an explosive detonated near him and his body flew up into the air. When he hit the ground, he had an awakening. It was as if his body and mind exploded into a billion pieces and his soul merged with everything around him. Every soldier on the battlefield and he were connected. Friend and foe were all a singularity. He suddenly realized that there was no separate Bart, that he was one with everything, and that he was all there was. The experience lingered for a while, but it wasn't permanent. After the war, he started trying to learn more about what had happened to him. He studied with several teachers but failed to recreate the experience, until one teacher offered a single word to him: "Simplify." Bart didn't know what that meant, but eventually the idea exploded inside him and it was as if he was back on the battlefield. He was everywhere and nowhere. He couldn't explain the power of what was happening, but in that instant everything became clear. In the spiritual vernacular, he realized who/what he was – the fullness, the emptiness, the totality of Being. He returned home to his family and tried to explain what had happened, but no one understood. In an effort to find a community, he began offering spiritual retreats near his home in North Carolina. People started showing up. They would gather every week and talk about their own experiences or attempts at awakening, and Bart would guide them toward this new consciousness.

I was so moved by his story that I wrote to the director of the documentary to see if I could get in touch with Bart, who seemed, in the film at least, to be the real thing. The next thing I knew, he called me. We spoke for a short while, then he asked me if I would read his screenplay. I thought, *Why would a guy who has been enlightened want to show me his screenplay?* I felt he was going in the wrong direction, and that awakening should have freed him from wanting to make movies. But I agreed to read his screenplay, which was actually very good, although it had nothing to do with spirituality and everything to do with a love story in Vietnam. An authentic dialogue began between us, one that quickly moved into the realm of non-dualistic teaching. Bart invited me to come visit him at his family's retreat on the Chesapeake Bay. I didn't know what to expect, but I liked the idea of spending one-on-one time with him, and accepted his offer.

I was surprised that Bart turned out to be so human, so open and easygoing. There were no teacherly pretentions. I was totally disarmed, and we talked for three solid days. I felt like I was speaking with someone I had known all my life. There was no sense of getting to know each other – just an instant and profound friendship. There was no mystical jargon, no need to translate Sanskrit or Tibetan terms into some English equivalent. It was a straightforward conversation about the essence of human life.

"There is nothing you can do to be awakened," Bart kept saying to me. He told me I had no control over it, which was a frustrating thing to hear. I wanted to believe that I could somehow attain it, that I could make myself worthy of it. "That's not the way it works," he said. "Then why do anything? I asked, "Why sit and meditate?" He responded with something Rudi would have said, that you don't know when it's going to happen, but you have to keep doing the work. You have to keep knocking at the door to demonstrate your commitment. In the biblical sense, "Ask, and it will be given unto you; seek, and you shall find; knock, and the door will be opened unto you."

Months later, when I attended one of Bart's gatherings in Raleigh, North Carolina, I was very taken by the people assembled there. I loved their stories and their sincerity. Many claimed to have been awakened and others were sincerely seeking. I felt like a wannabe, but was glad to have discovered them. It felt like we were speaking the same language. What I loved most was the idea that these were people from all walks of life, and that many of them who shared their stories of awakening didn't seem separated from the day-to-day reality of human existence. They just seemed to know *something*, to embody *something*, that joined them together more than set them apart.

In October of 2009, Bart invited me to speak at one of his Raleigh meetings. I was surprised because all the other speakers were acknowledged to be awakened and I wasn't sure what I could offer. "Just tell your story," he said. Bart also gave me an opportunity to introduce my meditation practice to the group. It felt odd giving an introductory meditation class to this group of awakened people, but they were all very respectful. Then we sat and did an open-eyed meditation, which was an important experience for me, because I felt that many of these awakened people were still somewhat incomplete. I could see that some of their heart chakras were closed, that their third eyes weren't open, that their navel chakras were limited. I didn't know what to make of it. I didn't understand how a person could be awakened and yet still incomplete. It would take me years to make sense of this.

The following year, Bart invited me to come back and speak to the group again. I was still hesitant, but decided I would simply continue to represent myself as the token "unenlightened" guy. Two weeks before that trip, I made a profound change in my life. After 44 years of daily meditation, I decided to stop meditating. I figured that if I wasn't awakened after 44 years of sitting, it wasn't going to happen, or I was simply on the wrong track. But then I had an astounding realization, that the very person who was sitting, trying, reaching, wanting – that guy himself was the problem. The goal of meditation wasn't to awaken the person but to move *beyond* the person, the ego mind wanting attainment, freedom and specialness. Not that sitting had been wrong. It demonstrated a true commitment to the essence of spiritual awakening. But it was wrong-headed. Bruce could never have an awakening. Bruce was the problem. Bruce wanting a result was the problem. I guess the Guys Upstairs, as Rudi called them, wanted some demonstration of commitment, and 44 years of sitting did that. I continued teaching, but only by sharing what was going on in my journey. I also still had the capacity to transmit shaktipat. I could still send healing and loving energies to people and saw no reason to stop.

So I went back to North Carolina as the "unenlightened non-meditator" and gave another talk about my studies with Rudi, kundalini yoga and energy work. Several of the awakened people approached me afterward and said, "Do you realize that you're already awakened?" "No, I'm not," I said. "And if I am, I shouldn't need anyone to tell me. What good is it if I don't know it for myself?"

After that, I realized I had arrived at a place where it no longer mattered whether I was "awakened" or not. There was nothing in me that was struggling with it anymore. I just didn't care. I didn't need it. I simply accepted that there was nothing I could do to attain it. I figured, *It will happen when it happens.* Or not. Either way, I will continue to live my life, trying to be as open and available to each moment as I can be.

The second morning of the retreat, I went to hear a talk by a guy named Paul Hedderman, who has a website called *Zen Bitch Slap.* With a name like that for a website, why would anyone go to his workshop? But I felt compelled. Paul is a tall, lean man who speaks at enormous velocity with a thick New York accent. Words, sentences, thoughts, concepts rush forth in a torrent. And as he talked that day, something weird happened to me. I kept trying to conceptualize what he was saying, but I couldn't do it. His words registered such absolute and irrefutable truth that I couldn't resist them or get out of their way. It was all making sense, but I couldn't put any of it into context. So I stopped trying and just listened. Words flowed through me like a river. When the talk was over, I couldn't find the person who had been reacting to what Paul had said. There was no "Bruce" left. Bruce had been washed out of the equation. It was as if I could have been anyone or everyone in the room. A collective being. I had no attachment to me, to personal history. It was like waking up after a nap and having to remember who you are. Only, you're no one. You're like a newborn baby, staring out of the crib. It was an absence and a presence at the same time. The moment was so simple and invisible that it would have been easy to dismiss – except there was no one there to do that, nobody left to embrace it or push it away. There was only… this. There was nothing other than This.

This!

There's no event or day that something ever happened to a "me." It's a story in the world of appearances. It's like, here we're at a retreat and everyone is talking about the ocean, but we're all sitting here

as individual waves. You can hear the beauty of the ocean over and over and over again – it's just going to flip you out more and more as a wave. But the sense of being a wave is the act of denial of the oceanness. To study the ocean, the best the wave can do is, "I hope I can get an experience one day of what the ocean is really like." All the while, while it's longing for this one-day mythical event, it's the ocean all along. It doesn't have to know anything more about the ocean. It just has to realize it's not a wave.

Paul Hedderman, Self-Inquiry Group Retreat
October 3, 2010

After the talk I went up to Paul, to hug him and say thank you. I told him something had happened. "Great, man," he said. "Great!" Then, as I tried to figure out what the hell had happened, he moved on to someone else. I felt extremely present, like I needed to go back and convey to Paul the magnitude of the experience. You can't simply thank the person who just totally transformed your life. I went back, hugged him again, and said, "Something happened!" And he just glowed. He started laughing, and, hugging me, said, "Congratulations." Then I walked over to Bart. "Bart, I think it happened." He started crying. All the people around me started crying. And I still couldn't even say what had happened because there was no "I" to say it. There was only This.

At first, I felt like a fraud. What had happened was so minuscule – like blowing a piece of dust off a table – that I couldn't understand the celebration. I thought, *Certainly that couldn't have really been "it."* It was probably just a precursor to something huge around the corner. "No," said Bart, "it's nothing but that. Once the last speck of you has been blown away, there is nothing left. You are free."

I didn't feel free. I was still very present, just not as Bruce. Now there was just this walking, talking, seeing, hearing, thinking Presence. That afternoon I felt strange listening to other enlightened people speaking, so I just wandered around on my own. Individual people found me and struck up conversations. That was okay. There was no "me" there to resist or reject it.

Then I went back to Bart's house, and we talked late into the night. He affirmed and confirmed everything that was happening. I retraced my long journey back to the LSD trip and realized it had taken me all these years to assimilate the dissolution that had occurred that day. It was a slow unraveling that had just been completed. The last piece, it seemed, had fallen away.

I imagined sharing this amazing news with everyone when I returned to LA, but as I stepped off the plane, all of Bruce's old thought patterns surged forward like some alien force. They danced around for a while and then disappeared. My friend Julie picked me up at the airport. I could barely speak. She appeared to me like a phantom, a robot playing the role of Julie – and playing it beautifully, totally unaware of what she was doing.

Then I got home and saw Blanche. We kissed and I knew she wasn't really kissing "me" because I wasn't there. I was reminded of the moment when Rudi asked who I was looking at and I said "You," and he said that wasn't possible because he wasn't there. That was my experience. Suddenly I felt like I wasn't there. I felt like I was performing the role of Bruce, which I think I did convincingly. But then the weight of that responsibility took hold and I wanted to run. Saying "I" seems to misrepresent the experience. It's more like "he," in the third person. "He" sat down and ate some food at the kitchen table. "He" got lost in the eating. "He" looked at the newspaper, the arts section, and "he" felt some comfort in that old habit. But "he" didn't want to read anything. Focusing the mind was painful for "him."

The third person expression felt odd and unnatural, and there was a strong need to return to the "I." I excused myself and went to my office, to be alone. I had a deep sense of confusion about what should come next, although I knew that I didn't want to speak to anyone. The idea of carrying on a conversation seemed impossible. I tried answering emails. Somehow that flowed easily. I got out a folder of family photos and began looking through them – and I shuddered. Nothing in me felt any relationship to these people. I knew them. I knew their pains, their joys. But they somehow seemed like phantoms. I knew they weren't really who they thought they were, but I also knew that they totally believed they were the people they pretended to be. I sensed that I was now living a fiction that I would be expected to embrace, but wasn't sure if I would be able to do that. I wanted to hide, to stay in my office or even leave the country. I understood why Eckhart Tolle sat on a park bench for so long after his awakening. *How is it possible to re-enter the world after such an experience?* I realized how psychotic it all seemed. I wondered why this state of mind could possibly be worth seeking or finding, but at the same time had to acknowledge that it was profound and exceedingly real. It connected me to something vast, or at least eliminated the barriers that separated me from vastness. All distinctions and separations melted.

When I came out of the office, I decided I needed to talk to Blanche. She knew something was different. I tried to explain what had happened, what I was going through. She had been doing spiritual work with me for so many years, which meant she wasn't unprepared for something like this to unfold. Still, she was a bit threatened by my announcement. Lying in bed that night, Blanche asked, "What does this mean for us? How is this going to work now that you're not Bruce? Will you still love me?" The answer that came out was, "I love you more than Bruce ever did." And it was absolutely true. The love pouring out of me was enormous. It was so overwhelming that I couldn't sleep.

Bart reassured me that this phase would pass, that the newness would mellow into a simple state of knowing, trust and well-being. And after about six weeks, that's exactly what happened. Eventually I realized that Bruce *hadn't* been eliminated. He had just been reabsorbed into the larger Self. I remember driving down a crowded street and getting only green lights. *Okay, this is what happens when you wake up, when you're in flow, when you have moved beyond Bruce.* At that exact second, with that very thought, I hit a red light. The universe spoke. Pride goeth before a fall, and red lights happen if you think you've arrived at any kind of special or exalted state. Accepting life as it is, embracing both red lights and green lights, accepting what is, or simply not reacting to perceived benefit or punishment, is more the answer. The question will always be, "Who is it that is reacting? Who is feeling special (or unworthy)?" As long as there's "someone" there, there's more awakening to come.

Twenty-Five

Being – *Ghost the Musical*

I tried to explain what had happened to me. It didn't play well. Most people didn't have a clue what I was talking about, and intelligent friends who were Buddhists or had similar practices said, "No, it doesn't work like that. You can't be enlightened like that. Whatever you have is nice, but it's not enlightenment." "Maybe not," I said. "Maybe it's enlightenment. Maybe it's something else. I don't know."

Then something started to happen, something Paul Hedderman called "selfing." Selfing is when the remnants of the old self arise. In my case, he referred to it as "Brucing." Bruce would come up and express himself very clearly. I was put off by that at first, because I didn't want to be Bruce again. Something in "me" would get disturbed and say, "Get out!" And Bruce would leave. Just like that. *Wow!* I thought. *Bruce is no longer in control.*

I started to philosophize, sometimes using scientific principles. We're told that light is both a particle and a wave, at the same time. That makes no sense to most people. How can it be both a particle and a wave simultaneously? Scientists say it depends on how you observe it. If you observe it one way, it's a wave. If you observe it another way, it's a particle. I began to think that Bruce was a particle and non-Bruce was a wave – but really, we were the same thing. We were this little particle and this vast ocean of being that somehow operated as a whole. Bruce didn't have to die or disappear. He was still making himself known, but he was working in tandem with something much bigger. In a sense, I knew this after my LSD trip but had no vocabulary for it. It only took nearly five decades to make any sense. Whether this dovetailed with other people's experiences of awakening or enlightenment, I had no idea. But it was certainly *my* truth.

Blanche and I took a cruise with Joshua, Evanne and Ari around Northern Europe. We were to board the ship in Amsterdam and spend several days there in the museums and walking around the canals. The morning of the cruise, it was announced that an intestinal norovirus had been found on the ship and that they wanted to alert passengers that we would have to take precautions on board to keep healthy, like not serving ourselves from buffet lines, washing our hands a lot, that kind of thing. Joshua and Evanne looked unusually concerned. We tried to persuade them that if we were cautious, there would be no problem. I was surprised to see Joshua so worried, but I didn't know Evanne well enough and feared she might back out. They disappeared for a stressful half hour. Joshua finally reappeared and seemed relieved. They had decided to go. Blanche and I were so grateful, and we all boarded the ship. We were placed at a very central table at dinner that night, overlooking everything. It was very stately and seemed singled out and special. Before we started eating, Joshua said he and Evanne needed to explain to us why they were so concerned about getting on the ship with an infection circulating on board. They explained that they had needed to call her doctor to get approval for their travel because, in fact, there were actually three of them boarding the ship. Evanne was pregnant.

It's hard to express this kind of life-changing moment. I had made sacrifices in my life to get married and have children, the joys of which were, and remain, overwhelming. But the experience of having a grandchild took me by surprise. There was a sense of fulfillment and wholeness that I had never known before. The delight on everyone's faces was luminous, but the feeling I had inside could have flooded the universe. Everything aligned for me in that moment. Every choice I had ever made was affirmed in that instant. I felt I was in alignment with God, and God was smiling.

The remainder of the cruise was like a completion, a blessing. We visited Berlin and saw the Brandenburg Gate, the bunker where Hitler died, and the remains of the Berlin Wall. We visited St. Petersburg and saw where the Russian Revolution had begun and the throne where the Czars had once sat and governed an empire. I thought of Mark and our childhood fascination with Russian history. I was now touching the throne. World history and personal history were coming together. Everywhere seemed magical and at peace. Soon I would have a grandchild. Perfection was possible. Then the virus hit full force and every one of us, except Evanne, got sick. It was virulent, coming out both ends. We might be the first people to ever lose weight on a cruise.

Various people over the years had proposed the idea of turning *Ghost* into a musical, but I had never been interested. I just couldn't see Sam singing "Ditto" as a meaningful musical moment. But then I was approached by two producers, Colin Ingram (based in London, where for years he had worked with Cameron Mackintosh) and David Garfinkle, who was in the middle of producing *Spider-Man* on Broadway. Their ideas for *Ghost* were unexpectedly smart. I enjoyed their vision for turning the movie into a Broadway or West End show. During a visit to see me at the farmhouse in Bear Hollow, we got so engrossed in sharing ideas that they missed their train back to New York and had to spend the night. The next morning, I committed fully to collaborating with them. Suddenly I was writing a musical. Visions of Broadway and Times Square were dancing in my head. I remembered sixty years earlier, choosing the pageant instead of hunting frogs at summer day camp. I remembered *Candide*, *The King and I* and *West Side Story*. I felt a sense of flowering. But to start things off, we needed songs.

We approached a lot of composers and lyricists, but most of them didn't get the world of *Ghost*. I went to see Bee Gee Barry Gibb at his estate in southern Florida. He sat on a kind of throne as we spoke and told us he wanted to use Bee Gees songs and just plug them into the show. It felt so lazy, so wrong, that I couldn't wait to get out of there. Other lyricists I met with also failed to deliver anything with insight or imaginative clarity that would enhance or deepen the movie. In the end, even though I had never written a song in my life, I decided that *I* could write better songs than any of these guys. I sat down and wrote lyrics to twenty-five songs over the next few months. I showed early versions to a few people, including Jerry Zucker, who seemed enthralled by what was unfolding. It was enough to keep me going. Even Colin and David seemed impressed. One day they called and said they wanted me to meet with two songwriter/composers who had expressed interest in what I was doing. One was Dave Stewart of the Eurythmics, whose song "Sweet Dreams (Are Made of This)," with Annie Lennox, was among my favorites. The other was Glen Ballard, who had never paired up with Dave before but wanted to do so on *Ghost*. He had co-written and produced Alanis Morissette's *Jagged Little Pill* and Michael Jackson's "Man in the Mirror."

We had our first meeting at Dave's house. When I showed up, about six months after my awakening, there was no Bruce. But there was a strange sense that Bruce was necessary because Bruce was who they had to relate to. Without Bruce, I was uncertain about how to fill the moment. It was a little bit like finding stories on the way to a pitch meeting, trusting that something would be delivered. I just relaxed and the work took over. The writing began to flow through the three of us. Bruce had nothing to do with it. It just happened. And I realized that everything "just happens." We think we're the doers, but we're not. We are what happens. There's no need to worry about any of it – it's happening within us, through us, and in spite of us, so you might as well sit back and enjoy it. Glen was especially connected to the spiritual universe and expressed a joyful openness and a level of moment-to-moment acceptance that opened my heart. We quickly melded. Dave was a more unique presence, and I wasn't sure how to connect to him. He was very kind but sort of all over the place, very talkative, full of endless ideas and creativity, and somewhat socially awkward. I realized that the way to connect to Dave was through his music. It became a clear and direct path to his heart.

The producers began by having Dave and Glen put some of my lyrics to music. I'll never forget sitting in Dave's office and hearing my words sung for the first time. It was a transcendent experience for me. Within a few months they had written great music for all my songs and we had a full album's worth of music. Suddenly, as if out of the ether, Bruce was a songwriter.

We auditioned singers to do run-throughs and staged readings, and rewrote the show's book to fit musical demands. The only thing we didn't have yet was a director. We met with a lot of prospects, and one of them, Matthew Warchus, stood out. He had directed *Lord of the Rings* in London and *God of Carnage* on Broadway, and went on to create the musical of *Matilda* and head The Old Vic in London. At our lunch together he talked about the magic he felt would be needed in the show, the illusions of Sam walking through a solid door and the subway ghost levitating people. He communicated a true sense of delight in how the stage would fill with images that no one had ever seen before in live theater. I was enthralled. So were the producers.

I desperately wanted to be part of the rehearsal experience, and the producers flew me to London in early 2011, but when I arrived it turned out that Matthew wasn't really interested in having me around. I had learned in Hollywood that some directors feel that having a writer in the room can complicate things, but I thought it would be different in theater. I promised to keep my mouth shut and be a fly on the wall. I sat at the farthest end of the production table, just beyond the props people. If I had a thought or a concern I would express it to Matthew privately, out of earshot of anyone in the cast or on the crew.

My silence deepened my sense of presence, the non-Bruce entity simply observing, experiencing, witnessing the world of theater. I loved every moment of it. My silence seemed to have an influence on people in the room. Eventually they started coming over to rub my head or give me a kiss. For me, the rehearsal space was imbued with joy and light. I loved seeing all the dancers and singers learn their routines. I had so much love for all of them, and I think they could feel it. Soon Matthew started asking for my opinion about things out loud, with everyone around, and we developed a wonderful relationship. I started talking more with the cast and crew. Just being in the presence of so much ongoing creativity was enriching.

Movies always seem to happen at such speed. You get the shot and move on. Once it's over, mostly you never see anyone again. The theater experience gives you time to breathe, to deepen and expand. People become part of your life. We spent months together on *Ghost*. They don't feed you in the theater like they do on a Hollywood set, with catering nearby so you can rush back and be shooting in an hour. In the theater world you eat a real lunch. It's collegial.

One afternoon, Matthew approached me at the back of the auditorium. He had a serious look on his face and said we needed to talk. He told me that he really liked all of my songs, but – and it was a long "but" – we have two of the best songwriters in the world working on this show. Why not give them a chance to play with the songs? Let's see what they could do. I was taken aback. I had fallen in love with every lyric I had written and even appreciated some of the new ones that arose as the production evolved. But the idea of turning the songs completely over to Dave and Glen surprised me. They were certainly better and more experienced songwriters than me, but these were *my* songs. At the same time, I knew Matthew was right. Why should I hold on to anything at this point? We were all working together to make the best show possible, so I agreed – and never once regretted it. I did miss sharing my lyrics with a mass audience (though many remain), but the newly expanded and re-invented versions were more vibrant than anything I had written.

It was a real teaching moment. I embraced letting go in a way I had never done before. The collective shared experience became more important to me than any kind of personal ownership. I had no need to be a focal point. It was thrilling simply to be there and be one with this creation. "Doing" occurred on occasion, but "just being" was the operating concept during the creation of the show. It felt like awakening in practice. *Ghost the Musical* offered that experience.

Back in LA, I got a call from Joshua that Evanne was in labor. Then we didn't hear anything for five hours. And all I could think was, *Bruce isn't here, so who is it that's so worried?* I came up with a theory that the universe was worried. Not so much worried, but rooting for the success of this birth. I feel that there's a rooting

factor in the universe that wants the best for all of us and cares about us profoundly. Maybe I'm wrong, but it sure felt right at the time. It felt very real to me.

Thalia Sky Rubin was born, and Blanche, Ari, and I rushed over to the hospital. Right away I experienced total Presence with her. No obstruction. No filter. Instantly, I was introduced to what has become one of the most remarkable relationships of my life. Everything I experienced on the cruise ship exploded into something more real and concrete than any movie or play I could produce. A human being. She was, and is, such an imprint of the miraculous for me that just conjuring her in my mind fills me to this moment with waves of ongoing gratitude. Nothing one can build or create in life equals the pure wonder of birth.

It's hard to explain how deeply Blanche and I were impacted by Thalia's arrival. I wanted nothing else but to be near her. The idea that something completes you is certainly overused, but that's how I felt. Although my gay life had been sublimated for many years, it was still an undercurrent and I sometimes wondered if I had denied a central part of my being. But watching Thalia learn to crawl around the Northridge house and then romping around the fields of Bear Hollow was like the ultimate pot of gold. She was the end of the rainbow that appeared on her parents' wedding day in our backyard.

Ghost the Musical moved out of the rehearsal hall and we went to Manchester for an out-of-town run at the Opera House. Before the show, Matthew got up on stage and explained to the audience that this was a preview and that things could go wrong. He apologized in advance. Then the show began, and nothing went wrong. Paul Kieve's magic all worked. Sam actually did walk through doors.

When the curtains came down, the entire theater erupted into an explosion of riotous applause. For me, it was a blessing and a curse. The blessing was that we had created something that audiences really loved. The curse was that I now really cared about the success of the show. Bruce cared about the show. As we started to move toward the opening night in London, I began having a lot of anxiety about the outcome. *Brucing* was in full force.

Ghost opened in London at the Piccadilly Theatre on July 19, 2011, to what I heard were mostly positive reviews. After having learned my lesson from the movie business, I decided not to read what the critics thought. I began projecting having a hit play running in London for decades and opening on Broadway in the near future. I was living in the pumped-up space of my own mind filling me with a giddy pleasure. I had made it yet again. My career had triumphed. As I learned almost immediately, that's a dangerous place to reside.

Blanche, Ari and I took a relaxing trip to the Isle of Man right after the show opened. On the second morning, there I was looking at *The New York Times* website and saw a headline in the theater section about something "haunted." I didn't know what it was, so I clicked on the link and read a review of *Ghost*. Ben Brantley, the *Times'* chief theater critic, had seen the show in London. And he hated it. *Hated* it! I sensed that I had set myself up for this moment when I wrote the movie *Ghost* and Molly feared getting a bad review for her pottery exhibit. Sam tried to calm her down, saying, "*The New York Times* is some frustrated little critic with pimples on his ass who flunked out of art school. Who cares what *The New York Times* thinks?" This was clearly payback. It was a horrible, overwhelming moment with huge ongoing implications for my emotional and spiritual life. Suddenly the entire future of the play and my fantasy for its wild success collapsed into nothingness. I was certain that no producer in their right mind would ever open the show on Broadway, knowing in advance that *The New York Times* theater critic hated it. I sensed it was the death knell for both the show and my baronial life, and I fell into an instant and deep depression.

Blanche, Ari, and I went out for dinner that night. I wasn't good company. They knew about the review but seemed totally unfazed by it. At one point, Ari told me to stop being so negative about everything. Blanche agreed with him. And I lost it. At that moment, I tumbled headfirst into an abyss. It felt like everything had come to an end. The promise of *Ghost* on Broadway evaporated. The future of the show traveling around the world evaporated. After all, *The New York Times* had spoken. I felt totally undermined, deeply lost. And whatever claim I had to awakening was completely gone. And I was ashamed of that. Of course, I realized that the scale of my depression over a bad review was absurd. But there I was. This moment on the Isle of Man was a shock. It was also my introduction to a pattern of spiritual shocks that would lift me up to amazing heights and then abruptly abandon me to total despair. This oscillation would occur repeatedly over the next decade, as I realized, over and over, how attached I was to the experience of bliss. My attachment to the "I" that desired bliss is also the "I" that experienced its yin/yang opposite: despair. Attaching to one automatically encompassed the other. Learning to let go of all attachment seemed to be the lesson, and it was harder than I had ever imagined. *The New York Times* taught me that. Ben Brantley had become my teacher.

The hardest part for me was coming back to the States and teaching meditation. I had to say something. And I found that the only thing I could do was be honest. In the end, that's all any of us can do. Usually when I teach a meditation class – and I've been doing this for a long time now – the teacher shows up. This time, the teacher didn't show up. I felt like a pathetic little kid sitting there, trying to explain himself away. It was humiliating. It was as if my core had disappeared.

Desperate for guidance, I realized that even for someone devoted to the meditative journey and spiritual awakening, it's good to have someone to share your journey with. I decided to go back into therapy, something I hadn't done since high school. But I wanted a Jungian therapist, someone who could understand my metaphysical as well as worldly struggles. I found someone who lived a few miles from Bear Hollow and who became a refuge for me. Mostly now she's my comforter, my confessor, my confidant. Many people on the spiritual path think they're beyond the need for therapeutic help, and that may be true. But I'm not one of them. I am grateful for her counseling.

Blanche and I were also struggling, debating the need to remain in two homes. With *Ghost the Musical* likely disappearing as a source of income, I was open to moving back to LA, but she wanted to stay in Bear Hollow and be near her horses and the friends we had made. Getting a marriage counselor turned out to be a valuable move. We connected with a brilliant listener, someone who allowed Blanche and I to voice things that we had struggled to express to one another. It wasn't confrontational – it was a revelation. It's amazing how much doesn't get said when a couple is raising two children, living in two homes, caring for three dogs, five horses, and two birds. We talked and talked. The counselor helped us find ourselves on the same page. We couldn't have done it alone.

I mention our therapy only to express what a gift it is when blocked words are finally allowed to be spoken. I remember the head of a studio telling me he would never go to therapy. Why would he ever want to share such private things with anyone? It's none of their business. I can tell you from personal experience that had this person shared any of their hidden venom and let it flow constructively, decades of punishing behavior inflicted on innocent and often wounded souls might have been avoided. While I am a big spokesman for sitting still, meditating and looking inward, I'm also a promoter of any therapeutic help that can guide us through the confusion and darkness of human life. Human beings are always in such endless and often mindless motion that they can't resolve the inner issues that knock us off balance. Therapy helps us in the outer world. Meditation guides us inside. The combination is a gift. Talk to your therapist. Listen to yourself. I tell my students: STOP, SIT, STAY. It's as if our minds are like distracted dogs. We need to stop what we're doing. Sit still. Stay put when the mind gets anxious and wants to run after a bone. It's only by staying longer than your mind wants to sit in one place that the secrets, the joy, the insight and love begin to arise inside. You need to give it time.

A year or so before working on the musical, one of my students suggested that I begin recording my class talks, which I delivered after each session. The hundreds of them, now on YouTube, document much of my spiritual journey, particularly the dark periods after London, and capture some of the devastation of that time, a period of loss and grief, real or imagined. Interestingly, the dark episodes after the *Ghost* opening had a transformative aspect. Although I felt like I was facing death and loss, I also realized it wasn't Bruce facing death. It wasn't personal. It was universal. I was the entire human race facing the Inevitable. The word "impermanence" shot through my system. It was an elemental Buddhist experience. We *all* face total annihilation. Nothing lasts. This experience was another step in the waking-up process.

During that period of loss and annihilation, it felt like I had two seconds to choose how to die. That's what it feels like to face impermanence. It's paralyzing and absolute. It's undeniable. It's the real, ultimate truth. No matter what your mind or story tell you, it's the thing you have been fearing and avoiding from the beginning. I wasn't sure how to handle such a magnitude of terror, the opening to so much truth. I was staring at the end of all things. And it was just projections from a bad review that had caused all this suffering.

I know it sounds like madness, but I have spoken with many people whose dark journeys have been set off by much smaller things.

It's interesting how quickly one can move from the existential terror of death and meaninglessness to sublime hope and the illusion of renewed happiness. For me, it all happened with a phone call, when Colin Ingram and David Garfinkle reached out. They had found the courage and money to open *Ghost the Musical* on Broadway. Nothing in me expected that to happen, not after the *New York Times* review. Instantly, in a microsecond, I felt a kind of rebirth, a new beginning. It was an amazing lesson in just how quickly the truth of impermanence disappears in the distraction of your show opening on Broadway. I recommend it to all awakened souls or spiritual seekers looking for the bliss of worldly distraction.

The process of creating the new version of *Ghost the Musical* was similar to what we had done in London – only faster. There was less of a learning curve. It felt more industrial, more Hollywood. We rebuilt the show on the stage of the Lunt-Fontanne Theater, just steps from Times Square. We had a massive billboard on Broadway and huge sign covering the theater marquee. There was a dreamlike sense of fulfillment seeing *Ghost the Musical* ten stories high in brilliant lights. It was like the moment I discovered theater at the age of four, watching my mom in *Mary Poppins* on stage – only now I was in the heart and center of the theater world. My own play was opening on Broadway. I couldn't have dreamed a better dream. Until the press preview.

I don't know why I went. I had seen the show a hundred times by now, but walked into the theater for the second act. I was told things were going well. I was standing in the back of the auditorium when suddenly, near the end of the show, the entire set went black. Something mechanical had failed. This had never happened before. The play stopped and a voice came over the loudspeaker telling people to remain in their seats. Twenty minutes went by. All I could think was, *Why tonight? Why the press preview?* Whatever aura the play may have cast over the audience, and most importantly the critics, evaporated.

I went back to my apartment that night almost stumbling along the street. It was like being back on the Isle of Man after reading Ben Brantley's review. I told Blanche what had happened, and she hugged me. I got into bed, staring quietly into the abyss yet again, and fell asleep. In the middle of the night, I woke up with a sense that God was laughing at me. But it wasn't a derogatory laugh. It was like God was letting me in on the joke. I suddenly understood that the blackout on stage was so brilliantly contrived, so perfect and focused, that this was no mishap, no sleight of hand. It was God at work. It was the universe smiling. In the end, life takes everything away. Everything. It's impermanent. Enjoy the ride – then let go. I felt a strange kind of connection to the totality of being. There had never been a promise of total and unending success. If anything, I was lucky to be given such a wonderful ride.

This time, I managed to stick to my self-promise in London and not read the reviews. I didn't have to. I could intuit them from the people around me, the way they avoided eye contact, the way they held their heads. But the truth is, the amazing fact is, I'd had a play on Broadway. I had enjoyed success and I had smelled failure. I had tasted such a cornucopia of life experience that there was nothing left to do but feel grateful. *Ghost the Musical* closed after about a year. It had a sweet run and continues to play around the world. But the real joy is that I was exposed to such breadth of worldly experience. Creating the musical helped me reach an enormous depth of joy and suffering. It opened doors for me.

Twenty-Six

Knowing Nothing – Grandkids

Our financial advisor called and said that without a Broadway hit, I should rethink our two homes on two coasts. If we sold our Northridge home, he said, we could stay in Bear Hollow for thirteen more years and would then be broke. On the other hand, we could live in Northridge comfortably for the rest of our lives. The decision seemed obvious. Except for one thing. Evanne was pregnant again and she and Joshua were moving to Seattle. The idea that Thalia would have a sibling was overwhelming. The news that they were moving to Seattle was unsettling, but Joshua explained that he had a good job opportunity there.

Blanche and I had actually been exploring the idea of selling Bear Hollow for a while, and used our weekly therapy sessions to share the complexity and pain surrounding the idea of letting go of a home that had enriched our lives for so many years. But the financial burden was a reality, and having another grandchild was the tipping point. With great sadness but clear heads, we put Bear Hollow on the market. It sold very quickly. The sale was especially hard for Blanche, since she loved having her horses on the property and we loved the community we had built there. We ended up trading Bear Hollow for a rental near Seattle, close to the kids. We continued to commute, flying south to Northridge every month to visit family and teach class. Two months after moving, Elijah Orion was born. Life felt complete.

Living in the Seattle area was a joy. My friend Rona from second grade and another friend, Barbara Boster, lived there. Shortly after arriving, we learned that Barbara was dying of cancer. She was the first of Rudi's students to leave this world, and the grace and good nature she brought to the process was an important lesson for me. Her last word to us as we said goodbye for the final time, accompanied by a gentle wave of the hand and a huge smile, was "Tootaloo!" A perfect farewell. Shortly after Barbara's passing, Joshua discovered that his job was ending and his rental house was being sold. He found a new job and house for his family in San Anselmo, just north of San Francisco, and Blanche and I a house in San Rafael, fifteen minutes from theirs. We flew down and had a look. It was perfect – full of light, with huge windows that gave us a majestic view of the world around us.

My friend Larry, who has always been like a second brother to me, was living in neighboring Oakland, and was an especially welcoming presence to our new homestead. I loved that we were able to be "queer" together and that our dialogue over the decades allowed for an honesty I still hadn't found in my day-to-day life. Another Detroiter from the 678 West Warren circle, Arnold Kessler, also lived nearby with his wife, Leonie. Around this time my friend Mark left his position at the Getty Museum and went back to school at Cal State Northridge, walking distance from our LA home, where he ended up living for seven years. I never imagined we would be roommates again, and having him there whenever we came back was great fun. When he graduated, he bought a home in Palm Desert. We all gathered once a year around our birthdays, mostly at Larry's Oakland home. It completed a circle.

I made one more film – my last – while living in San Rafael. Disturbed by the separation of children from their parents at the Mexican/US border after the election of Donald Trump, I decided I needed to do something to stop it. All I really knew how to do was make movies. How hard could it be to make a one-minute PSA on my iPhone? I recruited Andrew Wagner, head of the directing program at the American Film Institute, and Robert Dalva, editor of *The Black Stallion* and *Jurassic Park 3*, to assist me as volunteer crew members with the project. Peter Coyote came on board as our narrator. It was a grueling experience on every level, and may be one of the best things I have ever done – though it changed nothing. People like Sherry Lansing, former president of Paramount, Art Agnos, former mayor of San Francisco, and actress Eva Longoria all got behind the film, but we made little headway in getting the film seen. Even so, I could feel in my bones and psyche that it was the right thing to do. Sometimes that's the only payback we get.

I had imagined we would live in San Rafael for many years, but then Joshua and Evanne surprised us once more. They decided to move again. Joshua's career as a video game writer was evolving and he was working with clients all over the world. It made more sense for him to move east. I didn't want to move again and figured we would just head back to Northridge, and I was sure Blanche was on the same page as me. But the truth was that she didn't want to spend the rest of her life in Los Angeles. She loved the East Coast. It was her home. She was born on Long Island and had spent summers going to camp in the Hudson Valley. When we got a call from Joshua saying they had found a house in Red Hook, NY, just twenty minutes from Bear Hollow, I could feel the earth shaking. Blanche's eyes lit up. She had devoted much of her life to following me, and I could feel that it was my turn to follow her. So, for the third time in six years, we followed our grandchildren and moved back to the East Coast. It was, I insisted, the last time we would ever do that.

We bought a place fifteen minutes from Joshua and Evanne's new home. As soon as we walked inside, Blanche and I both had the feeling that it was the right house for us. The entrance was full of light coming from a window above the staircase, filling the area with an uplifting illumination. The walls were all varying shades of gray, very different from the off-white walls we'd always had. The ceilings in the living room were coffered, strangely regal and lovely. Upstairs there was a sprawling room that could be used for my office and a classroom combined.

Leaving California was surprisingly freeing. We emptied out two houses, San Rafael and Northridge, taking only what would fit into a single home smaller than any we had lived in since DeKalb. It was amazing how easy and liberating it was to give things away, especially having recently carted so much of it across the country. Students and friends were grateful for the sudden bounty. The Academy of Motion Picture Arts and Sciences Library took box upon box of my scripts, and the Academy Museum took a bag of disturbingly realistic rubber arms and feet that I had grabbed from the hospital scene in *Jacob's Ladder*. Still, we had two truckloads of furniture and art (a truck from each home) that needed to make the cross-country trip, along with Blanche's one surviving horse, Max. Before we left both houses, I prostrated myself and kissed the lawns of our Northridge and San Rafael homes, thanking the universe for having provided me and my family with such blessings. I had done the same thing at the holy temples of India decades earlier. I have found that full-bodied prostrations of gratitude, although very un-Western, are supremely humbling and satisfying. I don't think one can say thank you often or deeply enough. Just before we moved, Blanche and I celebrated our fiftieth wedding anniversary. We went out for dinner, just the two of us. Sometimes arranged marriages work.

Shortly after moving back to New York, *Ghost the Musical* opened in Paris and Madrid, and we were flown to both cities to support the show. Productions have played all over the world and enabled us to travel to many places we might never have visited: Australia, South Korea, Russia, Japan. We even created a smaller, more intimate version of the show for schools and independent theaters. It was a gift that kept delivering. A production in LA at the Pantages Theater was especially joyful, allowing me to share it with friends and colleagues there. After one performance, while walking out of the theater, I was stopped by Shirley Jones, star of the movie *Oklahoma!*, who told me how much she loved the show. I never imagined that the star of one of my favorite musicals would be praising *my* musical, or that I would ever have even created a musical. It was one of those pinch-yourself moments that make you wonder about the nature of reality.

I discovered photography in our last years in California. It all happened unexpectedly when I was hiking in the hills around San Rafael and stumbled upon a road covered in bird droppings. They looked, strangely enough, like a Jackson Pollack painting in the middle of the street. I snapped a photo. Walking home I began to see all sorts of other unexpected images – rusting mailboxes, scratches on cars – and took photos of them too. I realized that I was, at this late stage of life, really beginning to see. It was a visual awakening. There was a world all around me that I had never bothered to look at: street curbs, trash cans inside and out, soap dishes – you name it. It was all beautiful to me, just waiting to be discovered. I sensed that my still images had stories of their own, and my assistant of many years, Ann Cameron, put some of them on Instagram, adding brief descriptions. It felt like photography was replacing writing for me.

Before leaving San Rafael, Joe Ruben, my director friend from *Sleeping With the Enemy*, said that his daughter Kate had an art gallery in San Francisco called The Laundry, and that she would love to see my work. She came over to our house and instantly loved my photos, but, more importantly, noticed all of Blanche's paintings and pottery displayed around the house as well. She was struck by the artistic thrust of our marriage and said that she wanted to do a show that combined both of our work. In May 2019, we opened at The Laundry in San Francisco. Our first ever art exhibition in fifty years of marriage. It felt important to be perceived as equals, Blanche and I, sharing our art with the world. The show, which Katie lovingly titled "An Artful Marriage," gently closed the door on our West Coast life.

Twenty-Seven

Mortality – Clarity

Many years ago, I had a strange vision. Climbing up a mountain, I was surprised to see Jesus standing at the top, his arms spread wide, a love radiating from him that surpassed any experience of love I had ever known. One would think I would have rushed forward to embrace and be embraced by him, but I turned and ran the other way as fast as I could. The love I was feeling was overwhelming, annihilating. I sensed then that it was God's love that finally dismantles us, that takes away all we have, all we hold onto, all we believe in. I wanted to accept it, but, in truth, I wasn't ready for so much love.

The spiritual question became, "Why am I running from this love? Who is this person so afraid of annihilation, even though I was living in a world that wouldn't last?" It was clear that this frightened person was *me*. I was the source of my own suffering. My fear of death was at the core of my spiritual journey. Years later, when I had my awakening in North Carolina, it felt like a true arrival, that the personal me was gone, that I was simply an expression, an emblem of God's love. That we *all* are. But that was challenged in my later years. It's easy to be an awakened consciousness when life is easy, but then old age descends. Experiencing pain and staring into the portal of death alters and deepens the spiritual equation. It's easy to let go of your mind/body/self when sitting on your front porch gazing at the lawn. It's hard to be at peace when your body is drowning, or on fire, or nailed to a cross. That's another level of detachment and spiritual work. I began to learn about all this in Red Hook.

Stuck at home during the pandemic for two years, I began to feel more mortal than ever. My mom had died at 74. She was reaching for a glass in a cupboard and had a brain aneurysm. Two days later, gathered around her in the hospital, my family and I collectively pulled the plug on her rich and joyous life. It was heartbreaking. Now, in Red Hook, finding myself three years past the age when she died, I felt vulnerable.

One Covid afternoon, I was driving to a doctor's appointment across the Hudson River in Kingston when suddenly a massive wild turkey crashed directly into my car's windshield. It was explosive. My car swerved wildly. For a moment, I thought, *Well... this is it... this is how I die.* Glass was everywhere, including stuck in my skin. Then, unexpectedly, everything went into slow-motion and I became totally clear-headed. Somehow, I had been able to avoid swerving into passing cars or crashing into a forest of trees. I pulled off to the side of the road and breathed deeply, happy to be alive. Rather than wait for road service, I continued driving the five miles to the doctor's office. Peering out of the bottom of the shattered window, I made it to the parking lot, then arranged for towing and windshield replacement as I sat there. All I could think was: *This is a wake-up call.*

Endings can be sudden. Stay alert. You aren't special. Even *you* can die – perhaps in the very next instant. Not that I hadn't had these thoughts my whole life, but this was immediate and loud. It crashed in on me. It has always surprised me how little anyone faces or embraces the existential truth, even people obsessed with death and endings, like yours truly. My encounter with the turkey opened my eyes. It was time to confront unfinished business. I was getting old quickly and didn't want to leave this world with things undone, incomplete or unsaid.

Blanche, too, was aging. She'd had a horseback riding accident years before during a family cruise that docked in Jamaica, and was in a coma for a week. The two of us were evacuated to Florida. She recovered, but without a sense of smell and an experience of depression that was hard to overcome. Her hearing was also beginning to fade. Socializing became difficult and isolating. We were diminishing, or as I have recently come to put it, "evaporating." Both of us were joining the ranks of the elderly with our own versions of discomfort and a growing awareness of memory loss. I couldn't remember things from past years, even months – people I had met, places I had been. Blanche couldn't remember why she had walked into the room or recall the movie we had seen the night before. It was clear that in Red Hook, we had entered the endgame. It was time to enjoy the beauty around us and prepare for the uncertainty and wonder of each moment ahead.

Shortly after the turkey smashed into my car, I came out to my students as gay. A strange cause and effect, but there it was. It had taken a lifetime to share my hidden sexuality with people other than Blanche, Larry, Mark and Rudi. Even my kids were in their twenties before I told them. Living as a gay man wasn't part of my day-to-day life and never fit into casual conversation. But as I approached the end of this life, I felt it was essential that I open up all the hidden chambers of my being. I didn't want to die a closeted gay man, or a closeted anything. I didn't want to leave this life with secrets. Of course, everyone has been gracious and my coming out never turned into the kind of feared rejection that imprisoned me as a boy and most of my adult years. I have felt a new level of freedom in just being myself. Even so, this book may shock some people. My apologies to those who may feel betrayed by my decades of silence.

I have been learning to share the dark parts of my life journey, my career journey, my spiritual journey. I have tried to express them in my teaching and relationships as best I could. The painful or frightening experiences I have had – the very public failure of some of my films, the loss of loved ones, the reception of the musical – I was always honest about. But now, in Red Hook, something new was happening. The door to a deeper and more profound sense of darkness and despair had begun to open. I know that it's there for us all. I would love to think that after years of teaching about the infinite joy of being, I could sustain the joy and bliss until the end. But it's interesting to witness what happens when the mind and body that build and reinforce your story begin to dissolve. There is gradually nothing left to distract you from existential truth. All sense of security and assurance that held you together falls apart. How do you operate from that place? How do you relate to a world that no longer makes sense to you? How do you teach?

For a while I felt like a phony, a failure. But at the same time, I sensed that I was learning more from my dissolution than I had ever learned before. I became deeply aware of the underlying fear that awaits us all and the pain that so often accompanies our final journey. I experienced emotional and physical suffering, but I was also aware of great joy and bliss. The lesson of this alternating joy and fear appeared to be: don't grab hold of either, don't run from nothingness or rush toward bliss. Look for the middle ground, the space between fearing and hoping, running away and grabbing hold. Try to find rest there. The struggle arises when you get caught by the opposites in the world. When that happens, ask yourself: who is it that is reacting to all this drama? That person, the one endlessly repeating your story, is the source of your torment. Let go of the storyteller. When your inner voice starts to tell you things you don't want to hear, just say, "Nope." You have that power. Don't react. Reactivity is a programmed event. It can be positive or negative.

Reacting with love and compassion builds character. Reacting with annoyance and anger builds suffering. A lifetime of small reactions will define you as a person. Massive reactions, something I refer to as "nuclear reactions," can destroy your life. When you see yourself reacting negatively to old patterns and thoughts, just say, "Nope." It will give you enormous control over your life.

We live in a world of opposites – yin and yang, pleasure and pain. We're here simply to witness and experience them. Learning to witness takes a lifetime. The desire to hold on to joy and the instinct to recoil from fear is how our drama unfolds. We tend to be unconscious, reactionary beings, building lives we often don't want and can't move beyond. Meditation helps us to detach, to simply observe, to witness it all. It's called "the path to liberation" for a reason. It frees us from ourselves. Being still, saying, "Nope," is great practice. Instead of grabbing hold of everything that arises, we learn to let go. Rudi taught that this simple effort of surrender, of letting go, was the work of a lifetime. More than I ever imagined, that has proven to be true for me.

When I had my awakening in North Carolina, I thought it was a graduation, a kind of PhD in spiritual attainment. Only later did I learn that it was actually something much less grand. It was a graduation, yes – but from kindergarten into first grade. My first-grade awakening felt like an ultimate state, a simple awareness that there was no one, no person to awaken, that the ego mind and the Totality of Existence are not separate, but actually one and the same. I thought that awakening to this truth would be the end of spiritual effort and practice. But now, as a first grader, I realized that there was no end to spiritual work. When you awaken, you realize that there isn't any "you" doing the work. It's happening by itself. Life, our lives, are simply and miraculously happening. But that sublime awareness doesn't take away the pain and the experience of suffering. It's an awakening to a new level of consciousness. It's the beginning of second grade.

Following several operations for a degenerative spine, I began to discover pain. I also have diabetic neuropathy, for which there is little treatment. About five years ago a friend left an unfinished marijuana joint in our house. I hadn't had a single psychedelic drug in over fifty years. Rudi told me early on that if I ever took LSD or smoked marijuana again, I couldn't come back to his class. That was pretty specific, and I abandoned mind-altering drugs in favor of the meditative path. But meditation didn't help me with neuropathy. And so, having a joint lying around and being unable to sleep for many nights because of incessant pain, I smoked grass for the first time in half a century. It was exceptionally revealing. I immediately began rising upward into higher and higher planes of existence. It felt just like LSD, only this time the Guys Upstairs were evaluating my life journey and checking off a long list of achievements and stumbles over the past seventy-plus years.

They checked off my leaving a comfortable job at NBC and heading to India in search of a teacher. There was a check for meeting and marrying Blanche, a check for meeting Rudi, a check for leaving the Whitney and joining the ashram, a check for leaving DeKalb and moving to Hollywood. I sensed that I was passing my life review. It felt like a bardo experience, with the universe saying, "Good… good… good… okay… not bad." It was at this point that I sensed I might be in my final moments, that I might be leaving this world. I got up and walked into the bathroom where Blanche was getting ready for bed and told her I thought I was dying and that I loved her and wanted to say goodbye. She looked at me, knowing I was high, and smiled. She told me she loved me too. Then I went back to the bedroom and lay down, ready to depart. I was sailing higher and higher into some vast and unknown cosmos. It felt bigger than LSD. But then something deep inside me said quietly, "I'm not ready to die." And a voice arose. It said, "Really? You don't want to die? That's okay. You don't have to die. Just say that you want to live." And so I did. "I want to live." And immediately I was descending, returning back into my body, my life. I hovered over it, then was lowered into a kind of comforting dream state, followed by sleep. I woke up in the morning totally free of my neuropathy, a respite that lasted several months. I was very grateful to still be in the world. In fact, during the journey a voice told me that the neuropathy was just a ploy to get me high so I would check in with the powers that be. I sensed that it wasn't something I should do regularly, that the check-in was complete. I was in good hands.

Over the last few years in Red Hook, my spiritual journey has intensified. The beauty has been endless. In the best of moments, I have felt myself to be a flower that has waited decades to bloom, filling the world with a sweet aroma. But then the petals fall to the ground, withering into nothing. It took me a while to understand that actually I wasn't a flower, I was a plant, and the plant – vast in size and scope, the source of everything – was bigger than I ever imagined. When the pain starts, it's a cosmic reminder to stop, sit, stay. I have to surrender. I have to let go.

Rudi used to say that pain was God's love. I always sensed that this was true, but I didn't fully understand it. Following one major surgery on my spine, I had levels of pain that the narcotics offered me didn't cure. I begged doctors to give me more morphine, but they said I had taken all that was allowed. They had nothing else to offer. I was sleepless for a week, until a cortisone shot magically relieved the suffering. As I recuperated, I noticed a profound side effect that seemed to come out of nowhere. My heart was dazzlingly open. I wasn't sure of the cause, but it did seem to reflect Rudi's teaching. The pain had opened my heart chakra to levels unknown. The real beneficiary of this opening was Blanche. As much as I had always loved her, even after my awakening, this new depth was beyond anything I had known. This light, her light, just poured through me. My gratitude for even knowing her, let alone having spent a life

with her, was overpowering. All of this just adds to the mystery of this journey we are on. Why pain is God's gift still eludes me, but the experience was undeniable.

When I hear spiritual teachers talking about transcendence and endless bliss, I wonder whether they have experienced neuropathic pain, a degenerative spine, night after night of sleeplessness. I wonder if they have had children or family who were suffering and unreachable, and how their bliss plays out in the face of a loved one's horror. I could not and do not deny the possibility of a love that transcends all understanding, but I know that arriving at that place is profoundly challenged by true suffering. Daniel Subkoff, a dear friend, once said that the moment he accidentally smashed his thumb in the door of a taxi, twenty years of Buddhist practice flew out the window. That speaks to me. It's easy to talk about bliss, but smashed fingers can alter the dialogue.

I think the hardest part of the spiritual journey is the need to acknowledge and embrace darkness, emptiness and even meaninglessness, as part of the whole. So many of us reach for the light because we're frightened. We can't admit to ourselves that we have created spiritual personas that deny darkness. What I discovered for myself is that all I had done was lock the darkness in the basement, closed the door, and said, "You don't exist. I don't have to deal with you." But as you get older – or, more specifically, as you arrive at greater levels of clarity and awakening – one of the things you realize is that the darkness in the basement is very real. And then it's no longer silent. It's banging on the door, usually in the middle of the night, when you're sound asleep, when the pain arises and can't be hidden. You wake up in white-knuckled fear with an awareness of something unnameable that you don't want to deal with.

So what do you do? My answer is simple but perhaps hard to accept: open the basement door, because the thing you're running from is the very thing you have to run *toward*. The thing you are most afraid of is the thing you must accept most deeply. The spiritual life that many are using to escape fear is programmed to lead you to a direct confrontation. You can't escape yourself. You can't escape the totality of Self. It's not possible. Simon and Garfunkel wrote a song about this. "Hello darkness, my old friend." Start singing.

One final truth has dawned on me during my Red Hook journey. It may be the most important in all my years of sitting and teaching. After more than fifty years of spiritual pursuit, I have come to realize that I know nothing. Why, you may wonder, have I wasted my time reading this book or listening to Bruce's spiritual pronouncements if this is true, if this is all he has to say? But let me assure you, the journey to knowing nothing appears to be at the core of the human adventure, and so, to me, it's a story worth telling. It hasn't been an easy ride, but I wouldn't trade it for the world. Every philosophical and spiritual truth that I embraced has begun to evaporate. My own narrative is crashing on the shore as the ocean behind it reveals its power. I'm finding myself without a story – or at least, I'm watching the story being dismantled. It may seem odd to document this unraveling, but I felt compelled, indeed instructed, to pass it along, to offer some insight that may help others on their own journey into evaporation and knowing nothing. We don't evaporate gently or easily. It's overwhelming, this dissolving process. You can open to it or fight it. You can embrace existential truth or look the other way.

At one point, recently, I decided to stop teaching. I questioned how one can offer meaninglessness and knowing nothing to students as a core concept, a central lesson in the spiritual textbook. For six months in Red Hook, I had no students. And in all honesty, I enjoyed it. After nearly fifty years of weekly classes, it was good to have Sundays alone with Blanche and family. I probably wouldn't have returned to teaching except that a voice began speaking quietly inside me. It said, simply, "It's not about you." I've heard that before, but it was especially loud and clear this time. I somehow sensed that knowing nothing, the emptying out of knowledge, had left me strangely lighter. The word "enlightened" percolated in my brain, not as an attainment of anything but as a dropping off, the loss of held thoughts and beliefs. Enlightenment was an emptying out, a freeing oneself from knowledge. Something was still there, but it had nothing to do with me or my experiences. It repeated, "It's not about you." It was very clear. I went back to teaching.

Many of the people I know have little or no idea what I mean when I talk about the spiritual universe. That's okay. We don't need to know exactly, just that there is something looking out for us. The more I look at existence and the nothingness that precedes it, the more I am aware of something arising from the core emptiness of existence, something we humans call love. I've watched it happen many times now. Somehow, rising out of the great abyss, love, miraculously, is the first thing to appear. It's quickly followed by something we call beauty and truth. They all emerge and are perhaps the same thing. It appears to be the source of all that is, and seems to envelop us and dance inside us for our entire journey – whether we perceive it or not. That sensitivity has led me to a very simple understanding about how to live your life. You can try to awaken and transcend the world as we know it. Awakening has its perks. But it's not for everyone. Westerners, especially, don't like to meditate, don't like to sit.

There is, however, an ancient teaching, central to every religion on the planet, that can serve every human being in the deepest possible way.

Be a good person. Be nice. Be kind.

That seems to me to be the totality of what I have learned in this lifetime.

Do unto others as you would have them do unto you.

Embracing kindness and working to manifest it is, for me, all that needs to be taught. Our hearts are a road map. They offer directions for making kindness happen. Opening your heart, your mind, your gut, helps find the guidance we all need to live a good and kind life. It's like a personal GPS. It will take you where you need to go and help you learn that we are all connected, that empathy and compassion are the very foundations underlying our lives. Becoming attached or addicted to the outer world and losing touch with our inner selves is disorienting and causes people to suffer needlessly. Finding the source of kindness within can change it all. Even if you don't find it, just being kind will take care of your journey. That, anyway, is what my life has taught me. That is what LSD taught me, what more than fifty years of meditating and teaching has taught me, what three decades in Hollywood has taught me, what being married and raising children has taught me, what "enlightenment" has taught me.

Be a good person. Be nice. Be kind.

There you go. It's all that needs to be said.

Twenty-Eight

Love – It's Only a Movie

At one point I considered writing a musical about my life, mostly because I thought it would be more fun than a book – for me and for the audience. But then I decided I needed to write everything down so I could cobble together the essence of the show. Thus, this book. I don't know if I will ever write the musical, but I did write one song for *Ghost the Musical* that in many ways is a love letter to Blanche. It's impossible to stress enough how empty my life would have been had I not met her and had the blessing of her love on this wonderful journey. Writing a love story, a musical with song and dance about our life together, seemed a perfect way to celebrate the joy I feel in having known her, in having spent a life with her. But in case this musical never happens, I want to share some of it – or the lyrics at least. This is for Blanche.

"I've Always Loved You"

Before you were born
Before time began
Before I could walk
Before you could stand
Before there were stars
Before the sun rose

Before darkness fell
Before all of those
I loved you
I always loved you

From the very first moment
And even before
There was only love
Love and nothing more

Before there was a world
Before heaven and earth
Before my own life
Before my own birth
Before I found you
Before you had a name
Before we were here
I was filled with this flame
I loved you
I always loved you

From the very first moment
And even before
There was only love
Love and nothing more

Before I could laugh
Before you could crawl
Before I could catch you
Before you could fall
Before there was hope
Before there was fear

Before love arose
It was already here
I loved you
I've always loved you
I've always – loved you

If the musical gets written or ever comes to Broadway or a theater near you, go see it. Even though you already know the story, it should be fun.

Old age, I have discovered, is when a lifetime of spiritual practice comes in handy. My home in Red Hook has been a true proving ground for me. It's my Goldilocks space – not too grand, not too small. Just right. I am endlessly grateful for it, and, with luck, I will end my journey here. We shall see. Mostly, to quote *Candide*, all I want is to make my garden grow.

When I was young and would go to the movies with my parents, I would get so caught up in the movie that I couldn't bear it. I would start crying. My mother would hug me and say, "Honey, it's only a movie."

It helped when she did that. I could step back from the story and look at what was actually happening. I was with an audience, not being chased or under attack in any way. The safety I felt at that moment was enormous. It was so helpful to be reminded that I was just sitting in the theater, an observer, not inside the story, and that everything was fine.

Sit back and relax. It's all okay. Enjoy the ride. And in my mom's most loving and comforting voice, "It's only a movie."

Love to you all.

www.ingramcontent.com/pod-product-compliance
Lightning Source LLC
Chambersburg PA
CBHW070124080526
44586CB00015B/1554